Bear Necessities of Politics and Power

Iratus Ursus Major

Iratus Ursus Major

Contents

To my husband, who has been my greatest sounding board and supporter.

To my Twitter followers who have fostered a community with me.

And to caffeine, the substance which has kept me awake far more than I should be allowed to in any way or form.

Thank you to you all.

Acknowledgements

To Everyone Who Made This Book P ossible.

No book is truly a solo endeavour, and *Bear Necessities Of Politics and Power* is no exception. It's a testament to the power of collaboration and the collective effort of a remarkable group of people. I've been incredibly fortunate to have you all supporting me through this process, and I owe a huge debt of gratitude to each and every one of you. This book is as much yours as it is mine.

First and foremost, my heartfelt thanks to Pea Channon, whose tireless work in proofreading and editing helped shape this book into something coherent and possibly even elegant at times. Your keen eye and dedication have been invaluable.

To Reece Dinsdale, Carol Vorderman, Baroness Jenny Jones, and Sacha Coward, who took to Twitter to help promote this project, you all have been absolute legends, rallying support and spreading the word when it mattered most.

Beki Jane, your advice on the layout of the book jacket was instrumental in ensuring it looked sharp and professional—thank you for your creative insight and for helping to bring the visual side of the book to life.

A massive thank you to everyone who took the time to test-read chapters and provide thoughtful feedback, especially:

- Tamara Jarvis

- Joe (Viking Dane)

- Nathan Dennis
- Vicki "The Cat's Mother"
- Seonaid Dawn
- Andrew Godsell
- Sue "Topsys Cat Mum"
- Jane Remain
- Jack Janglebones
- Jenny Wrenn
- Ceinwen McMillan
- Kathy Trevelyan
- Nicky Busst
- Caroline Scott
- The Woke Lady Snowwhite of The Catbiscuits
- "Retired and Mostly Happy"
- Jezebel
- Girlyswot Spider
- Withnail Jones
- Russ Jones
- Matthew Watts
- James Graham
- Mike Barron

- Jen Ben
- Chris Moran
- Carol Evans
- Donna Donut
- Colin Grimes
- Picky Lilly
- Cathy Beesley
- Rainbow Chazer
- Lord Sir Andrew Harris OBE
- Andy Burge
- Gary Gilligan
- John Walker
- Polly
- Mariken
- Hagrid Grohl
- Jamie
- Julia Tanner
- Melanie Isabella
- Avril Silk
- Iain Stewart
- Anne-Laure Donskoy

Your comments, insights, and encouragement were a constant source of inspiration and motivation. Each of you brought a unique perspective that helped shape this book, and I'm so grateful for your time and feedback.

Finally, to anyone I may have inadvertently missed—you know who you are, and your support hasn't gone unnoticed. Whether through a comment, a kind word, or a thoughtful critique, you've all been part of this journey, and I genuinely appreciate each and every one of you. This book is as much yours as it is mine.

Introduction

A quick heads-up if you've picked up this book expecting a grand, definitive political theory: you're in the wrong place (and you might want to return it before you spill tea on it). This is not an academic manual that will unlock the mysteries of global politics, and it won't earn you a PhD. What it *will* do is offer my personal way of making sense of the tangled, confusing, and often downright absurd world of politics—particularly in the UK, though we'll glance at a few other places along the way. It's a version I've pieced together over years of watching, questioning, ranting, and occasionally laughing at the absurdity of it all.

If you've ever been called a "dirty commie" or a "fascist" on Twitter[1] (and that's just in the last 24 hours), or maybe you've thrown those words around without entirely understanding their weight, but this book is for you. Words matter, especially in politics, and right now, they're being flung around with reckless abandon. People often throw out accusations like confetti without grasping what they truly mean. Understanding these terms is crucial—not just to win your next Twitter spat, but because when we misuse these words, we dull their meaning and power. And let me tell you, history shows us that when people aren't paying attention to the language of politics, the worst ideologies can quietly slip back in.

---

1. Yes, I am fully aware that it's called "X" now, and no, I will not call it that.

And while I'll touch on a few other parts of the world, this book is very much about the political landscape here in the UK—where, if you listen closely, you can hear echoes of the same dangerous trends we've seen before. People bandying about terms like "fascism" and "socialism" without a second thought, while dangerous ideologies are creeping into mainstream conversations. It's enough to scare the bejesus out of anyone who knows a bit of history—and if it doesn't worry you, well, this book might just change that.

Now, I'm not naïve. I don't think this little bit of noise will stop the darker turns of history from repeating themselves. This book isn't here to fix the world. But if it makes a few people stop and think about the words they're using and the importance of standing up against dangerous political trends, I'll call that a win. We've all got a role to play, and while this might only be a small part of the bigger fight, every bit helps.

As you dive into these pages, feel free to approach this book however you like. Skim, skip chapters, or flip to the glossary to decode any "-ism" that piques your interest. It's not exactly a beach read (unless your idea of beach reading involves political philosophy), but it could be a handy reference when trying to make sense of today's chaos. One note: despite all the doom and gloom, I do still hold on to hope. The truth is, we've faced hard times before, and ordinary people have stood up, pushed back, and made real change happen. That's the heart of democracy: the power of people. If enough of us refuse to accept extremism, refuse to be apathetic, and refuse to misuse the words that define our political landscape, then we can push back against history repeating itself.

You'll meet a few familiar faces along the way—some global figures, yes, but many with particular relevance to Britain. There's Machiavelli, who understood the game of power better than most, and Marx, who tried to peel back the layers of capitalism. Hobbes will remind you why life without government might be "nasty, brutish, and short." Then there's Rand, whose individualistic ideas have found surprising followers here, even in a country where collective action gave birth to the NHS. And, of course, we'll spend some time in the 20th century because Britain's political history has its own share of infamous characters who've shaped today's debates—whether you like it or not.

So no, this book won't solve all the world's problems, and it's definitely not the last word on anything. But if I've done my job, it'll help make sense of the political chaos we're living through in the UK, give you a deeper understanding of the words we're throwing around so carelessly, and maybe even make you chuckle a bit in the process.

Thank you for supporting me by buying this book. I appreciate every single one of you who's taken the time to read it. My hope is that you walk away from these pages having learned something, thought a bit more deeply, and, above all, laughed—because we could all use a bit of that right now.

— Iratus Ursus Major

Political Theory
A Quick and Dirty Introduction

"All political theories assume, of course, that most individuals are very ignorant. Those who plead for liberty differ from the rest in that they include among the ignorant themselves as well as the wisest. Compared with the totality of knowledge continually utilised in the evolution of a dynamic civilisation, the difference between the knowledge that the wisest and the most ignorant individual can deliberately employ is comparatively insignificant."

Friedrich Hayek

L et's start with a story. Imagine a room packed with politicians, all dressed to the nines—suits perfectly pressed, ties neatly straightened, and expressions of utmost seriousness on their faces. They're gathered in Westminster, Washington, or perhaps Brussels, ready to tackle the latest global crises—climate change, wealth inequality, the erosion of democratic institutions. The agenda is jam-packed with issues that could affect the lives of millions, maybe billions. And yet, instead of diving headfirst into these crises, they spend the next three hours embroiled in a heated debate about what constitutes a sandwich. Does it need to have two slices of bread? Can a hot dog count? Must it be open-faced? Should we even be entertaining the totally anarchic notion of wraps? Yes, this is the state of political discourse in the 21st century.[1]? Yes, this is the state of political discourse in the 21st century.

It's easy to laugh (or more likely shake your head) at the absurdity of this image, but behind the humour lies a sobering reality: while the trivial dominates headlines, the true crises of our time—inequality, climate change, the dismantling of democratic systems—are often left on the sidelines, drowned out by the noise of meaningless squabbles. And herein lies the problem: the issues that shape our lives, and frequently the quality of our future, are decided not in grand debates about justice or equality but in political arenas where distraction often outweighs substance.

Now, you might wonder, as an average citizen who already endures endless debates about Brexit, austerity, NHS cuts, and even the seemingly frivolous controversy over whether pineapple belongs on pizza, why should you care about political theory?

Because, dear reader, it's absolutely everywhere, and it permeates *everything*. You might not realise it, but political theory is the invisible force shaping almost every conversation (or Twitter argument) we have about governance, power, and society. Every time you hear a politician wax poetic about *"freedom"* or a pundit on the television bluster about *"democracy,"* you're really hearing a mangled, second-hand version of centuries-old debates. These debates are rooted in political theory, but—here's the thing—the people speaking about them often have about as much understanding of the subject as they do the intricacies of quantum physics. In other words, not much at all.

---

1. The answer is no. A wrap is just a lazy sandwich.

Take the constant chatter about *"sovereignty*[2] *"*during the Brexit debate, for example. Politicians love to throw that word around as though it's a magic wand capable of solving all of Britain's ills, but ask them to define it in any detail, and you'll quickly realise they're just rehashing something they kind-of-sort-of-half-remember from a GCSE history lesson (which they possibly failed). And then, of course, there's *"freedom."* You've heard it a million times, usually in the context of someone demanding the freedom to do something—*anything*—normally without consequence. But freedom, as we'll see, is far more complex than people give it credit for. It's not just the right to do whatever you please; it's also about the responsibilities that come with it, a nuance often lost on those who seem to think *"freedom"* means *"I get my way."*

Political theory isn't just an academic exercise for philosophers cloistered in ivory towers. It's the foundation of every policy decision, every piece of legislation, and every debate about what kind of society we want to live in. Whether you're arguing with your mates about the fairness of progressive taxation, wondering why the housing crisis has persisted for well over a decade, or debating whether the latest government overreach constitutes an attack on your personal liberties—guess what? You're engaging with political theory.

Now, I get it. You're probably thinking, *"I'm just trying to get through my day without having a full-blown, panic-laden existential crisis. Why do I need to care about this stuff?"* Well, because it pretty much shapes everything around you. The policies that decide how much tax you pay, how affordable (or not) your rent[3] is, how your local schools are funded, and yes, even whether your neighbour can erect a flagpole taller than your house, are all based on political ideas that have been debated for centuries. And here's the best part: even if you don't care about

---

2. Or even "Sovrinity" if we want to really get the message across.

3. It's a universal truth that no one's rent or mortgage is ever affordable.

political theory, rest assured, political theory cares about *you*. It's shaping your world, whether you're paying attention or not.

It's woven into every argument you see on TV, from the self-righteous rant about *"freedom"* on Question Time to the incoherent rambles of populist politicians claiming they're *"giving the power back to the people"* while simultaneously trampling over the very democratic institutions they claim to protect. Whether it's capitalism, socialism, neoliberalism, or the latest brand of authoritarian nationalism[4] masquerading as a populist uprising, all of these movements are underpinned by political theories that have been debated, contested, and reinterpreted for centuries.

And here's where things get interesting: political theory doesn't just help us understand how we got here but also gives us the tools to think critically about how to make things better. It's not just about dissecting the mess that politicians have made (although that's certainly a big part of it); it's about figuring out how we can do things differently. Why is it that despite decades of economic growth, wealth inequality has only worsened? Why are public services collapsing under the weight of austerity while billionaires get tax cuts? Why do governments so often seem to prioritise the interests of corporations over the needs of the people they're supposed to serve? Political theory offers the framework to understand these contradictions—and, if we're lucky, figure out how to fix them.

Locke vs. Hobbes (Or, The Cage Match of the Ages)

Now, imagine two of political theory's biggest heavyweights, John Locke and Thomas Hobbes, somehow transported to the present day for a no-holds-barred debate on the state of modern politics. They find themselves on a debate stage—probably in a half-empty conference room in some decaying Westminster

---

4. Read: Probably Racist.

building, where the flickering lights and the faint smell of budget cuts linger.

Looking back with a smug grin, Hobbes begins: "Well, Locke, your grand ideals of liberty and natural rights have done it again. Just look at the state of things! Populist movements everywhere, governments barely hanging on, and people running riot under the delusion that their voice matters. You give them too much freedom, let them vote on things they don't understand, and what do you get? The collapse of rational governance, waves of mass hysteria, and leaders whose only qualification is shouting the loudest."

Locke rolls his eyes. "Oh please, Hobbes. Don't pretend this is the fault of liberty. If anything, the mess we're in today is a result of bad leadership and opportunists who prey on fear. Populism isn't a failure of democracy—it's a symptom of leaders who stopped listening to the people long ago. The rise of populist figures isn't about too much freedom; it's about a system where the elite grew too comfortable, and now they're paying the price for ignoring the frustrations of the people they were supposed to serve."

Hobbes scoffs, leaning forward. "Ah, yes. The 'people.' You always were the idealist, Locke. The idea that people—*the masses*—are capable of rational thought en masse is laughable. What have we actually seen? A bunch of people convinced by demagogues that the way forward is to dismantle everything, to throw their lot in with charlatans who promise them the moon while leading them straight into ruin. Democracy, in your sense of the word, is nothing but mob rule in a nicer suit."

Locke, smirking, shoots back: "I'll admit, populist leaders have done a good job of exploiting people's fears, but that's not the fault of liberty. It's a failure of the political class—the same class that dismissed real grievances for years. When people don't feel heard, they turn to anyone who promises to shake things up. The problem isn't that the people are wrong to want change; it's that they've been fed lies by those who exploit their trust. If governments had been doing their jobs—actually representing their citizens, rather than protecting their own interests—these movements wouldn't have gained traction."

Hobbes, laughing darkly: "There's your problem, Locke—trust. You think governance can run on goodwill and accountability. But people aren't looking for competent leadership; they're looking for the next loudmouth who tells them what they want to hear. Look at the rise of these populist movements! They promise everything, deliver chaos, and leave countries more divided than ever. You think this is liberty? This is the result of unchecked freedom, where any crackpot can claim the mantle of leadership as long as they've got enough social media followers."

Locke, with a steady gaze: "Hobbes, you always underestimate people. Yes, populism thrives in the cracks left by bad governance, but that doesn't mean people are inherently irrational. They want to be heard, and when they aren't, they turn to anyone who acknowledges their pain. The failure isn't in giving people too much freedom; the failure is in political leaders not being accountable. These populist figures are dangerous, yes, but they only thrive because the institutions meant to safeguard democracy were hollowed out—leaders stopped representing their citizens and started ruling like they were untouchable."

Hobbes raises an eyebrow, clearly unimpressed. "So your solution is more of this freedom, this grand experiment in 'accountability'? Have you seen what happens when you give people too much of a voice? They dismantle the very systems that protect them. You talk of rebuilding institutions as if that's enough, but trust me, Locke, what this world needs is more control, not less. Strong authority is the only way to prevent these populists from ripping apart the foundations of society. The more freedom you give people, the more they'll tear things down."

Locke sighs but doesn't waver. "You see, Hobbes, that's where you've always been wrong. The answer isn't to tighten control—it's to rebuild trust in democratic institutions. People aren't asking for chaos. They're asking for leaders who care, who will listen to their concerns and govern with integrity. The rise of populism is a result of leadership that took the people for granted, that ignored their struggles while enriching themselves. If we restore that trust—if we give people honest, principled leadership—they won't turn to demagogues. They'll turn to democracy."

Hobbes grins, leaning back again. "Oh, yes. Democracy—the fairy tale that keeps disappointing you, yet you keep believing. Look at the mess we're in! The political elite you defend is just as corrupt as the populists. People don't want trust, Locke, they want results. And if they can't get them, they'll burn the whole system down. That's why strong leadership is what this world needs—firm control to prevent the chaos from spreading any further. Otherwise, we'll be stuck watching this slow-motion train wreck of democracy collapse under its own weight."

Locke, more determined now: "The wreck isn't inevitable, Hobbes. Populism may have exposed the rot, but it hasn't destroyed democracy. It's not too late to rebuild. The solution isn't more authoritarianism; it's better leadership. Strong institutions, real accountability, and leaders who actually serve the people—that's what will save democracy, not the iron fist you're so eager to clench."

And so, the debate rages on. Locke defends the virtues of freedom, trust, and the need for honest leadership, while Hobbes remains steadfast in his belief that only strong, authoritarian control can prevent further chaos. In the background, the rise of populism looms like a spectre—a political reality born of desperation, fear, and the failure of institutions that once held firm.

Fundamental Concepts in Political Theory (Or, Why Your Neighbour Thinks Their Vote Matters)

Now that we've watched Locke and Hobbes squabble with the requisite flashbacks to that one conversation you had on Twitter that evokes very similar feelings, just with more swearing and someone being called a strong name for female genitals, it's time to break down some key concepts.

Power

Power isn't just about who can shout the loudest (though that certainly helps in some political circles[5]). In theory, power is the ability to influence people or situations—whether through force, persuasion, wealth, or the much-loved *"strongly-worded letter."* Every political system, no matter how chaotic or seemingly democratic, requires power to function. The issue, of course, is that power is a double-edged sword. It can be used to protect rights and promote the common good, or it can become a tool of oppression and manipulation[6], hoarded by the elite and doled out only when convenient. You know, like free Wi-Fi in public spaces—when you really need it, it's nowhere to be found.

Power can be subtle, or it can be overt. It might manifest as a politician giving a speech that sways public opinion or a country using its military to, erm... *"liberate"* another nation—often with dubious intentions. The real question isn't just who holds power, *but how they wield it.* Do they exercise it for the good of society or simply to maintain their own position? That's where things get murky.

---

5. I'm looking at you, Mr Gullis.

6. "Responsible use of power" might be the biggest political oxymoron of all time.

Authority

Power only becomes authority when people actually recognise it as legitimate. It's one thing to have power; it's completely another to have the consent of the governed to use it. Think of it like this: the tax office demanding your money has authority. You may grumble noisily about it, but you (usually) pay your taxes[7] because you recognise the government's legal right to collect them. On the other hand, your neighbour demanding you stop parking in front of their house does *not* have authority, no matter how many notes they leave on your windshield[8]. Just because they're *loud* doesn't mean they're *legitimate*.

Authority is crucial for any functioning government, but it's also exceedingly fragile. The moment people stop recognising a government's right to rule, authority crumbles rather spectacularly. This leads to protests, civil disobedience, and, if things get really out of hand, full-blown revolutions. In modern times, authority isn't just about formal institutions either; it's also tied to public perception. A politician might have the *legal* right to govern, but if the public loses trust in their legitimacy—well, let's just say their tenure becomes shakier than a Tory leadership contest.

Legitimacy

This is the secret sauce that turns raw power into authority. Without legitimacy, even the most powerful rulers will find themselves facing pesky problems like protests, coups, or, in today's world, social media storms that do irreparable damage to their credibility. Legitimacy is what makes authority *stick*.

---

7. Unless you're the Chancellor of the Exchequer for a brief period during which you're investigated and then pay a fine which is more than most people will earn in their lifetimes, but hey-ho.

8. Your neighbour's inflatable flamingo also lacks legitimacy.

It's why even when we don't particularly like a leader, we still (mostly) accept their rule, as long as we believe in the fairness of the system that put them there.

Think of legitimacy as the political equivalent of Teflon[9]. When a leader has legitimacy, criticism and opposition slide off them more easily. Without it, everything sticks—scandals, missteps, and the inevitable grumblings of opposition. Legitimacy often comes from different sources: democratic elections, legal frameworks, or even traditional authority, as with monarchies (although their legitimacy is increasingly based on whether they behave well in the tabloids). It's the belief that those in power have a *right* to be there, even if they occasionally fumble things (looking at you, Liz and Rishi).

Sovereignty

Then, of course, we have sovereignty - the one word that makes every politician sound important and authoritative, especially during a debate about Brexit[10]. In its simplest terms, sovereignty is the idea that a state has absolute authority over its territory and people. It's the right to govern without interference from external powers, which, in the Brexit era, became a rallying cry for those who believed the UK was being *"controlled*[11] *"* by the EU. Spoiler: sovereignty doesn't mean doing whatever you want without consequences. It's not a magic shield somehow that blocks bad things from happening.

In reality, sovereignty is less about *isolationism* and more about *negotiation*. In an interconnected world, no country operates in

---

9. Legitimacy does have its limits—especially when those in charge can't tell the difference between governing and self-serving photo ops.

10. It can also make whole sections of the public positively tumescent with excitement and/or rage.

11. It was not.

a vacuum. So, while Brexiters may have dreamed of a glorious return to full sovereignty, the reality has been a little less sunlit uplands and a lot more paperwork, tariffs, and queues straight from the bowels of Dante's worst nightmare leading to Dover. At its core, sovereignty is about making decisions for your nation - just don't be surprised when the rest of the world has a say in how those decisions impact them.

Sovereignty, in the hands of nationalist movements, has become a tool for inflating fears and fostering division. Across Europe, far-right parties have manipulated the concept of sovereignty to push their agendas, often framing the idea as synonymous with reclaiming national identity and shutting out external influences. Leaders like Marine Le Pen in France and Viktor Orbán in Hungary have effectively weaponised sovereignty, suggesting that the nation's ability to make decisions independently is under siege by the European Union, immigrants, or global elites. The irony, of course, is that these movements don't seek to expand the freedoms of the people but rather to consolidate power for themselves.

In the UK, the Brexit campaign's cries for "taking back control" were a direct manifestation of this same rhetoric. The notion of sovereignty was sold as the ultimate prize, a return to some golden age of British autonomy, but the realities that followed have shown the complexities of global interdependence. Far from being a straightforward assertion of power, sovereignty in the modern era often requires negotiation and compromise with other nations and organisations. Yet nationalist movements across the continent persist in exploiting this idea, capitalising on public discontent and fear, much as the Brexit campaign did in the UK.

The Social Contract

Finally, we come to the Social Contract —a concept that's a favourite of philosophers but also somehow remains completely and utterly ignored by most of today's politicians. The idea is simple really: we, the people[12], agree to follow the laws and live peacefully under a government in exchange for protection and the safeguarding of our rights. It's an unwritten deal that's supposed to ensure mutual benefit. The government keeps us safe and provides basic services, and in return, we don't, you know, start rioting in the streets.

Of course, like any contract, it can be broken. When governments fail to hold up their end of the deal—like, say, failing to provide functioning healthcare, trashing the economy, or, I don't know, spending £40,000 on wallpaper for their Downing Street flat or driving the economy straight into a wall only to be outlasted by a lettuce—people start to question whether they should keep their part of the bargain. At its core, the social contract is about trust, and when trust is lost, society risks breaking down. So, perhaps the next time a politician mentions *"hard-working families"*, *"making hard decisions"* or *"doing what's best for the country,"* it's worth considering how well they're actually holding up their end of the deal.

These are the key concepts that underpin much of political theory, and though they might seem abstract at first glance, they influence everything from your right to vote to the legitimacy of the government collecting your taxes. By understanding these fundamental ideas, you're already one step ahead of most politicians—though that's not saying much these days.

Global Discontent: The US, Europe, and the Far-Right's Political Rebirth

Let's take a detour across the Atlantic for a moment. If you've been paying any attention to the political chaos in the United States, you'll know that it has become the epicentre of modern democratic dysfunction. On one side, you have Kamala Harris, the Democratic nominee for President—sharp, competent, and

---

12. Also: Voters

often maligned for not being *"charismatic enough,"* which is apparently the new requirement for fixing centuries of systemic inequality. On the other side, like the political equivalent of a bad sequel, you have Donald Trump making a grand return as the Republican nominee, still clinging to his MAGA[13] hat and the same recycled populist slogans from his first run[14]. Yes, the political system that gave us reality TV stars as presidents hasn't learned its lesson.

But let's not pretend this is just about one man and his tweets. Trump's rise—and now his turgid and noisy resurgence—wasn't a fluke. It was the product of years of brewing discontent, a boiling over of frustration with political elites, stagnant wages, and the steady erosion of the middle class. Sound familiar? It's not altogether *that* different from the frustrations that drove Brexit, except in this case, it's wrapped in the Stars and Stripes and comes with a side of conspiracy theories about stolen elections[15].

Trump's brand of populism—loud, abrasive, and *terrifyingly* effective—has capitalised on the fears of those who feel left behind by globalisation. He promises to *"drain the swamp,"* but conveniently leaves out the part where he's spent his entire career swimming in that very swamp. But here's the thing to really keep in mind: Trump's resurgence isn't just a quirk of American politics. The rise of the far-right is a global phenomenon, and it's spreading like a particularly virulent strain of political flu.

Take a look at Europe. In France, Marine Le Pen and her far-right National Rally party have steadily gained traction,

---

13. Make America Great Again – though "Great" in my mind has a slightly less orange tinge about it.

14. Because apparently, four years of chaos and a failed insurrection attempt weren't *quite* enough for some voters.

15. And as I'm editing this book, it now also comes with Lassie and Garfield being prepared for the dinner table if you're a migrant.

despite being the political equivalent of trying to bring back flared jeans—no one asked for it, but somehow, here we are. Le Pen, like Trump, taps into fears about immigration, economic insecurity, and national identity. The message is clear: *"We're under attack, and only strong, authoritarian leadership can save us."* It's a message that resonates across borders. Viktor Orbán in Hungary has built his own brand of *"illiberal democracy,"* which is really just code for *"democracy without the democracy part."* In Italy, the Brothers of Italy party, led by Giorgia Meloni, has rapidly risen to power, pushing a hardline nationalist agenda. And let's not forget Poland's Law and Justice Party, which has been steadily chipping away at democratic institutions under the guise of preserving *"traditional values."*

What do all of these movements have in common? They thrive on fear—fear of the *"other,"* fear of losing national identity, fear of change. And they sell the same simple, seductive solution: give us power, and we'll take care of everything. It's Hobbesian authoritarianism with a modern populist twist. They frame themselves as the defenders of *"freedom,"* but what they're really offering is the freedom to submit to their version of national greatness, where dissent is quashed, and democracy is an inconvenience.

In the US, Trump has spent years railing against *"fake news"* and completely undermining trust in democratic institutions. If you tell people long enough that their government is corrupt, that the media lies, that their elections are rigged—eventually, they'll believe you. And once you've convinced enough people that democracy doesn't work, it's a short leap to authoritarianism. Trump's candidacy in 2024 isn't just a run for office—it's an assault on the very principles that underpin the American political system. And while Harris represents a counter-narrative of inclusion and progress, the reality is that her campaign will have to navigate an electorate that's been bombarded with years of populist rhetoric and division.

But it's not just about the US. Europe is seeing a similar erosion of democratic norms as the far-right gains ground. These movements may wave the banner of *"national sovereignty"* or *"traditional values,"* but make no mistake—they are symptoms of the same disease: a deep mistrust of established institutions, coupled with a desire for strongman politics that promises easy answers to complex problems.

Whether it's Trump in the US or Le Pen in France, the rise of the far-right isn't some passing phase. It's the political consequence of years of economic inequality, cultural anxiety, and the failure of centrist parties to address the needs of ordinary people. And if you think the UK is immune, just take a look at the current state of British politics. The last fourteen years of Conservative governments shifting increasingly to the right may have been just the opening act, but the far-right's appeal is far from fading—in fact, it's gaining strength and influence following our most recent elections.

So why does this matter? Because these movements, whether in the US, Europe, or the UK, challenge the very core of democratic theory. They twist the principles of freedom and sovereignty into tools for division, offering strong leadership at the expense of personal liberty and democratic accountability. And while they promise to protect "the people," what they really deliver is a consolidation of power that benefits the few while leaving the rest to fend for themselves.

Why Political Theory Matters Even More Now

And so we come back to our initial question - why should you care about political theory, again? It's not just for those with a PhD in philosophy or the insufferable talking heads on political talk shows. In reality, political theory is the blueprint for how societies function—or, more often, how they *fail* to function. The evidence can be found in the silent hand guiding of the laws that govern your everyday life all the way through to the larger forces that shape global politics.

Political theory matters because it is the lens through which we can critically examine not just what's happening now, but *why* it's happening and *what could be done differently*. It helps you see past the surface of the endless, deafening noise—be it from Brexit debates, climate summits, or Twitter meltdowns—and forces you to ask the deeper questions. Why does populism seem to be gaining ground? Why does inequality persist, even in so-called advanced democracies? Why do governments so often fail to solve even the most basic problems, like housing, healthcare, and wealth inequality?

These aren't just policy failures; they're failures of political design. Political theory gives us the framework to understand that what we're seeing today—the political chaos, the rise of authoritarianism, the disillusionment with democracy—isn't random. It's the predictable outcome of systems designed to benefit a select few while paying lip service to the rest of us. Whether it's Brexit, the rise of nationalism across Europe, or the steady erosion of democratic norms in places like the U.S., these developments all have their roots in the structure of power, authority, and legitimacy. Political theory unravels that structure, showing us where it's gone wrong and, critically, where it could be fixed.

Take Brexit as an example. It's easy to blame the whole debacle as a referendum gone awry, but it was so much more than this - it was the culmination of decades of discontent with political elites, economic inequality, and the gradual alienation of working-class communities. Political theory helps us understand that Brexit wasn't a flash in the pan—it was a symptom of deeper fractures within the political system, fractures that had been widening for years. It forces us to confront uncomfortable truths: the liberal democratic model isn't as invincible as we like to think, and unchecked populism can destabilise even the most established institutions.

And while political theory might not offer immediate solutions—after all, Hobbes and Locke have been arguing for centuries[16] —it does provide the intellectual tools to navigate the chaos. Understanding concepts like power, authority, legitimacy, and sovereignty won't magically fix the system, but it gives you the critical insight to see when a government is overstepping its bounds or when it's failing to uphold the social contract. It shows you that political decisions aren't made in a vacuum; they're the result of historical, economic, and social forces that are deeply embedded in political structures. Recognising these patterns can help you anticipate political trends and, perhaps, fight back against them when necessary.

Political theory also matters because it arms you with the ability to engage in meaningful political discourse. It helps you rise above the shouting matches that dominate social media or family dinner tables and ask the more pressing questions: Why is this policy being implemented in this way? Who benefits from this decision? What power structures are being reinforced, and which ones are being dismantled?

In a world where political literacy is often limited to soundbites and slogans, understanding the theory behind the practice is not just helpful—it's essential. We live in a time where authoritarianism is creeping into democracies under the guise of *"strong leadership,"* where the far-right waves the banner of *"freedom"* while pushing for ever-greater state control and where progressive movements struggle to challenge entrenched power dynamics. Political theory is the toolset that allows you to cut through the rhetoric and understand the forces at play.

Understanding political theory also equips you with the ability to critique the system effectively. Rather than simply reacting to the latest scandal or policy blunder, you can question the underlying assumptions that keep failing us. Why do neoliberal economic policies continue to dominate, even as they exacerbate inequality? Why does the illusion of democracy persist

---

16. And I do sometimes believe that their undying souls are being channelled occasionally into Twitter spats.

when so many people feel disenfranchised? Why does the idea of sovereignty still hold so much appeal, even when we're more interconnected than ever?[17]

Political theory forces us to confront the uncomfortable reality that most political systems, as they currently exist, are designed to preserve power for the few, not to serve the many. It challenges the status quo by asking not just whether a system works but for whom it works. By digging into the theories that underpin our institutions, you gain the clarity to see when they are being twisted to serve private interests over public good. You begin to understand why governments cling to outdated models of governance, even when they're clearly failing to address modern problems like climate change or technological surveillance.

And yes, political theory can also help you win arguments at family dinners[18]. In a world where rhetoric has replaced reason and populism masquerades as leadership, political theory isn't just a relic of academic discourse—it's the tool we need to understand, challenge, and ultimately rebuild the systems that shape our lives. The ideas that once laid the foundations of empires might just help us reconstruct what's been broken and create a society that finally serves the many, not the few. The next time someone insists that we need to return to *"traditional values"* or that *"strong leadership"* is the answer to all our problems, you'll be equipped to dismantle their arguments with a well-placed critique of authoritarianism or a pointed reminder that nostalgia for an imagined past is rarely a solution for present-day issues.

---

17. Most importantly, you'll be able to respond with a meaningful answer to Bob-Bunchanumbers on Twitter exactly why you are not, in fact, a Commie or Marxist.

18. And if nothing else, you can always use your knowledge of political theory to politely shut down that one relative who insists we should all live in a "benevolent dictatorship" run by billionaires.

Ancient Political Thought

Where It All Started

"A good decision is based on knowledge and not numbers"

Plato

Welcome, dear reader, to our political tour through the ancient powerhouses of political theory: Greece and Rome—two civilisations that, despite their historical grandeur and intellectual contributions, often struggled to manage the messy reality of human governance. These societies gave us the foundational ideas of democracy, republics, and civic virtue—concepts that, for better or worse, still underpin much of modern political discourse today[1]. But let's not get too idealistic. For every lofty philosophical debate about justice and the *"good life,"* there was a not-so-lofty political scandal, power grab, or outright catastrophe.

So, as we wade through the philosophical wreckage, I invite you to imagine the chaos behind these supposedly sophisticated political systems. Please mind the philosophical debris scattered

---

1. Also, Spaghetti and Koftas.

about—remnants of great ideas that were as often ignored as they were revered—and let's dive into one of the most influential, yet paradoxically dysfunctional, attempts to organise society: Classical Greece, where democracy was born, flourished briefly, and then spent much of its life in critical condition. So grab your metaphorical toga[2], because we're heading straight into the birthplace of democracy—Athens—where the concept of people-powered governance was conceived, tried out, and nearly fell apart under the weight of its own contradictions. It's here that we first see the daring, often experimental, ideas about self-governance and civic duty, ideas that were groundbreaking for their time but often mismanaged in ways that should feel all too familiar to anyone observing modern politics.

Athens – The Birthplace of Democracy (And a Few Bad Decisions)

Imagine the scene: It's a warm afternoon in classical Athens. The sun glints off the Parthenon, olive trees sway in the breeze, and a group of Athenian citizens—*free men only, of course*—gathers in the Assembly to decide the future of their city. Democracy, or at least the Athenian version of it, is in full swing. This isn't your average representative democracy, mind you. In fact, it's not representative at all. Every single political decision, from declaring war to determining whether your neighbour should be exiled for being a bit too annoying at dinner parties[3], is made directly by the citizens themselves. There are no MPs, no intermediaries—just you and your fellow Athenians, voting by a show of hands. It sounds like pure and total chaos, doesn't it?

---

2. And keep it wrapped nice and tightly at all times.

3. Or whether he really should be allowed to keep that damned blow up flamingo.

This is direct democracy, Greek-style. The idea that every eligible citizen had not just the right but the obligation to participate in political life was revolutionary for its time. Decisions weren't made behind closed doors by a privileged few—they were made in the open, in the Agora, with full public visibility. Of course, this system only applied to a small subset of the population—women, slaves, and foreigners need not apply. But for those who did qualify, it was the ultimate form of people-powered governance.

In modern Greece, the concept of direct democracy still resonates, though it now lives mostly in the realm of symbolic political ideals. The modern Greek state is a parliamentary democracy, where elected representatives make decisions on behalf of the people. Yet, during the 2015 Greek debt crisis, the Athenian spirit of direct democracy made an appearance when the government held a referendum asking citizens whether to accept the harsh bailout conditions imposed by the European Union. In a move reminiscent of their ancient ancestors, the Greek people voted "Oχι," outright rejecting the austerity measures—though, much like in ancient Athens, the will of the people didn't prevent political reality from taking a sharp turn in the opposite direction shortly afterward.

In both ancient and modern times, we see the inherent tensions of democracy: the desire for citizen control versus the complexities of governance. It raises the question: can a democratic system truly function when the stakes are so high and the issues so complex? Ancient Athens was the cradle of democracy, but also the cradle of its inherent contradictions.

Direct Democracy:

Now, let's just give this a bit more thought—no MPs to dodge blame, no layers of bureaucracy to hide behind. Every free adult male (I really must stress the exclusionary nature of this system) gathered in the Assembly to vote on everything. That's right—*everything*. From foreign policy decisions to whether or not bin day should be on a Tuesday[4] or a Thursday. It sounds like democracy in its purest form. And in some ways, it was—though whether that's a good thing is up for debate. After all, letting the masses directly vote on complex issues tends to get a bit... chaotic[5]. Or as we might say today, the ultimate town hall meeting from hell.

In modern Greece, that same democratic impulse persists, though somewhat tempered by centuries of political evolution. But let's not delude ourselves—there's something both charming and terrifying about a system that could exile its most troublesome citizens by popular vote. Imagine applying that today: the next time a political scandal breaks, instead of a Twitter storm, we'd all just cast a vote to exile the offender to some distant island—perhaps a modern-day Crete.

Rotational Leadership:

Rather than trusting elections to consistently choose the best leaders (we've all seen how *that* goes), the Athenians came up with an ingenious—if slightly alarming—solution: leadership by lottery. Yup, you read that right. Athenian officials weren't elected based on their qualifications, charisma, or experience. Instead, they were randomly selected by lot. The theory behind this was that it would prevent corruption and ensure that everyone had an equal chance to mess things up equally. It was democracy's version of the lottery—except instead of winning money and a nice article in the Sun, you won the unenviable job of running the city.

It's as if Athens decided that the best way to run a city-state was by pulling names out of a hat—kind of like running a modern multi-billion-pound corporation by randomly selecting the

---

4. I vote Tuesday.

5. We've all seen how well Referenda tend to go, right?

CEO from the list of employees who didn't call in sick that week.

Contrast this with modern Greece, where leaders are still elected—though not necessarily trusted any more than their ancient counterparts. While modern democracies have moved past the lottery system (barely), the Athenians might have been onto something. After all, when you see how well some of today's elections turn out, you start to wonder if picking leaders by sticking your name into a hat might not be such a bad idea after all[6]. At least then you'd get the thrill of knowing your leader wasn't some career politician—just some poor sap who happened to have their number drawn.

Public Debate:

The Athenians didn't just vote—they debated. In fact, the ability to speak well in public was considered one of the most important civic virtues. If you thought Twitter spats were brutal, try defending your policies in the Agora against a philosophical giant like Socrates, who, as far as we can tell, spent most of his time publicly dismantling people's arguments with merciless precision. Public debate was democracy in action, and if you couldn't hold your own, you might as well have stayed home.

In modern Greece, the spirit of public debate remains strong, though it's now more likely to take place in parliament than the Agora. The fiery debates over austerity measures and EU bailouts in the last decade felt eerily similar to the intense public discourse that characterised Athenian politics. The stakes, too, were just as high—though the consequences of a poor argument today are more likely to result in a Twitter pile-on than being ostracised for a decade.

---

6. Especially when considering both Liz "The Lettuce" Truss and Rishi Sunak's track record.

Rome – Where Politics Got Practical (And Occasionally Stabby)

Now, let's leave the philosophical musings of Athens behind and pop over to Rome, where the toga-clad political class didn't waste much time theorising about governance—they were far too busy figuring out how to *actually* make it work. Well, sort of. If Athens was the birthplace of democracy, Rome was the birthplace of bureaucracy. The Romans didn't have time for the lofty ideals of direct democracy. They were more focused on building roads, expanding an empire, and conquering anyone who looked at them funny. This wasn't about theory for them; it was about power, practicality, and occasionally stabbing your political rival in the back. Literally[7].

Much like modern Italy, where political drama still unfolds regularly on the national stage, ancient Rome's politics were equally theatrical. Today's Italian politicians may not brandish daggers in the Senate, but they certainly do know how to make and break alliances with dizzying speed, channelling the spirit of their Roman forebears with a bit less bloodshed. After all, Italy's modern political scene still carries shades of its ancient past, with shifting coalitions, short-lived governments, and a Senate that is not exactly known for its efficiency.

Republicanism:

Forget democracy in the Athenian sense—Rome was all about the Republic. This meant the rule of law, mixed government, and *civic virtue* (which, in practice, translated to *"don't get too comfortable with power, because someone will likely stab you in the Senate if you do"*). In theory, this sounds noble, but in reality, it was more like an ancient version of *Game of Thrones*, except with fewer dragons and more backstabbing senators

---

7. I really, really hope that I don't have to expand at some point on what I meant by the stabbing of people.

(though roughly the same amount of breasts). While the Republic promised balance and a shared sense of responsibility, it also provided a perfect stage for power-hungry politicians who knew how to manipulate the system.

In modern Italy, the echoes of Roman republicanism are still felt. Italy, a republic since the fall of the monarchy in 1946, has a similarly complex political structure, full of checks and balances meant to prevent anyone from gaining too much control. But as we've seen with the meteoric rise of populist parties like the Five Star Movement and Lega Nord, as well as the current prominence of Giorgia Meloni's Brothers of Italy party, the dance between democratic ideals and power politics continues. Much like in ancient Rome, modern Italy's political scene often feels like a delicate balancing act—except now, instead of senators with daggers, we have coalition governments that can collapse with just the tiniest of nudges.

The Senate:

Speaking of senators, let's talk about the Roman Senate—the real seat of power in the Republic. The Senate was dominated by wealthy patricians, the elite class who believed they were naturally superior to everyone else because, well, they were richer and, therefore, clearly better[8]. The Senate was supposed to provide a stabilising influence, offering wisdom and guidance for the Republic. In reality, it was just as corrupt, power-hungry, and self-serving as any modern-day parliament you can think of.

Fast forward to modern Italy, and you'll see that while the Senate no longer deals in backstabbing (at least not literally), it remains a symbol of political gridlock and inefficiency. Much like its Roman predecessor, the Italian Senate is often criticised for being out of touch with the everyday struggles of ordinary citizens, instead serving the interests of those with power and

---

8. Some might say not much has changed.

wealth. And, just as in ancient Rome, it's often the place where political careers are made—or destroyed—depending on how well you can navigate the treacherous waters of political alliances.

Consuls and Assemblies:

The Romans, ever the pragmatists, believed that concentrating too much power in the hands of one person was a recipe for disaster—after all, they had a front-row seat to the fall of tyrants like Tarquin the Proud[9]. So, instead of putting all their faith in a single leader, they had two consuls who shared power, ensuring that no one got too comfortable (or tyrannical). The consuls were elected for just one year—hardly enough time to wreak havoc—while the Assemblies gave the plebs something to do. The plebeian class could vote, but only on the issues that the Senate allowed them to, ensuring that the ruling elites always had the final say.

It's a bit like modern Italian politics, where coalition governments form and dissolve with such regularity that keeping track of who's in charge feels like a national sport. Italy has had over 65 governments since 1946—proof that the Romans were onto something when they decided to limit the time any one person could hold power. Like the Romans, modern Italy maintains a system designed to distribute power and prevent authoritarian rule, but the sheer number of coalitions and short-lived governments make it seem like the political equivalent of juggling—except with more players and fewer clear rules.

In both ancient and modern Italy, the tension between the ideal of power-sharing and the reality of political manoeuvring has always been palpable. Whether in the ancient Senate or the

---

9. I shit you not, this was an actual person who went by the fancier name of Lucius Tarquinius Superbus (which is the perfect name for a cat if there ever was one.)

modern Italian parliament, politics is as much about alliances and survival as it is about serving the people.

The Philosophers: Now Let's Meet the Cast

The philosophical stars of the ancient world weren't just great thinkers; they were the political commentators and architects of their time, offering us everything from utopian dreams to searing critiques of human nature and governance. Each one contributed to the political thought we still grapple with today. But don't be fooled—they weren't just having coffee-fuelled debates about justice in ivory towers; they were deeply involved in shaping how societies understood power, authority, and morality. Let's take a stroll through some of the most influential minds in ancient political thought.

Plato: The Dreamer

Plato wasn't just a philosopher—he was an idealist with grand visions of how society *ought* to be, as opposed to how it *was*. In his famous work, *The Republic*, Plato lays out a vision of a perfectly ordered society where everyone knows their place, and governance is in the hands of the wisest: the philosopher-kings. Think of him as the ancient world's version of a political idealist who truly believed that society could, and should, be led by those who understood the deeper truths of justice and morality. In many ways, Plato's ideas were less a reflection of what was possible and more a blueprint for what could be if humanity ever managed to transcend its flaws.

- Philosopher-Kings: According to Plato, philosophers—those who have ascended from the shadows of ignorance to understand the Forms[10] (particularly

---

10. Plato's theory of the forms is worth a look into, but fair warning, it's very wishy-washy and I wonder whether he had been consuming... something, when he worked them up.

the Form of the Good)—are the only ones wise and virtuous enough to rule. It's a radical departure from the democracy of his day, which he considered chaotic and easily corrupted by the passions of the masses. In Plato's eyes, the philosopher-king is a ruler who is *above* personal ambition, governing solely in pursuit of the common good. It's as if he imagined that we could entrust today's political systems to an elite intellectual class who, like benevolent overseers, would make decisions purely based on reason, untethered from the messy desires of everyday people.

- The Tripartite Soul and Society: Plato believed that both the human soul and society itself were divided into three distinct parts, each with its own role. In the human soul, these were reason (which should rule), spirit (which supports reason), and appetite (which must be controlled). He saw society in much the same way, with rulers (the philosophers), warriors (the guardians or defenders of the state), and producers (the workers who provide for the material needs of the city). For Plato, justice was about each part of society—and the soul—doing its appropriate role and not meddling in the affairs of others. A bit like saying, *"Stay in your lane, and everything will run smoothly."*

Of course, Plato's ideas, while ambitious, have been criticised for being undemocratic and elitist. His philosopher-kings sound good in theory, but can we really trust those with supposed *"higher knowledge"* to govern us? After all, history is filled to overflowing with intellectuals who turned tyrants once they gained just a little too much power. Modern Greece, with its troubled relationship with democracy in the face of economic crises, is a far cry from Plato's utopia—and a reminder that even philosopher-kings can't control the tides of global finance.

Aristotle: The Pragmatist

Where Plato was the dreamy idealist, Aristotle, his student, was firmly grounded in reality. If Plato was up in the clouds thinking about perfect societies, Aristotle was on the ground, asking, *"How can we make this work in the real world?"* His political theory was less about crafting utopias and more about understanding what worked best given human nature's limitations. Aristotle's emphasis on empirical observation and common sense[11] brought political thought back to earth, focusing on what was practical, achievable, and just in the governance of actual states.

- The Polity: Aristotle's ideal form of government wasn't some unattainable utopia ruled by philosopher-kings. Instead, he advocated for a mixed system—a combination of democracy and oligarchy that avoided the excesses of both. Aristotle argued that the best government is one that serves the middle class, the group he believed was most likely to keep the state stable and balanced. He understood that extreme wealth or poverty in a society would lead to strife, and thus, the polity represented his effort to create a stable, moderate political structure that neither catered to the elite nor gave in to the mob[12]. Think of it as the political equivalent of a well-balanced cocktail—strong enough to get the job done, but not so strong that you wake up regretting your choices.

- Virtue Ethics and Leadership: Unlike Plato's focus on philosopher-kings, Aristotle believed that the health of a society depended not on who ruled but on the moral

---

11. No, not the Esther McVey brand of "common sense", actual common sense.

12. If this was known in the fourth century BC, how are we still struggling to realise that poverty = bad.

character of its citizens and leaders. Good governance, according to Aristotle, comes from virtuous leaders who act for the good of the whole, rather than personal gain. It's a noble idea, but one that seems almost laughably quaint in today's world of corruption scandals and corporate lobbyists. Aristotle believed that a state was only as virtuous as its citizens—and that a just society was one where people cultivated *eudaimonia*, or human flourishing, through virtuous living.

Aristotle's practical approach resonates today, especially when we consider modern Italy, where political leaders are constantly balancing competing factions, coalitions, and popular demands. Italy's recent political landscape, with its frequent elections and shifting alliances, is a far cry from Aristotle's balanced polity, but his insistence on the middle class as the stabilising force might give us pause as we witness the growing divide between the wealthy and the struggling across Europe.

Cicero: The Orator

Jumping forward to Rome, we meet Cicero, the statesman and philosopher who was part rhetorician, part politician, and full-time defender of republican ideals. Cicero was deeply influenced by Greek thought, especially the ideas of Plato and Aristotle, but he merged these with distinctly Roman practicality. He was a tireless advocate for the rule of law, civic virtue, and the idea that certain laws were universal—grounded not in the whims of rulers but in *natural law*[13], derived from reason and justice. Cicero believed in the balance of power and was deeply concerned with the erosion of the Roman Republic, which he witnessed firsthand.

- Mixed Government: Like Aristotle, Cicero champi-

---

13. And no, this is not the Natural Law that the Mango Carter bunch think they're referring to when donning their tin-foil hats.

oned the idea of a balanced government—a mix of democracy, aristocracy, and monarchy. This was intended to prevent any one faction from gaining total control and to ensure that power was distributed in a way that kept the state stable. Cicero's mixed government can be seen as a precursor to modern checks and balances, where different branches of government work together (or, as often happens, against each other) to keep any one person or group from dominating. If he were around today, Cicero would probably be on CNN warning about the dangers of populism and the need to preserve the Republic.

- Civic Virtue: For Cicero, the wellbeing of the state rested on the virtue of its citizens. He believed that the health of a republic depended on the moral integrity and active participation of the people. If citizens neglected their civic duties or allowed corruption to flourish, the republic would fall. For Cicero, politics wasn't just about power—it was about justice, virtue, and the common good. The problem, of course, was that Cicero's lofty ideals were constantly undermined by the reality of Roman politics, where ambition and self-interest usually won the day.

In modern Italy, where political leaders often rely on populism and opportunistic alliances, Cicero's insistence on civic virtue and balanced governance might seem like a distant dream. Yet, his warning about the fragility of republics in the face of corruption and apathy feels strikingly relevant as Italy grapples with its own political instability and the rise of far-right movements.

Each of these philosophers, from Plato's idealism to Cicero's Roman pragmatism, offers lessons that still resonate today. Their writings are more than just historical footnotes—they're blueprints (and sometimes cautionary tales) for how we think about power, governance, and the role of citizens in shaping so-

ciety. They may not have had all the answers, but their questions
are just as important now as they were thousands of years ago.

Final Stop: Relevance Today (Or, Why We're Still Talking About These Dead Philosophers)

So, why do these ancient thinkers still matter[14]? Why, in a world
dominated by Brexit hangovers, populist leaders, and crises over
climate change, are we still discussing philosophers who lived
thousands of years ago in togas and sandals? The answer is
surprisingly simple: these ancient philosophers laid the intellectual foundations for almost everything we know about political
theory today. Whether it's Plato's utopian dreaming, Aristotle's
balanced governance, or Cicero's insistence on the rule of law,
their ideas have shaped modern politics in ways we often take
for granted.

Take the United States Constitution, for example. The
Founding Fathers weren't just influenced by Enlightenment
thinkers—they were directly inspired by Cicero and Aristotle. The system of checks and balances that defines American
governance today is a direct nod to the Roman Republic and
Aristotle's belief in mixed government—a structure designed
to prevent any one branch from becoming too powerful. Fear
of tyranny, whether from a monarch or a demagogue, was a
preoccupation of both Aristotle and Cicero, and the Founding
Fathers sought to mitigate those dangers by distributing power
carefully.

But let's not get too caught up in America. Here in the UK,
we don't have to look far to see the relevance of these ancient
ideas. For instance, Plato's fears about democracy devolving
into mob rule became eerily real during the Brexit referendum.
Plato, ever the sceptic of democracy, worried that the masses,

---

14. Or rather, why have you had to read through nearly 4,000 words of me
nattering on endlessly.

driven by emotion and manipulated by demagogues, would make disastrous decisions[15]. The referendum and its chaotic aftermath—fuelled by misinformation, emotional appeals to sovereignty, and populist rhetoric—would be a perfect case study for Plato's concerns. The promises of Brexit—a simpler, more sovereign Britain—quickly gave way to economic uncertainty and political turmoil, much of which we're still trying to navigate today.

Then there's the rise of populism across the world. Right across the world, we're seeing a worrying resurgence of demagogues who stoke fear and resentment, offering simplistic solutions to complex issues. This was exactly the kind of leadership that Aristotle warned about. Aristotle believed that a healthy state must avoid the extremes of tyranny and mob rule, advocating for a middle ground—a polity that serves the common good, not just the whims of a charismatic leader or the emotional outbursts of the masses. The current political climate, with its polarised debates and rise of nationalist movements, shows that Aristotle's warnings about the fragility of balanced governance are just as relevant now as they were in ancient Greece.

But let's bring this back to the present day here in the UK, where the Labour Party is now in power after the Conservatives' long reign was finally cut short in the recent general election. After years of austerity measures, Brexit upheavals, and the mishandling of public services, the UK finds itself in a moment of profound political change. Keir Starmer's Labour government has promised to rebuild public trust, invest in the NHS, and address the growing economic divide—echoing Cicero's concerns for civic virtue and the idea that the health of a republic depends on the moral integrity of its leaders and active participation from its citizens.

While Labour's rise to power may signal a shift in policy and tone, the ancient concerns about governance remain. Brexit's

---

15. No shit, Sherlock.

long shadow still looms over the country, with questions of sovereignty, trade, and international relations far from settled. The UK, much like ancient Rome in its later days, is grappling with internal divisions, regional autonomy, and a sense of national identity that has been severely tested. Scotland's push for another independence referendum brings us back to Aristotle's warnings about the dangers of fragmentation within a polity. Aristotle believed that when different regions or factions begin to pursue their own interests at the expense of the whole, the unity of the state is at risk—something that the UK is currently navigating with great difficulty.

In many ways, the challenges the UK faces now are exactly the kinds of issues that Plato, Aristotle, and Cicero were trying to address. Plato's fear of populism, Aristotle's emphasis on moderation, and Cicero's insistence on the rule of law and civic responsibility all resonate in today's political landscape. As Labour seeks to rebuild the country after years of division, the ancient debates about how to balance power, maintain justice, and preserve unity are as pressing as ever.

So, let's go back to the original question of why we're still talking about these dead philosophers. Because they gave us the tools to think critically about our political systems and to ask the right questions: How do we prevent democracy from being undermined by populist rhetoric? How do we ensure that our leaders act for the common good, not just their own self-interest? And how do we navigate the complexities of a fractured political landscape while maintaining a sense of shared purpose?

Political theory may have started in the dusty streets of Athens and Rome, but its legacy continues to shape our world[16]. These ancient philosophers didn't have all the answers (as evidenced by the fact that we're still debating many of the same issues),

---

16. And that's why, 2,000 years later, we're still reading dead guys in togas—and realising they had more to say about today's problems than we'd like to admit.

but they laid the foundation for us to keep asking the important questions. And as the UK moves forward, grappling with the realities of post-Brexit politics, regional autonomy, and the fight against inequality, their insights are more relevant than ever.

Medieval Political Thought

Where It All Fell Apart

"The Study of philosophy is not that we may know what men have thought, but what the truth of things is."

St. Thomas Aquinas

N ow, after that slapdash tour into ancient political thoughts, let's set our time machine to a little bit into the future to the grand and intricate saga of medieval political thought, a time when political power was woven from the very fabric of divinity and swordplay. Imagine a world where the church spires loom tall over every town and the castle walls encircle the very heart of authority. The landscape is not just physical but ideological, shaped by a near-unshakable belief in the divine order. In this world, to question the king was not simply to challenge a man, but to defy the very will of God Himself—a risk few were willing to take[1].

---

1. Understandable, considering that even your stew getting burnt was God punishing you – and that's when you hadn't even done anything wrong!

The Middle Ages were more than just an era of knights, kings, and crusades[2]; they were a period of profound tension between earthly power and heavenly authority, where political legitimacy wasn't merely a matter of governance but of divine favour. It was a time when monarchs ruled by God's grace, and the Pope, as God's earthly representative, had the power to legitimise or topple entire kingdoms. The concept of divine right meant that kings wielded their power with the authority of heaven, and to defy them was not just an act of rebellion but an act of heresy. In many ways, politics during this era was a spiritual battleground as much as it was a secular one.

Just imagine the complexity: on one hand, monarchs striving to maintain their grip on the throne through military might, alliances, and the occasional strategic marriage; on the other, religious leaders wielding the threat of excommunication like a political weapon. To be cast out from the Church was not just a personal condemnation—it could destabilise entire realms, leaving rulers isolated and vulnerable. And let's not forget the nobility, ever so eager to expand their influence through a web of vassalage, treaties, and, of course, the sharp edge of a well-placed dagger[3].

And yet, amidst the grandeur and violence, there was also a fragile, delicate balance that underpinned medieval political life. At its core was the belief that society was an organic, hierarchical whole, with every class—be they king, knight, or peasant—playing a role in maintaining order. It was a world obsessed with social harmony, built on the idea that each stratum of society had its place, ordained by God, in the great chain of being. Upset this balance, and chaos would *surely* follow.

We're about to embark on a semi-epic journey through this tangled web of monarchy, feudalism, and religious authority.

---

2. And many, many diseases and back-to-back apocalypses.

3. Whiffs of the previous chapter coming through here.

Prepare to witness political philosophies that were as much about maintaining cosmic order as they were about maintaining control over territory. Kings drew their power from God's divine will, and the Church's influence stretched across continents, subjugating even the most powerful rulers to its will. To question either was not just dangerous; it was unthinkable.

So, strap on your metaphorical armour and prepare to traverse a world where divine favour, military strength, and feudal allegiances delightfully intertwined to form the very fabric of medieval political life. A world where power was both material and metaphysical, and where the stakes were nothing less than the salvation of one's soul.

The Epic Struggle: Church vs. State

If you think politics today is a bunfight of epic proportions, you should have *seen* medieval Europe in action. The relationship between the Church and the monarchy wasn't just a political partnership; it was more like a dysfunctional marriage, complete with whispered plots, power struggles, and the occasional full-blown betrayal. At the heart of medieval political life was the age-old question: who *really* held the ultimate authority—the king, anointed by God to rule over earthly matters, or the Pope, God's official rep, who wielded the spiritual power to decide the fate of kings, kingdoms, and everyone else?[4]

The Church wasn't merely concerned with saving souls; it was one of *the* most powerful political forces in Europe, often wielding more influence than kings. The Pope was the medieval equivalent of a political kingmaker. He had the power to excommunicate rulers, effectively severing their ties with God and leaving them politically isolated. The Pope could also deny or annul royal marriages, which was pretty much like vetoing your ruler's succession plans in medieval terms. And when it came

---

4. Spoiler alert: They were both convinced they were in charge.

to anointing kings, the Pope's approval was the final stamp of legitimacy. Imagine the Pope as your overly meddling in-law[5], constantly sticking his nose into the state's business but with the added ability to damn you to eternal fire. Nice.

The kings, on the other hand, weren't exactly powerless. They claimed their authority through the doctrine of divine right, but it came with strings attached—namely, the Church's approval. If a monarch fell out of favour with the Pope, he could quickly find his rule crumbling. Without the Church's blessing, rebellious barons might question his legitimacy, and before you know it, the crown is looking awfully shaky. For medieval rulers, the Church wasn't just an ally; it was a necessary partner in maintaining control. You could have all the knights and castles in the world, but without the Pope's favour, you might find yourself playing a rather perilous game of *"king or sinner?"*

The power struggle between Church and state wasn't just about who got the best seat at banquets—it was about the very nature of authority. Who held sway over the souls of the people? Who could claim the ultimate right to rule? The Pope, with his heavenly mandate, or the king, God's chosen ruler on Earth? This conflict was at the heart of medieval political life, culminating in epic confrontations like the Investiture Controversy—that time when Pope Gregory VII and Emperor Henry IV engaged in political theatre so dramatic, it makes *Love Island* look positively tame. At its core, it was a power struggle over who got to appoint bishops: the Pope (because, well, God) or the Emperor (because, naturally, swords).

Things escalated when Henry, assuming he was the main character, defied Pope Gregory's authority. In response, Gregory excommunicated him—essentially telling the Emperor, "You're not invited to heaven, hun." Not to be outdone, Henry retaliated by calling Gregory a "false monk" and trying to replace him.

---

5. No, really, darling, you should marry him. It's what God wants. And if you don't, well... let's just say I hope you like hellfire.

This all led to Henry's infamous Walk to Canossa, where he spent three days grovelling outside Gregory's residence, waiting in the snow for forgiveness—a reminder that even emperors sometimes need a good PR recovery plan. It wasn't just about crowns and sceptres; this was a battle over who held the keys to both earthly power and eternal salvation.

Fast forward to the modern era, and while the battle between Church and state has evolved, the echoes of this medieval struggle still persist. Today, the separation of Church and state is enshrined in many democracies, particularly in Western Europe, where the role of religion in politics has been drastically reduced. In the UK, for example, the Church of England exists but plays a largely ceremonial (and very misunderstood) role, while the monarchy, stripped of most real political power, watches from the sidelines. The idea that the Pope could excommunicate the Prime Minister and throw Parliament into chaos now seems ridiculous—but in the Middle Ages, that's *exactly* what could have happened – and it did.

However, the tension between religious authority and state power hasn't disappeared entirely. In countries like the United States, religious leaders still wield significant influence, particularly in matters like abortion rights, same-sex marriage, and education policies. Even in the UK, though far more secular, religion can still creep into political discourse, particularly in debates over immigration or moral policies. The question of who holds the moral high ground, much like in the Middle Ages, is still up for debate—just with far fewer excommunications[6] and so many more parliamentary votes.

---

6. These days, being excommunicated by the Pope just means you won't get a Christmas card from the Vatican. Less fire, more "I'm very disappointed in you."

The (Very Convenient) Divine Right of Kings

"Hear Ye, Hear Ye, my good people! Gather close, for today we speak of the sacred and most holy truth: the divine right of our beloved king to rule over us all. For did not the Almighty Himself, in all His wisdom and infinite grace, part the very heavens and place upon the royal brow that gleaming crown of legitimacy? Yes, it is true, for kings are not mere men like thee and me. Nay, they are chosen—handpicked—by the Lord Almighty, for it is written that the king's authority comes not from the squabbles of men, but from the divine will of God Himself! And who, I ask, amongst thee dares to question the will of God[7] ? Who among ye, humble as you are, could ever dream of contesting the decisions of the Divine? Raise not thy hand, for to question the king is to question the very foundations of heaven. And that, dear peasants, would be most unwise."

Now, all this divine right business wasn't just a convenient tool for kings to keep the common folk in line—it was pretty much the ideological bedrock of medieval political thought. According to this sacred doctrine, kings ruled because they had indeed been *chosen by God*[8] . No elections, no campaigns, and certainly no pesky votes from the peasants. Instead, monarchs were believed to have been divinely selected to reign, anointed by both the Church and the heavens above. This granted them absolute authority over their subjects and an unassailable claim to power. And, as one might expect, this came with all the perks of a royal lifestyle, free from the inconvenience of having to justify their decisions to mere mortals.

---

7. Let's be honest, back then, no one really had a choice but to nod along and hope they weren't struck by lightning—or worse, the king's soldiers.

8. I mean, how do you actually disprove this?

But here's where it gets truly interesting (or infuriating, depending on your perspective): The divine right of kings effectively gave monarchs carte blanche to do as they pleased. Whether it was raising taxes, declaring wars, or building themselves yet another lavish palace, kings could point to divine favour as justification for every decision they made[9]. After all, if God had chosen them, then surely their actions were part of His grand design, right? And if anyone dared to argue, well, they weren't just rebelling against the king, were they—they were rebelling against God's *will itself*.

Of course, this wasn't just about kings enjoying the fruits of unchecked power. The Church played its part too. Kings needed the Church's approval to maintain this celestial narrative. After all, what's a divine mandate without the endorsement of God's earthly representatives? The bishops and popes were more than happy to provide that endorsement—as long as the king stayed in line and remembered who had the power to bless (or curse) his reign. If a monarch got too big for his boots, the Pope always had the nuclear option: excommunication, which was essentially the medieval equivalent of being *"cancelled,"* but with a far more dramatic flair[10]. Not only would the excommunicated ruler lose the loyalty of his subjects, but he'd also be left pondering his eternal fate in the afterlife.

But let's not pretend it was all smooth sailing for the kings. Sure, there were some moral obligations that came with this divine favour. Kings were supposed to act justly and govern for the good of their people. They were expected to protect the Church, uphold the law (as much as it suited them), and wage the occasional holy war or two when required. But really, these moral expectations were more like guidelines than actual

---

9. "Yes, I am raising taxes to build that seventh castle. It's what God wants. Trust me."

10. Small suggestion: Can we refer to *"Cancel Culture"* as *"Excommunication Culture"* from now on? Please and thank you.

rules. After all, who was going to argue with a monarch backed by both the sword *and* the cross? The peasants? Hardly. The nobility? Well, only if they fancied a trip to the gallows.

The doctrine of divine right also came in handy when things went wrong. Was the harvest bad this year? Were there rumours of rebellion among the barons? Was the treasury looking a little thin after financing that really ill-advised war with the neighbouring kingdom? Fear not! It wasn't poor leadership or misguided policies—it was clearly a test from God[11]! Monarchs could frame any hardship or disaster as part of the divine plan, a way to remind their subjects that even when things were tough, their king was God's chosen leader, and to follow him was to follow the will of the Almighty.

And so, the peasants, with no other choice, would nod and accept their fate, all the while knowing that to challenge the divine right of kings was to risk eternal damnation. Absolutely no one wanted that, so the system endured for centuries. It was, in many ways, the ultimate power play—a fusion of politics and religion that ensured kings and the Church stayed in control, all while the masses toiled away, believing that every decree from the throne was not just law but divine decree.

But here's the thing: no one ever actually stopped to ask God whether He (or She) really wanted that particular monarch in charge. The divine right of kings was an entirely one-sided conversation, where the kings did the talking and conveniently assumed that God's response was always, *"Yes, absolutely. You, my child. Yes, the one with the hat and panoply of genetic disorders. You are the chosen one."*

---

11. And this was during a pretty bad period for her, so She was in a mood and not taking shit from anyone.

The Thinkers: Augustine and Aquinas – Saints with Swords

Medieval political thought wasn't all about kings sitting on gilded thrones or popes whispering divine instructions into the ears of monarchs. No, behind the throne (and occasionally in front of it) were the thinkers—the theologians who wrestled with the grand questions of human nature, divine order, and the purpose of earthly governments. Enter two of the most influential minds of the medieval world: Augustine and Thomas Aquinas. These men didn't just write about political theory—they shaped the way rulers and clergy alike thought about governance, justice, and the divine balance between heaven and earth. Their ideas, forged in the fires of philosophy and theology, would echo through the halls of medieval courts and beyond.

Augustine: The Pessimist with a Plan

Before he became the saintly father of Christian thought, Augustine of Hippo lived a rather colourful life that would make any reality TV star blush[12]. He spent his youth dabbling in pleasures of the flesh, embracing hedonism with the kind of enthusiasm usually reserved for a 24-hour feast. But after converting to Christianity, Augustine's worldview took a dramatic turn. He became the ultimate theological realist—perhaps the original political pessimist—believing that human nature was fundamentally flawed and that earthly governments, no matter how grand or righteous, were doomed to be imperfect reflections of a broken world.

In his magnum opus, *"City of God"*, Augustine painted a stark picture of two competing realms: the *City of Man*, where sin,

---

12. Though maybe not the Tangerine one – that one has no shame.

corruption, and ambition ruled[13] , and the *City of God*, a perfect, divine order that existed beyond the flawed reality of human governance. For Augustine, the best a government could hope to achieve was a kind of rough justice—a necessary evil that restrained humanity's worst impulses. No matter how hard kings or emperors tried, they would never achieve a perfect society, because, in Augustine's view, original sin had tainted every human institution.

- Earthly City vs. City of God: Augustine saw the world as divided between these two cities. The *City of Man* was governed by flawed, self-interested rulers who acted out of greed and ambition, while the *City of God* was a divine kingdom ruled by virtue and love. For Augustine, true Christians should pledge their loyalty not to earthly kings, but to the heavenly city, where eternal justice reigned. This perspective didn't exactly inspire confidence in earthly governments, but it did reinforce the idea that the Church had a divine role in guiding worldly rulers. After all, who better to nudge kings in the right direction than those who had one foot in the celestial city?

- Original Sin and Politics: Augustine's concept of *original sin* was political dynamite. If humans were inherently sinful, then no human institution—no matter how well-intentioned—could *ever* be free from corruption. Governments, Augustine argued, were a necessary evil designed to keep sinful human nature in check, but they were inherently flawed. This was a critical shift in medieval political thought, as it gave the Church a crucial role: it was the only institution capable of overcoming humanity's sinful tendencies, at least in theory[14] . The Church, therefore, had the divine knowledge needed to guide rulers and kings,

---

13. Like Westminster, but nicer.

making it indispensable in the political arena.

Thomas Aquinas: The Optimist Who Loved Aristotle

While Augustine was brooding over humanity's fallen state, along came Thomas Aquinas, with a much sunnier outlook on both human nature and political life. If Augustine was the pessimist who thought earthly power was inherently corrupt, Aquinas was the optimist[15] who believed that reason and divine will could actually coexist in a well-ordered society. Aquinas, a Dominican friar and philosopher, took many of Aristotle's ideas and gave them a Christian twist, merging Greek rationalism with Christian theology. The result? A political framework that not only emphasised moral duties but also allowed for a rational, orderly structure of governance. If Augustine was the medieval prophet of doom, Aquinas was its philosophical cheerleader.

- Natural Law: For Aquinas, the laws of the universe weren't just divine commands—they were based on *reason*. Drawing from Aristotle's natural law theory, Aquinas argued that human laws should be rooted in the eternal law of God, which governed the natural order. Any law that went against natural law, Aquinas argued, was no law at all. This was a radical idea in medieval times, suggesting that rulers couldn't just make any decree they pleased; their laws had to align with God's eternal truths. It's a bit like saying today's politicians can't just make up new rules—there's a higher order that they have to follow. Except instead of a UN Charter, Aquinas pointed to divine law.

- Just War Theory: In an era where everyone seemed to

---

15. Aquinas' optimism is like assuming your favourite politician can both act in your best interest and never lie... We'll wait.

be fighting someone else (usually with a holy banner flying above the battlefield), Aquinas developed his famous Just War Theory. War, he argued, could only be morally justified if it met certain criteria: it had to be declared by a legitimate authority (a king or pope), there had to be a *just cause* (such as defending the realm), and the violence used must be *proportional*. In other words, kings couldn't just throw armies around like toys—they had to have a moral justification for their campaigns. This was a big deal in medieval Europe, where knights and kings were often looking for any excuse to wage war. Aquinas's ideas would influence military ethics for centuries, even forming the basis for modern international law on warfare.

- Moral Obligations of Rulers: Aquinas believed that rulers had a *moral duty* to govern justly and for the *common good*. Tyranny, in his view, was a perversion of political authority and had to be resisted. Aquinas's optimism about human nature meant that he believed rulers could be virtuous and that societies could be governed by reason and morality. His writings laid the groundwork for later political thought, especially in the development of constitutional law and human rights.

Feudalism and the Divine Right of Kings: The Medieval Pyramid Scheme

Now, let's not forget about the real business model of the Middle Ages: *feudalism*. If you've ever wondered what it might have been like to live in a medieval pyramid scheme, feudalism was the answer—except instead of selling diet supplements and cosmetic products, it was all about land, loyalty, and military service. Here's how the scheme worked:

- King at the Top: At the very top was the king, who claimed *divine favour* and thus ultimate authority. He handed out vast amounts of land to his loyal nobles in exchange for their loyalty and, more importantly, their *military service*. The king got the land and soldiers, and the nobles got to rule their own little fiefdoms. Everybody (at the top) won.

- Nobles and Vassals: The nobles didn't stop there, though. They subdivided their land, granting it to vassals in exchange for loyalty and service. This feudal hierarchy continued downward until you reached the serfs, who actually worked the land, doing all the labour in exchange for a tiny patch to call their own[16]
.

- Land for Loyalty: In essence, feudalism was less about governance and more about survival in a fragmented world. Land was the currency of power, and the king's ability to distribute it kept the system running. In return, the nobles provided knights and soldiers, ensuring that the kingdom had a functioning military—well, most of the time.

The Legacy of Medieval Political Thought

At first glance, the political structures of the Middle Ages might seem like relics of a distant past—feudal hierarchies, kings ruling by divine right, and a Church with the power to anoint monarchs or excommunicate them. Yet, as archaic as these structures may seem, their influence still permeates our political and social systems today, albeit in subtler forms.

Take feudalism, for example. While we no longer exchange land for loyalty and military service[17], the hierarchical nature of

---

16. Spoiler: the serfs did *not* win in this arrangement.

17. Most of us don't anyway.

feudal society—where everyone had their place, from kings to serfs—finds echoes in modern institutions. Think about the way corporate structures work today: CEOs at the top, middle management in the middle, and the workers at the bottom doing the heavy lifting. The idea of loyalty to superiors and knowing one's place in a hierarchy is still deeply embedded in the modern workplace, albeit dressed up in terms like *"team dynamics"* and *"corporate ladders."* Much like the medieval serfs who were expected to labour for their lords in exchange for protection, workers today often put in long hours for the promise of a paycheque and the vague hope of climbing that ladder to a better position.

Additionally, the legacy of the divine right of kings might sound even more absurd in today's democratic age. Who could imagine the Prime Minister claiming that their authority comes directly from God? And yet, the concept of sovereignty, which was once wrapped in divine legitimacy, still underpins so much of modern political discourse. In the UK, discussions about sovereignty came roaring back during the Brexit debates, as political leaders invoked the idea of reclaiming control from the European Union. Though no one was claiming divine favour, the underlying question of who holds legitimate authority—and by what right—remains a key issue in modern politics.

Moreover, the UK's constitutional monarchy still carries traces of the medieval world. While the monarchy today is largely ceremonial, the monarch's symbolic role as the head of state, and the reverence many hold for the institution, harks back to centuries of royal authority. The Queen or King may no longer wield the power of life and death over their subjects, but the pomp and ceremony surrounding the Crown—including the coronation, which involves anointing the monarch with holy oil[18] —keeps the faint echo of the divine right alive, even if only in a symbolic sense.

---

18. And a cheeky Bank holiday.

As we moved beyond the Middle Ages, the influence of the Church on political life began to falter and wane, but its role in shaping moral and ethical discourse remains significant. The Church may no longer have the power to excommunicate a politician[19], but questions of morality, particularly those framed by religious belief, still feature in public debates. In the UK, for example, the Church of England plays a role in the national conversation, from its involvement in House of Lords debates to its commentary on issues like immigration, social justice, and poverty. Though the political power of the Church has diminished, its influence over cultural and moral discourse continues to shape policy and public opinion.

The slow decline of theocratic and feudal systems in the UK paved the way for the rise of secular ideas that began to chip away at the authority of the monarchy and the Church alike. This shift became particularly evident during the English Civil War and the subsequent Glorious Revolution[20], which challenged the absolute power of the monarchy and laid the foundations for constitutional government. These events, while far removed from the Middle Ages, were direct responses to the legacy of medieval political thought, particularly the notion that authority, whether divine or secular, must be accountable to the people.

Today's political landscape, with its focus on representative democracy, human rights, and checks on power, owes much to the gradual evolution of ideas that began in the medieval period. The medieval struggle between Church and state, the attempts to balance earthly and divine power, and the gradual move towards more accountable governance have all left their mark. Even as the modern world embraces secularism and democra-

---

19. Though I would be keen to see what Justin Welby would do if he did have this sort of power.

20. The Glorious Revolution: where the British decided they'd quite like their monarchs to have a *bit* less divine wrath and a *bit* more Parliamentary oversight.

cy, the debates about authority, legitimacy, and the balance of power between rulers and the ruled remain as relevant as ever.

Before we leave the Middle Ages behind, let's remember this: medieval politics wasn't just about kings sitting on thrones or bishops wielding crosses. It was about power—how it's acquired, justified, and maintained. The fusion of divine and earthly authority, the creation of rigid hierarchies, and the constant balancing act between rulers and the ruled are themes that have never truly left us. The medieval world may have been cloaked in the language of religion and royal grandeur, but at its heart were the same political struggles we see today. Power, in all its divine, earthly, and occasionally absurd forms, remains the ultimate game.

Secular Political Thought

Where It All Pulled Itself Together Again (Sort Of)

> "Men should be either treated generously or destroyed, because they take revenge for slight injuries - for heavy ones they cannot."
>
> Niccolò Machiavelli

P icture a bustling Renaissance café, tucked away on a cobbled street in Florence. The walls are adorned with rich frescoes, depicting scenes from ancient Rome, while heavy velvet drapes frame the windows, casting a soft glow over the polished wooden tables. The scent of freshly ground coffee beans mingles with the warm aroma of baking bread and the faint sweetness of burning candles. It's the 16th century, but there's an air of revolution in the air—not just in the arts and sciences, but in politics and philosophy. This isn't your run-of-the-mill café, and the company is anything but ordinary.

Seated at a corner table are four of the greatest minds of political thought, drawn together by a shared passion for ideas, but divided in their visions of the world. Machiavelli, ever the pragmatist, sits back, drumming his fingers on the table impatiently, his dark eyes scanning the room as though assessing everyone's usefulness. He sips wine, red and bold—perfectly matching his take-no-prisoners philosophy. Next to him sits John Locke, the idealist, gesticulating passionately as he explains his belief in natural rights. Locke's drink of choice is, of course, a refined cup of tea, a reflection of his measured optimism. Across from him, Hobbes sits in the shadows, grumbling about the futility of it all, his hands wrapped around a dark ale, as if preparing to drown his pessimism. And at the end of the table is Rousseau, leaning forward with a dreamy, almost fervent look in his eyes. A glass of wine, but lighter than Machiavelli's, sits before him as he awaits his moment to wax lyrical about the general will.

The café buzzes around them—merchants, poets, and scholars pass through, but the real drama is unfolding at their table.

Machiavelli: "Power, gentlemen. The world is nothing without it. Rulers who cling to virtue and morality over necessity? They don't survive. One must be feared to be respected. Politics isn't about being loved; it's about being effective."

He taps his fingers impatiently on his wine glass, as if waiting for the others to catch up to the grim realities of the world he so effortlessly accepts. Machiavelli, after all, knows the game of politics is ruthless—he wrote the rulebook.

Locke (sighing): "You see, Niccolò, that's where you miss the point. Power without consent is tyranny. A ruler who governs through fear governs in chains, not strength. The natural state of man is one of liberty, life, and property. Government exists to protect these rights, not to crush them."

Locke's voice is calm, but there's a passion underlying his words—a quiet, but unshakable conviction that the purpose of governance is to uplift, not suppress. He believes in the goodness of man, in a system where freedom and rights are intrinsic, not granted by rulers. A deep believer in social contracts, Locke can't help but see Machiavelli's realism as a dark view of humanity.

Hobbes (grumbling): "Liberty? Rights? Mere fantasies, Locke. You're naïve. Man is inherently selfish and brutish. Without a strong sovereign—a Leviathan—to keep them in check, they'll tear each other apart. Life is nasty, brutish, and short without order. Forget your social contracts. What's needed is power. Control. Absolute authority."

Hobbes shifts uncomfortably in his seat, his voice low and foreboding. He has seen what chaos looks like, and he's not eager to return to it. In Hobbes's world, order is sacred, and only a powerful, unyielding government can keep society from descending into anarchy. He looks at Locke with a kind of bemused irritation, as though Locke's hope for humanity is a quaint, but misguided, relic of the past.

Rousseau (leaning forward with a twinkle in his eye): "Ah, you all overthink it. It's simple. The people must govern themselves through the general will. Only when individuals come together, surrendering their individual desires to the collective good, can they find true freedom. You speak of liberty, Locke, but what you miss is that true liberty is found not in individualism, but in collective action."

Rousseau's voice is impassioned, full of conviction. To him, society isn't built on protecting individual rights but on finding harmony in collective unity. He glances around the table, confident that his vision of democracy—where the people themselves rule—will prevail. It's an idealistic, almost utopian vision of the world, but one he believes is worth fighting for.

The debate continues, growing more intense as each thinker elaborates on his views. Machiavelli argues that ideals are fine, but they must take a back seat to the realities of power and survival. Locke counters that power, if unchecked, will always lead to oppression, and that freedom is the only true foundation of a just society. Hobbes shakes his head, muttering about chaos and the natural state of man, while Rousseau insists that the answer lies in the people themselves—governance must come from the collective will, not from the top.

The conversation lingers, drifting from the practical to the philosophical, as they navigate their differing views on human nature, power, and governance. What unites them all, despite their deep disagreements, is the recognition that the world is no longer ruled by kings anointed by divine right, but by men who must grapple with how to balance secular power and individual freedom. Theirs is a debate that transcends time, and though the café may be Renaissance Florence, the ideas they're shaping will ripple through history into the very fabric of modern political systems.

As the conversation unfolds, it's easy to imagine how each thinker might view the politics of today. Would Machiavelli have a role advising political leaders on strategic manoeuvres? Would Locke be drafting human rights charters for the UN? And Hobbes? Perhaps he'd be writing the script for a dystopian Netflix series, showing the bleak consequences of too much freedom[1].

Timeline of Thought: The Evolution of Ideas

Let's take a step back and trace the slow, but inevitable, rise of modern thought after the exceptionally religious period that we discussed in the previous chapter. It was a journey that began with the dominance of the Church and monarchy and gradually gave way to secularism, individualism, and the principles of democracy. The shift didn't happen overnight—it was a slow burn over centuries, punctuated by both triumphs and tragedies. From the intellectual rebirth of the Renaissance to the revolutionary fervour of the Enlightenment, these key periods transformed the way we think about governance, society, and the individual.

---

1. Imagine this debate happening on Twitter today - Locke would be trending with #HumanRights, Hobbes with #LeviathanRules, and Machiavelli would probably be offering his services as a political consultant for whoever pays the most.

The Renaissance (14th to 17th centuries)

The Renaissance wasn't just an explosion of art and culture; it was a reawakening of ideas. Classical philosophy, humanism, and a renewed interest in science and reason began to challenge the centuries-old dominance of the divine right of kings and the Church's monopoly on truth. As Europe rediscovered the works of ancient Greece and Rome, thinkers began to emphasise human potential and the idea that man—rather than being subject to divine decree—had the capacity for reason and self-governance.

During this time, Machiavelli emerged as one of the most influential figures in political thought. In his work, *"The Prince"*, he offered a pragmatic and, some would argue, cynical view of politics, advocating for rulers to prioritise power and stability over morality. Machiavelli's ideas laid the groundwork for the modern understanding of statecraft—a sharp departure from the medieval notion that rulers derived their authority solely from God.

Meanwhile, Leonardo da Vinci was sketching his visions of the future, from flying machines to anatomical studies that put the Church's views on human nature to shame. This was also the period when Copernicus shook the very foundations of religious and scientific belief by daring to propose that the Earth revolves around the Sun—an idea that, at the time, seemed nothing short of blasphemous.

Elsewhere in the World: While Europe was busy rediscovering ancient philosophy, the Aztec Empire was flourishing in Mesoamerica. By the early 16th century, Tenochtitlán, the capital, was one of the largest cities in the world, with advanced systems of agriculture, trade, and architecture—until the Spanish arrived and, well, ruined everything.

The Enlightenment (17th to 18th centuries)

If the Renaissance was the spark, the Enlightenment was the bonfire that transformed not just Europe, but the world. With the rise of reason, science, and the pursuit of knowledge, political thought underwent a seismic shift towards individual rights, the role of government, and the rejection of traditional authority.

Philosophers such as Voltaire, Kant, and Diderot championed the idea that human beings could reason their way to a better society. They rejected the idea that kings ruled by divine right and instead argued that rational thought should govern political life. Voltaire's biting wit took aim at religious intolerance and monarchical tyranny, while Kant pondered the ethical implications of living in a world governed by reason, coining the famous phrase, *"Dare to know!"*

Meanwhile, Isaac Newton was busy redefining how we understand the universe, publishing his laws of motion and universal gravitation. Newton's work paralleled the Enlightenment's belief in natural law—the idea that the world, and by extension society, operated on knowable, rational principles. The concept of governance by consent began to take hold, with thinkers like John Locke arguing that governments must protect the natural rights of life, liberty, and property or risk being overthrown.

While Europe's intellectuals were debating reason, science, and individual rights, another radical shift was brewing in the world of commerce. The 17th century saw the rise of the Dutch East India Company, a corporation so powerful it could declare war, colonise lands, and negotiate treaties. Global trade routes were established, and the wealth of nations began to shift, laying the groundwork for modern capitalism.

Elsewhere in the World: While Enlightenment thinkers were busy philosophising about rights and reason, the Ming Dynasty was thriving in China. The Great Wall of China was fortified, and Zheng He's treasure fleets were charting new territories across the Indian Ocean and beyond. Meanwhile, Japan, under the Tokugawa shogunate, had just begun its policy of isolation, closing its borders to almost all foreigners for over two centuries.

Political Revolutions: American and French

By the late 18th century, Enlightenment ideas had gone from theory to reality in the form of two monumental revolutions: the American Revolution of 1776 and the French Revolution of 1789. These events weren't just political upheavals—they were direct manifestations of Enlightenment thought, where monarchies and feudal structures were rejected in favour of representative government, social contracts, and equality before the law.

The American Revolution was driven by Locke's ideals of natural rights and government by consent. Colonists rebelled against British rule, invoking the belief that government should serve the people, not exploit them. The resulting Declaration of Independence became a powerful expression of Enlightenment values, enshrining the right to life, liberty, and the pursuit of happiness.

Just over a decade later, the French Revolution turned these ideas into a bloody spectacle[2]. The French, inspired by thinkers like Rousseau and Montesquieu, sought to overthrow a corrupt monarchy and establish a republic based on the general will and popular sovereignty. The revolution gave birth to the Declaration of the Rights of Man and of the Citizen, which became a

---

2. The Enlightenment thinkers probably didn't envision their works inspiring revolutionaries to storm palaces with pitchforks and guillotines, but hey-ho, ideas have consequences.

beacon of hope for future democratic movements around the world.

And yet, as often happens, the aftermath of both revolutions was messier than their intellectual origins. In America, the Constitution emerged as a balancing act between liberty and governance, with federalism creating a system that allowed states to retain certain powers while central authority was strengthened. In France, the revolution descended into the Reign of Terror, where guillotines claimed the heads of those deemed enemies of the republic—including the very revolutionaries who had led the charge.

Elsewhere in the World: While the Americas and Europe were transforming politically, in India, the Maratha Empire was at its height, fighting against the growing influence of the British East India Company. The 18th century also saw the rise of Napoleon Bonaparte, who, though he claimed to champion the ideals of the French Revolution, crowned himself Emperor of the French in 1804.

Enlightenment hypocrisy, anyone?

Pragmatism vs. Idealism

And so, we return to our earlier conversation with our illustrious gentleman of the time. The café has grown quieter as the evening wears on, with the Renaissance thinkers now deep into their second round of drinks. The earlier conversation had explored the philosophical foundations of their ideas, but now, the discussion has narrowed in on a critical point: the tension between pragmatism and idealism.

The table is divided. Machiavelli sits back, more relaxed now, having asserted his views on power earlier. For him, it's obvious: rulers must do what it takes to survive. Locke, however, is becoming increasingly frustrated by Machiavelli's cold, detached view of humanity. Hobbes remains cynical, as ever, while Rousseau waits, poised to interject with his dream of a collective, harmonious society.

Machiavelli leans forward, his fingers tracing the rim of his wine glass as he speaks, his tone confident and assertive.

Machiavelli: "Governments, Locke, are not born from the idealism you preach. They are forged through action—decisive, sometimes ruthless action. You speak of rights, but rights are meaningless without power to protect them. The survival of the state is the first and only priority of a ruler. A government that hesitates in the face of threats—be they external or internal—will find itself overthrown. We cannot govern with morality alone. We must be practical."

Locke, always the idealist, sets down his tea and looks at Machiavelli with a mixture of sympathy and disdain. He cannot accept the notion that brute force or pragmatic ruthlessness should be the foundation of a government. To him, Machiavelli's philosophy seems like a relic of the past—a world dominated by tyrants.

Locke: "Niccolò, you mistake force for strength. Power without legitimacy is tyranny, and tyranny, while it may last for a time, is never sustainable. A government that does not protect the natural rights of its people—life, liberty, property—will ultimately fall. The consent of the governed is what gives a ruler their true authority, not the fear they inspire. Governments must serve their people, not rule over them."

Locke's idealism is clear, but Machiavelli looks unimpressed. To him, Locke's vision is naïve, too dependent on the goodwill of mankind—something Machiavelli doubts exists in any meaningful sense. Before Machiavelli can respond, Hobbes, who has been listening quietly, finally interjects with a weary sigh.

Hobbes (grumbling): "Neither of you seems to understand the true nature of mankind. Liberty? Consent? They are luxuries in a world ruled by self-interest and brutality. People are inherently selfish, and without a strong, central authority, society collapses into chaos. You speak of rights, Locke, but without a Leviathan to enforce order, those rights mean nothing. And as for you, Machiavelli, you underestimate the depths of human depravity. Even power, once gained, is never secure. Fear may maintain control for a time, but without a firm hand to uphold the law, we are all just animals fighting over scraps."

Hobbes leans back in his chair, his arms crossed, as though daring the others to argue with his bleak vision of human nature. He sees no space for idealism in governance—only control and the relentless pursuit of stability through absolute authority. To Hobbes, life without a strong state is nothing but a war of all against all.

Machiavelli, ever the strategist, gives a slight nod, acknowledging that Hobbes may have a point—though his own views lean more toward manipulation than Hobbes' stark imposition of control. But before he can respond, Rousseau jumps in, his eyes bright with passion, his voice full of conviction.

Rousseau: "You all miss the point! The purpose of government isn't to dominate or even to protect individual rights. It's to serve the common good. True freedom can only be found in the collective will of the people, where individuals set aside their selfish desires for the sake of the greater whole. Machiavelli, your realism leads only to tyranny; Locke, your individualism isolates us from one another; and Hobbes, your fear of chaos blinds you to the potential of humanity. Only when we work together, as a community, can we achieve true liberty."

Rousseau's vision is idealistic—almost utopian. He believes in a society where individuals willingly welcome and work with the general will, finding freedom in unity. His words are a stark contrast to Machiavelli's power politics, Locke's individual rights, and Hobbes' authoritarian vision. The idea that humans could willingly come together to govern themselves is, to Rousseau, the only way forward. But the other thinkers around the table seem sceptical, each caught in their own competing visions of governance.

Key Periods (Brief Comparative Timeline) and The Thinkers of the Time

The ideas of Renaissance and Enlightenment thinkers didn't fade away with the lifetimes of these four gentlemen. Their legacies extend far beyond their eras, laying the foundation for many of the political systems and conflicts we witness today. Let's take a closer look at how their ideas continue to shape the modern world.

Machiavelli

- *Historical Idea*: Pragmatic power, Realpolitik

- *Modern Impact*: Influences modern statecraft and political strategy

- *Ideological Movement*: *Political Realism* (or *Realpolitik*), a precursor to modern political realism and pragmatism in governance.

- *Modern Example*:

  ○ Vladimir Putin is often seen as practicing realpolitik in global relations.

  ○ The Conservative Party in the UK has historically adopted pragmatic approaches to maintaining power.

Machiavelli's work, particularly his treatise "The Prince", remains a defining text in the study of political strategy. His belief that pragmatism and cunning were more valuable than idealism in securing and maintaining power gave rise to what we now call Realpolitik—a political philosophy that prioritises the practical over the moral. Machiavelli argued that rulers should be prepared to use ruthlessness, deceit, and manipulation when necessary but also know when to appear virtuous to maintain public favour.

In today's world, Machiavelli's influence can be seen in the art of political strategy and diplomacy. Leaders still employ his lessons, especially in times of crisis, where the need to maintain power and stability often supersedes questions of morality. Think of the backroom deals, strategic compromises, and political spin we see in modern governments and elections[3]. Whether it's a national leader rallying support for a controversial policy or a political party manipulating the media narrative, the spirit of Machiavelli's ruthless pragmatism lives on.

Modern Impact: Statecraft, geopolitical strategy, and the relentless pursuit of national interests in the international arena owe a great deal to Machiavelli. Even in democratic states, political leaders frequently employ Realpolitik when negotiating foreign policy, particularly in tense international relations where morality takes a back seat to survival. The phrase *"the ends justify the means,"* although often misattributed to Machiavelli, sums up the mindset of many modern politicians.

Hobbes

- *Historical Idea*: Leviathan, sovereignty, control

- *Modern Impact*: Influences ideas of sovereignty, authoritarianism, and national security

- *Ideological Movement*: *Authoritarianism* and *Absolutism*, supporting the need for a strong, centralised power to maintain order and prevent chaos.

- *Modern Example*:

---

3. If Machiavelli were alive today, he'd be managing a political campaign or advising an authoritarian leader on how to stay in power despite tanking approval ratings.

- ○ Donald Trump's administration focused on national security and centralised power, echoing Hobbes' ideas.

- ○ Hungary's Fidesz Party under Viktor Orbán showcases authoritarian tendencies in line with Hobbesian thought.

Thomas Hobbes, with his famously bleak view of human nature, believed that the natural state of mankind was one of chaos and violence. To prevent society from collapsing into anarchy, Hobbes proposed that individuals must submit to an all-powerful sovereign, a Leviathan, who would wield absolute authority to maintain order. In Hobbes's mind, the only way to avoid the war of "every man against every man" was for citizens to surrender their rights to a sovereign who could enforce peace.

In the modern era, Hobbes's ideas about sovereignty and control have deeply influenced debates over authoritarianism and the role of the state in securing national security. The balance between individual freedom and state control remains a central issue in discussions about government surveillance, emergency powers, and the limits of civil liberties during crises. Hobbes's Leviathan finds a modern home in the rationale behind state interventions, where governments justify extreme measures in the name of national security—from the Patriot Act in the United States after 9/11 to emergency powers used during global pandemics.

Modern Impact: Hobbes's vision is alive and well in authoritarian governments, where control and security are prioritised over freedom[4]. Even in democracies, state sovereignty and the need for order are often cited in debates about surveillance, police powers, and the curtailment of civil liberties. When politicians

---

4. Hobbes would probably be a fan of modern surveillance states—after all, what's a bit of privacy invasion if it keeps society from descending into chaos?

justify state intervention on the grounds that "it's for your own protection," they're channelling Hobbes's Leviathan.

Locke

- *Historical Idea*: Natural rights, social contract

- *Modern Impact*: Shaped modern liberal democracies and constitutional law

- *Ideological Movement*: *Classical Liberalism*, advocating for individual rights, limited government, and constitutional democracy.

- *Modern Example*:

  - Angela Merkel's leadership in Germany balanced individual freedoms with state responsibilities, reflecting Locke's principles.

  - The Liberal Democrats in the UK advocate for individual rights and the social contract.

John Locke, often dubbed the *"father of liberalism,"* believed that human beings were born with natural rights—the rights to life, liberty, and property—that no government could take away. His concept of the social contract argued that governments only exist to protect these rights and derive their legitimacy from the consent of the governed. If a government failed in this duty, Locke argued, the people had the right to overthrow it.

Locke's ideas form the backbone of modern liberal democracies, influencing everything from the American Declaration of Independence to the UK's constitutional principles. His belief in the protection of individual rights underpins constitutional law and human rights frameworks around the world. Locke's ideas are at the core of debates on civil liberties, freedom of speech, and the role of government in ensuring justice and equality.

Modern Impact: Locke's vision is central to the functioning of liberal democracies, particularly in the Western world. Concepts like rule of law, government accountability, and individual freedoms are cornerstones of constitutional governance[5]. His ideas continue to shape debates on immigration, freedom of expression, and personal privacy—Locke would probably be arguing in favour of protecting individual liberties against government overreach in today's world.

Rousseau

- *Historical Idea*: General will, direct democracy

- *Modern Impact*: Influences participatory democracy and the use of referendums

- *Ideological Movement*: *Democratic Socialism* and *Populism*, stressing participatory democracy and the collective will of the people.

- *Modern Example*:

  - The Scottish National Party (SNP) advocating for independence is an example of Rousseau's idea of the general will, particularly through the use of referendums.

  - Bernie Sanders' grassroots campaigns are a modern embodiment of participatory democracy.

Jean-Jacques Rousseau, in contrast to Hobbes and Locke, believed that true freedom could only be found in direct democra-

---

5. Locke would definitely be leading human rights campaigns at the UN or writing scathing op-eds about government overreach in the Guardian.

cy, where individuals collectively shape the laws and policies that govern them. His idea of the general will[6] suggested that the will of the collective, if aligned with the common good, should guide society. While individual preferences might conflict with the general will, Rousseau believed that citizens should act in the interest of the common good—even if it meant sacrificing some personal desires.

In the modern world, Rousseau's ideas have influenced movements toward participatory democracy and referendums. From grassroots activism to national referendums like the Brexit vote, the notion of people directly influencing government decisions is rooted in Rousseau's philosophy. However, Rousseau's idealism also confronts the messy realities of modern politics, where the *"will of the people"* is often manipulated, and referendums can lead to divisive outcomes. The question of whether collective action truly represents the common good remains as relevant today as it was in Rousseau's time.

Modern Impact: Rousseau's ideas are evident in modern systems of direct democracy, where citizens have a say in policy through referendums and public consultations. His emphasis on the collective good has also influenced debates around climate change and social justice movements, where the argument is often framed around the need to sacrifice personal freedoms for the benefit of future generations.

The Legacy in Today's UK Politics

The political debates that shaped Renaissance and Enlightenment thought still ripple through the corridors of Westminster today. While the UK has long since moved away from monarchic absolutism and religious rule, the ideas of Machiavelli,

---

6. If Rousseau saw how direct democracy works in the age of social media, he might rethink that whole *"general will"* concept. After all, the internet hive mind isn't always known for its wisdom.

Hobbes, Locke, and Rousseau continue to influence modern British politics in profound ways. From Brexit to debates over national security, their philosophies can be felt in everything from the way leaders govern to how political parties craft their strategies.

Locke's Influence: The Champion of Rights and the Social Contract

John Locke's legacy is most evident in the foundations of the UK's constitutional system—even though the UK doesn't have a written constitution. Locke's emphasis on individual rights, government by consent, and the social contract is embedded in the fabric of parliamentary democracy. The belief that the role of the government is to protect citizens' fundamental rights—life, liberty, and property—underpins the UK's legal system and its democratic principles. This is visible in debates surrounding civil liberties, freedom of speech, and the role of the state in people's personal lives.

- Modern Equivalent: Locke's ideas resonate with modern UK political figures like Keir Starmer, who often emphasises protecting individual rights, ensuring equality, and holding the government accountable to the people. Starmer's arguments about protecting citizens from the overreach of the state, especially regarding civil liberties, echo Locke's vision of a government that must safeguard the rights of the people or risk losing legitimacy. Similarly, Caroline Lucas of the Green Party, with her emphasis on protecting the rights of individuals while promoting collective environmental responsibility, channels Locke's sense of balance between personal freedom and societal obligations.

Machiavelli's Influence: Pragmatic Politics and Realpolitik

Niccolò Machiavelli, ever the realist, argued that power and pragmatism are central to political success. His assertion that rulers must be willing to act immorally when necessary for the greater good is alive and well in modern UK politics, where political leaders and advisors frequently engage in Realpolitik—the strategic balancing act of power, influence, and public perception.

In today's UK political landscape, Machiavelli's ideas are clearly at play in the strategic manoeuvring of political parties. From spin doctors crafting campaign messages to the backroom deals that often define coalition-building, the Machiavellian idea that leaders must do what is necessary—whether morally right or not—resonates. The ruthless drive to win elections, dominate debates, and control narratives is the direct application of Machiavelli's principles.

- Modern Equivalent: A modern Machiavellian figure might be seen in Dominic Cummings, the former chief adviser to Boris Johnson. Cummings' unapologetically strategic approach to politics—particularly his role in the Vote Leave campaign—reflected a Machiavellian emphasis on winning at all costs, regardless of ethical concerns. His tactics, which some saw as manipulative, were often justified by their efficacy, much in the spirit of Machiavelli's belief that the ends justify the means.

Hobbes' Influence: Sovereignty and National Security

Thomas Hobbes, with his famously pessimistic view of human nature, believed that a strong, central authority—Leviathan—was necessary to prevent society from descending into chaos. In today's UK, Hobbes' ideas about sovereignty, order, and national security resonate in discussions about the state's role in maintaining control, especially in the face of external and internal threats.

Hobbes' belief in the necessity of a strong state is especially visible in debates over national security, counterterrorism laws, and police powers. Post-Brexit discussions about sovereignty, particularly the need to "take back control" from supranational bodies like the European Union, echo Hobbes' insistence that only a strong, sovereign state can ensure peace and stability. The growing debates around government surveillance, the role of the Home Office in immigration control, and the use of emergency powers during crises (e.g., COVID-19) are all manifestations of Hobbesian thought.

- Modern Equivalent: Suella Braverman, the twice-fired former Home Secretary, often embodies Hobbesian views, particularly in her emphasis on law and order and tight control over immigration. Her advocacy for strong border controls and tough stances on crime align with Hobbes' belief in the necessity of a strong state to prevent disorder. Similarly, during his tenure, Boris Johnson echoed Hobbesian ideas of sovereignty in his push for Brexit, rallying against the perceived loss of control to Brussels.

Rousseau's Influence: Participatory Democracy and the General Will

Jean-Jacques Rousseau believed that true freedom could only be found through direct democracy—where the general will of the people was paramount. His vision that the people themselves should shape laws and policies is evident in the rise of referendums, participatory democracy, and grassroots movements.

In modern UK politics, Rousseau's influence is most visible in the push for referendums and the belief that the will of the people must be directly consulted on critical national issues. The 2016 Brexit referendum is a prime example of Rousseau's philosophy in action. Advocates for direct democracy argue that citizens should have a say in shaping their own political futures, rather than leaving decisions solely to representatives.

However, as seen in the Brexit fallout, Rousseau's idealistic vision of the general will can sometimes clash with the messy realities of modern political life. The divisiveness of referendums and the challenge of interpreting what the "will of the people" truly means in a polarised society highlight the tensions in Rousseau's ideas when applied to today's complex political landscape.

- Modern Equivalent: Nigel Farage[7], with his constant championing of the will of the people during the Brexit campaign, embodies Rousseau's belief in the power of direct democracy. Farage's push for a people's vote on leaving the EU was deeply rooted in the idea that the general will—once expressed—must be respected, even in the face of institutional opposition. At the same time, leaders like Jeremy Corbyn have occasionally leaned into participatory politics, encouraging grassroots movements and promoting greater citizen involvement in political decision-making.

Through the lens of these four political philosophers, we can see the tensions and contradictions that continue to shape UK politics today. Whether it's the pragmatic manoeuvrings of Machiavelli, the security concerns of Hobbes, the rights-based arguments of Locke, or the participatory democracy espoused by Rousseau, the UK's political landscape remains a battleground of competing ideas—and none of them are going away anytime soon.

---

7. Yes, I did hear you drop your cup of tea dramatically to the floor at the comparison of Nigel Farage to one of the great thinkers of the secular era of politics, and no, I am not sorry.

A New Age, A New Debate

And so, before we leave this period, we return to our earlier conversation with our illustrious gentlemen of the time. The café has grown quieter as the evening deepens, with the secular ideas now weaving into the heart of their debate. The thinkers are more contemplative, their drinks half-finished, as they turn to the final question of how humanity will fare without the divine hand guiding governance.

Machiavelli, who has spent much of the conversation amused, now leans forward, tracing the rim of his glass as he speaks.Machiavelli: "So, we've cast aside God in favour of reason. But what have we gained? A world where power is no longer sanctified by the heavens, but still just as ruthless. The state will always be the ultimate authority, whether ordained by God or born of secular ideals. The rulers will do what they must, and the people will follow—either out of fear or necessity."

Locke, who has been patiently listening, sets down his cup of tea with a quiet smile, his tone measured but firm.Locke: "Niccolò, that's where you and I part ways. Secularism isn't just a change of crown for power—it's a new understanding of authority itself. Power now comes not from fear or divine right, but from the consent of the people. Secular governance gives us the chance to protect individual rights, to ensure that power serves the people, rather than ruling over them with an iron fist."

Hobbes, who has been nursing his ale, chuckles darkly before interjecting, his voice low and cynical.Hobbes: "Ah, Locke, ever the optimist. But without a higher authority to keep them in check, people will tear society apart. Secularism or not, humanity is brutish, self-serving. The Leviathan is still needed to enforce order. Strip away God, and you'll find that chaos is eager to fill the void. Power must be absolute, or it will crumble."

Locke opens his mouth to respond, but Rousseau, who has been watching the exchange with growing intensity, cuts in, his eyes alight with passion.Rousseau: "No, no! You all miss the point! Secularism frees us—not just from the church, but from the tyranny of kings! It's not about who holds power; it's about how the people come together to create it. True freedom doesn't come from rulers, but from the collective will of the people, from our unity. Secularism gives us the chance to find a new, harmonious way forward."

Machiavelli chuckles, swirling his wine before he leans back.Machiavelli: "Ah, Rousseau, ever the dreamer. And yet, who leads this harmonious society of yours? When it falters, as it inevitably will, who picks up the pieces? Power will always return to those who know how to wield it, not those who dream of utopias."

Locke shakes his head, but there's a warmth in his voice as he responds.Locke: "Perhaps, Niccolò, but it's a dream worth having. Secularism allows us to build something new, something better. We may stumble, but we now have the freedom to chart our own course. Power comes not from fear, but from the trust and reason of the people."

Hobbes grumbles, setting down his ale.Hobbes: "Trust? Reason? Locke, you and Rousseau are more alike than you think—both dreaming of a world that doesn't exist. Without authority, without control, society falls apart. Secularism doesn't save us from this; it merely shifts the seat of power."

Rousseau leans forward, undeterred, his voice rising with conviction.Rousseau: "But it does more than that, Hobbes! It gives us a chance to build a society where power is shared, where the people truly govern themselves. It is not perfect, no—but it is ours to shape, without the shadow of the church or the crown looming over us."

The conversation lingers in the air, the tension between pragmatism and idealism unresolved. The café feels still, as though even the walls are considering the weight of their words. Finally, Machiavelli shrugs and raises his glass, a smirk playing on his li ps.Machiavelli: "Well, gentlemen, one thing is clear. Secularism may have freed us from the divine, but it has not freed us from the questions of power and governance. We're still debating how to rule—and likely always will."

And with that, they each raise their glasses in a silent toast to the ongoing debate. Secularism has opened a new chapter, but the struggle for a just and balanced society, as they all know, is far from over.

Political Thought

A Retrospective and Wrap Up

"For long, history was mainly political history, and historical narrative was confined to an account of the most important crises in political life, or to an account of wars and great generals."
Michael Rostovtzeff

B efore we dive headfirst into the complex web of modern political systems, let's take a quick breather to reflect on the intellectual journey we've been on. We've walked through the grand halls of political thought, brushed shoulders with the greatest minds of the past, and even poked fun at the squabbles of long-dead philosophers. But what's the point of dragging you through these dusty debates if we don't stop to acknowledge how their ideas continue to shape the messy, chaotic world we call politics today?

This chapter is the bridge between ancient and medieval arguments about power and authority and the modern systems they helped spawn. It's a reminder that the conflicts between idealism and pragmatism, the tension between freedom and control, and the age-old question of who gets to rule haven't disappeared. Instead, these debates have evolved, becoming more complex and yet eerily familiar.

If there's one thing we've learned, it's that history doesn't repeat itself—not in the neat, circular way we sometimes imagine—but it certainly does rhyme. The ideas and power struggles that gripped ancient Athens, medieval kingdoms, and Renaissance courts are still with us, wrapped in new terminology and playing out on new stages. Modern political systems, whether they be liberal democracies, authoritarian regimes, or hybrid states, are, at their core, responses to the same fundamental dilemmas that occupied Plato, Machiavelli, Locke, and the rest of our philosophical company.

And if you're wondering why we're still grappling with the same problems centuries later—questions about sovereignty, individual rights, and how much power the state should wield—well, that's because these issues are as timeless as they are unresolvable[1]. Each generation reinterprets them, but the core questions remain the same, shaping political landscapes from Westminster to Washington, from the halls of the EU to the streets of Moscow.

So, before we charge into a discussion of modern political systems, let's pause for a moment. Let's appreciate how these ancient and medieval debates—these age-old tussles over justice, power, and freedom—have filtered down through the centuries to shape the structures, laws, and power struggles of today. In many ways, we're not as far removed from the political dramas of the past as we might think. The only difference is that our gladiators now argue in parliaments, on social media, or in the boardrooms of international organisations.

Revisiting the Foundations: Why Political Theory Matters More Than Ever

Let's take a quick stroll back to that first little argument between our old pals Locke and Hobbes—the one where Locke, ever

---

1. And good Lord, we have tried.

the optimist, clung to his belief that people, if left to their own devices, would generally behave reasonably. He argued that humans are endowed with natural rights, and that government exists to protect those rights, not to stifle them. Hobbes, on the other hand, famously grumbled about the brutish, nasty, and short nature of life without a powerful authority looming over us all. Hobbes believed that, left unchecked, human beings would descend into chaos, and only a strong, central authority could keep society from tearing itself apart.

Fast forward to today, and if you've been paying even the slightest bit of attention to the news over the last few decades, you'll notice something remarkable: these two figures may have been separated by centuries, but their arguments are alive and well. In fact, their debate has been playing out in real-time, with modern politicians picking sides—some shouting for freedom and individual rights, others insisting on control, order, and the need for strong government intervention. And nowhere was this more evident than during the saga that was Brexit.

I know, I know—Brexit. We're all weary of hearing about it, but bear with me[2]. The rhetoric of sovereignty and control, which defined the Leave campaign, was essentially a modern-day nod to Hobbesian thought. Sovereignty was presented as the ultimate safeguard against external forces—against chaos. The EU was framed as the cumbersome leviathan from which Britain needed to liberate itself, so it could regain control over its borders, laws, and trade policies. Hobbes would have been nodding in grim satisfaction[3]: when faced with uncertainty and external threats, the impulse to reassert centralised control is irresistible.

On the other side of the debate, however, were those who channelled Lockean ideals. The Remain campaign spoke of in-

---

2. See what I did there.

3. And a good point to note, when Hobbes is nodding in satisfaction, something has gone terribly, terribly wrong.

dividual rights, freedom of movement, and the protection of those hard-won liberties from oppressive bureaucratic structures. The EU was seen not as a beast to be tamed, but as a platform that safeguarded freedoms—freedoms which would be endangered by retreating into the sovereign, isolated state that Hobbes would have applauded.

Brexit was more than just a policy decision; it was an echo of the same fundamental questions that Locke and Hobbes debated centuries ago. On the one hand, we had the desire for sovereignty, control, and the protection of the state's power over its people—very Hobbesian indeed. On the other hand, we had the argument for individual rights, for collective agreements that transcended national boundaries, and for the idea that liberty thrives best when shared—very much in line with Locke's belief in government by consent.

The brilliance of their ongoing debate is that it never really goes away. Whether we're talking about Brexit, national security, health mandates, or the right to privacy, the tensions between freedom and control, individual rights and state sovereignty, are always bubbling just below the surface.

In fact, you could say that modern politics is just Locke vs. Hobbes 2.0, except now it's playing out in referendums, parliaments, and—no one would disagree—Twitter threads.

Classical Roots and Their Messy Legacy

Now, back to the Greeks and Romans—the architects of much of what we consider the bedrock of political theory and practice. Let's face it, the Greeks loved a good debate. Our Athenian friends gave the world direct democracy, that idealistic system where every citizen had a say in the decisions that governed the city-state. On paper, it sounds wonderful—empowering even—until you remember that ancient Athens was a society where citizens were often called to vote on everything from declaring war to managing trade, like whether or not they should launch a naval expedition for olive oil. The novelty of voting on every issue quickly wore off when people realised that democracy isn't always glamorous—it's often mundane, messy, and prone to gridlock.

The nightmare of direct democracy, as Athens came to realise, was that it's hard to govern when everyone's voice has equal weight on every decision. What began as a noble experiment soon revealed its cracks: populism, demagoguery, and mob rule could easily derail reasoned debate. In fact, Socrates' execution was a result of this very system, a tragic consequence of democracy gone wrong when the public, swayed by popular opinion, voted to condemn a man for asking too many uncomfortable questions.

And yet, we haven't entirely abandoned the Athenian dream. Modern democratic systems, including the UK's, proudly trace their roots back to Athens. The House of Commons may not resemble the chaotic assemblies of Athens in practice, but the principle of giving citizens a voice through representative democracy is a compromise—a middle ground between the messy direct democracy of Athens and the elite governance favoured by Plato's philosopher-kings. Instead of having the entire populace vote on every bill, we elect representatives to do the arguing for us (and sometimes the yelling too). This is how modern democracies attempt to balance inclusivity with efficiency—though even in this system, debates can drag on for what feels like an eternity (just look at any drawn-out parliamentary session on Brexit).

But while we've borrowed democratic ideals from the Greeks, our sense of pomp, tradition, and political theatre? That's all Roman. The House of Commons, with its ceremonial robes, archaic rituals, and occasional dramatic outbursts, bears more than a passing resemblance to the Roman Senate. The Romans perfected the art of combining governance with spectacle—after all, politics has always been a performance. The backroom deals, the politicking, the strategic alliances—Rome mastered all of it. And if you think modern politics is ruthless, just remember the assassination of Julius Caesar was essentially a Senate[4] squabble gone lethal.

And let's not forget the Romans' greatest contribution to governance: bureaucracy. The Romans understood that ruling an empire required more than just strong rulers; it needed systems, protocols, and endless scrolls of paperwork. The UK's complex legal system, civil service, and governmental structure owe a great deal to Rome's love of order and process, though we've swapped out scrolls for overly long emails and parliamentary memos.

Fast forward a few millennia, and while we don't gather in the Agora to vote on military campaigns, we're still grappling with the same core questions about representation, power, and the role of the citizen in governance. The dream of a government that reflects the will of the people remains as tantalising as it is elusive. While modern democracies like the UK have traded direct democracy for a more representative model, the tension between elite governance and populist sentiment never really goes away. Every so often, we catch a glimpse of that old Athenian spirit—whether it's in a referendum, an election, or even the odd town hall debate[5].

And while we're on the subject of governance, let's take a moment to reflect on the enduring legacy of the constitutional monarchy in the UK. Today, the Crown may seem like little more than a ceremonial institution, a symbol of national tradition trotted out for state occasions, but it wasn't so long ago that the monarch wielded serious political power. The idea of the divine right of kings—that rulers were chosen by God and therefore beyond reproach—still lingers in how we think about sovereignty and authority. Sure, we've relegated the monarchy

---

4. Or Parliamentary

5. Or from time to time a Twitter poll, which also shows us why this may not in fact be a great idea when we have the potential of an army of sex robots essentially making decisions for us.

to a largely symbolic role, but the history of Britain is filled with struggles between monarchical power and democratic governance.

The English Civil War, for example, was a bloody reminder of how monarchy and democracy don't always play nicely together. It's a tension that, while smoothed over with time, hasn't entirely disappeared. The existence of an unelected monarchy alongside a democratic Parliament speaks to this ongoing negotiation between tradition and modernity, between the weight of history and the demands of a democratic society.

While the English Civil War may seem like ancient history, the philosophical debates that underpinned it are far from over. The Crown's role may now be ceremonial, but the symbolic power of the monarchy persists, echoing those ancient battles between royal authority and popular sovereignty. The fact that the Queen (or King) still opens Parliament and remains a symbol of national unity shows that even as we embrace modern democracy, we're not quite ready to abandon the ceremonial power that once ruled Britain.

Medieval Authority and Its Shadows in Modern Politics

Now, let's pop back to the medieval period—a time when power was a curious cocktail of divine will and land ownership. Feudalism, the dominant political system, was less about governance and more of a glorified pyramid scheme, with kings perched at the top, nobles nestled comfortably in the middle, and the peasants—well, they were the base that propped up the entire structure. The whole system was stitched together with the idea of land for loyalty, with each level owing service to the one above it, all while claiming the divine right to rule. The divine right of kings was essentially the medieval equivalent of a lifetime pass to do as you pleased, backed by the claim that your authority came directly from God. And just to make sure no one got any funny ideas about rebellion, the Church was there to reinforce the notion that to defy the king was to defy God Himself.

Now, fast-forward to today[6]. We don't trade land for military service anymore—at least, not openly—and the absolute power of monarchs has been severely curtailed. But the echoes of medieval political structures are still with us, woven into the fabric of modern British politics. The most glaring example? The House of Lords. While it may not be the feudal system reanimated, its very existence is a reminder of how deeply rooted our political institutions are in hierarchical power structures. The Lords may no longer be bartering land, but the fact that it remains an unelected body, largely appointed by political or hereditary privilege, tells us that the tension between medieval hierarchy and modern democracy is far from resolved.

The House of Lords reform debate is a perennial fixture in UK politics, often framed as a conflict between the old world and the new. Should this institution, with its origins in feudal landownership and aristocracy, continue in its current form[7]? Should it become an elected body, reflecting the democratic values that are supposed to underpin modern governance? Or does its non-elected nature offer a stabilising counterbalance to the more political, partisan House of Commons? These are questions that continue to swirl around, reflecting the uneasy relationship between tradition and democracy that defines British politics.

And let's not forget the role of the Church. While its political power has dramatically diminished since the days when it could crown kings and excommunicate rebellious nobles, it still wields symbolic influence. The Bishops in the House of Lords, known as the Lords Spiritual, might not have the power to excom-

---

6. I know, I know – there is more jumping backwards and forwards than a B-Grade Sci-Fi.

7. Absobloodylutely not.

municate anyone these days, but their presence is a reminder that the intersection of religion and politics—so dominant in medieval times—still casts a shadow over modern governance. Their involvement in discussions on ethical and social issues, particularly those involving moral guidance (think debates on abortion or same-sex marriage), reveals the subtle, lingering influence of the Church in shaping British political life.

This influence, while far quieter than it was in medieval times, occasionally flares up, particularly in debates around education, social welfare, or moral issues where the Church's voice is still heard. And while we no longer have to fear being excommunicated[8] for challenging the Church's authority, the role of religion in public life—whether in the form of moral guidance or symbolic gestures—remains a topic that, every so often, bubbles to the surface.

The Renaissance and Enlightenment as Our Guiding Lights

And then came the Renaissance and Enlightenment, those eras when the Western world had its existential breakthrough: rulers didn't need to be anointed by God, and maybe, just maybe, human beings had intrinsic rights worth protecting. It was a dramatic pivot from the medieval mindset, where power was divinely ordained and ordinary people had little more than a feudal lord's mercy to depend on. Suddenly, the individual mattered, and the notion that power could derive from the people rather than from a higher power began to catch fire across Europe.

Of course, while these intellectual movements were sparking revolutions in thought, Machiavelli stepped in with a healthy

---

8. If excommunication were still a thing, some politicians might think twice before arguing with the Archbishop of Canterbury. On the plus side, it would make PMQs far more exciting.

dose of pragmatism. In his seminal work, *"The Prince, "*he ruthlessly dismantled the belief that virtue had much to do with effective rule. For Machiavelli, politics was not a moral endeavour
but a strategic one—leaders who clung to ethics were destined
to be overthrown by those who understood that power must be
maintained by whatever means necessary. And though Machiavelli wasn't offering a guidebook for tyrants (despite what his
critics might say or what may have accidentally happened), his
vision of Realpolitik still echoes in Westminster's halls, where
strategy and survival often come before idealism. Behind every
successful campaign, every backroom deal, and every calculated
policy shift is a little nod to Machiavelli's school of thought: it's
not enough to be good—you have to be *smart* about power.

On the other side of the coin were the optimists—Locke
and Rousseau, championing the radical idea that governments
should serve the people and protect their inherent rights. Locke,
the father of liberal democracy, believed in a social contract
where rulers derived their power from the consent of the governed. It was a seismic shift away from monarchic or divine rule
and towards individual liberty. His legacy can be seen across the
UK's legal and political institutions, from human rights protections to the principle of government accountability. When we
talk about constitutional law, free speech, or the need for checks
and balances, we're channelling Locke. His ideals are particularly visible in the ongoing efforts to reform state surveillance
laws, where the right to privacy and government transparency
often clash.

Meanwhile, Rousseau, with his lofty dreams of direct democracy and the general will, imagined a world where governance
was a truly collective act. For Rousseau, the ideal society was
one in which citizens came together to determine their collective
future, creating laws and policies that reflected the common
good. While the UK's parliamentary system is far removed from
Rousseau's dream of a self-governing society, his influence can
still be seen in the rise of referendums, grassroots movements,
and public consultations. For instance, the push for commu-

nity-driven policy—whether it's on local development projects or social issues—speaks to Rousseau's belief in collective decision-making.

Yet, Rousseau's ideas are not without their complications. The concept of direct democracy often struggles in a world where the "common good" is hard to pin down. As we see with debates around climate policy, for example, giving people a voice in governance can lead to polarisation. Rousseau's vision of a unified general will sometimes collide with the messy realities of public opinion, where individual interests and groupthink often get in the way of meaningful consensus. But his vision persists in the belief that people should have more direct influence over the decisions that shape their lives.

And then there's Hobbes, always lurking in the background, ready to remind us that left to their own devices, human beings can descend into chaos and conflict faster than you can say *"national emergency."* Hobbes' insistence on the need for a strong central authority to keep society from collapsing into a war of all against all is still highly relevant today. In debates about national security, law and order, and emergency powers, his belief in the Leviathan—the powerful state needed to maintain control—has modern implications. For instance, discussions about the expansion of police powers or counterterrorism measures often invoke a Hobbesian argument: that without a firm hand to maintain order, society risks falling into chaos.

While Hobbes' vision of control and order might seem at odds with Locke's or Rousseau's more democratic leanings, it's clear that we still live in a world where his ideas shape our approach to governance. The balancing act between freedom and security, between the rights of the individual and the authority of the state, is an ever-present feature of political debate, and one we're unlikely to resolve any time soon.

So, the Renaissance and Enlightenment didn't just give us fancy new ways of thinking about art and science—they laid the groundwork for how we approach power, freedom, and governance in the UK today. Machiavelli taught us the importance of pragmatism and power dynamics, Locke gave us liberty and the rule of law, Rousseau left us with the ideal of collective decision-making, and Hobbes reminded us that sometimes, we need a bit of authority to keep the whole thing from descending into chaos.

Threading Political Thought Together: The Modern Implications

So, where does all this leave us in the modern world? The political systems we see today, especially here in the UK, are the living embodiment of the ideas we've been discussing. Our parliamentary system is essentially Locke's dream—a balance of individual rights and government accountability, with a bit of Athenian democracy mixed in for good measure[9]. But don't be fooled into thinking we've outgrown the conflicts these thinkers wrestled with, far from it.

Consider the ongoing debates about national security and civil liberties—we're watching Locke and Hobbes square off yet again, only this time they're battling over surveillance technology, data privacy, and the power of the state to intrude in the name of security. We're still trying to balance freedom and control, rights and order, just as they did centuries ago. And while Machiavelli's ruthless pragmatism might seem at odds with the idealistic rhetoric of today's politicians, you can bet his strategic thinking is alive and well behind the scenes in every election campaign and political manoeuvre.

These age-old debates aren't just interesting thought exercises—they're embedded in the fabric of modern governance. Whether it's Locke's social contract at the heart of human rights law, Machiavelli's realpolitik guiding the manoeuvres of po-

---

9. At least we don't exile annoying citizens for ten years anymore. But imagine how peaceful Twitter would be if we did...

litical leaders, or Rousseau's populism surfacing in grassroots movements, the ideas of the past still frame the politics of today. The arguments, theories, and philosophies we've explored aren't relics of a bygone era—they're still shaping our laws, institutions, and social contracts right here, right now.

As we move into the next section of the book, it's time to shift our focus from the philosophies behind governance to the political movements that emerge from these ideas. Political movements are the vehicles through which these theories become action—how abstract ideas of freedom, equality, and power turn into real-world change. But what are political movements? What aren't they? And why should they matter to us? In this next section, we'll dive deep into the key players, the core ideologies, and the real-world implications of these movements and how they're so often so very, very misunderstood.

#IdeologyWars

The Great Political Tweet-Off

> "Taxes – you mean the government stealing **YOUR** money!!!"
>
> Bob-Bunchanumbers

I magine Twitter, where subtlety goes to die, and all the great minds of political philosophy have somehow found themselves in one giant, messy thread[1].

It's chaotic, it's messy, and everyone's got an opinion—but no one's really listening.

@LiberalLion (John Locke) Let's start with the basics: people are born free, equal, and with the right to life, liberty, and property. #Freedom #Democracy #Progress

@ConservaBurke (Edmund Burke) Whoa, slow down there. Progress is fine... as long as you don't destroy society in the process. Radical change is a one-way ticket to chaos. #TraditionMatters #FrenchRevolutionWasAMistake

@RedsForReal (Karl Marx) Property? That's cute, @LiberalLion. The *workers* should control the means of production

---

1. Just go with it, I never said this book was serious.

The whole system is rigged! Capitalism is exploitation, plain and simple. #ClassStruggle #WorkersUnite #Revolution

@FriedRich (Friedrich Hayek) And socialism is just a gateway to tyranny Central planning destroys individual freedom and innovation. The market knows best. Trust the invisible hand. #FreeMarkets #EconomicFreedom

@IronFistFascism (Benito Mussolini) Enough with your babbling about freedom and markets! The state is all that matters! National unity through strength, discipline, and absolute control. #StrengthThroughUnity #TheStateIsSupreme

@Anarchy4Life (Pierre-Joseph Proudhon) The state? Seriously? The only thing the state does is oppress! Real freedom is without rulers, without hierarchies. Smash the state. Trust in mutual aid and community. #AnarchyNow #NoGodsNoMasters

@GodsRuler (Calvin)I'm sorry, @Anarchy4Life, but your "freedom" sounds like chaos. Society must be governed by divine law. Theocracy is the only true form of governance #GodsPlan #ReligiousLaw

@ComradeLenin (Vladimir Lenin) Agreed, @RedsForReal but we need a vanguard party to guide the revolution. The people won't overthrow capitalism without leadership. #Proletariat #PowerToThePeople

@EcoRevolution (Greta Thunberg) If we don't get our act together, there won't *be* a world left for your revolutions or markets Climate change is the real threat, people. Time to act now! #ClimateCrisis #NoPlanetB

@NeolibForLife (Milton Friedman) Stop panicking, @EcoRevolution. The market can solve the climate crisis. Innovation, private sector investments, and carbon pricing will save us all #LetTheMarketFixIt #EconomicFreedom

@RoboLeader (Lee Kuan Yew) You're all missing the point. It's not the state or the market that will govern us—it's technology. We're heading for a technocratic future whether you like it or not #TechIsKing #TechnocracyRising

@LiveFree (Ayn Rand) Leave me out of your state-controlled fantasies, all of you are cucks The only morality is rational self-interest. The individual comes first, not the collective, and certainly not some authoritarian regime. #Objectivism #FreedomIsSelfish

@SocialSolidarity (Mikhail Bakunin)@LiveFree, @Anarchy4Life's got a point. All authority, including your beloved "free" markets, enslaves people. True freedom means solidarity and dismantling all systems of oppression #AnarchyNow #Revolution

@EcoRevolution (Greta Thunberg) Honestly, @SocialSolidarity, all of you are ignoring the planet Without radical environmental change, none of your ideologies will matter when the world burns. #ClimateJustice #SaveThePlanet

@LiberalLion (John Locke)I'm all for preserving the earth and our freedoms. But we have to balance liberty with responsible governance Let's not throw out the baby with the bathwater, @EcoRevolution. #ModerationInAllThings

@FriedRich (Friedrich Hayek)@LiberalLion finally making sense. A free society can find solutions without authoritarianism. Governments tend to mess things up #FreedomFirst #HayekKnowsBest

@IronFistFascism (Benito Mussolini) You all sound like weak, beta soy-boys It's about dominance, not freedom. The state must rule with an iron fist. #StrengthAboveAll

@ComradeLenin (Vladimir Lenin) The state exists to serve the revolution until we reach a classless society. Then we'll see

who's really in control, @IronFistFascism #ProletariatRising
#DownWithFascism

@NeolibForLife (Milton Friedman) All of this is irrelevant
without economic growth #JustSaying

@GodsRuler (Calvin) The only law that matters is God's law.
Your secular ideologies will fall without divine guidance #God-
AboveAll

@Anarchy4Life (Pierre-Joseph Proudhon) Power corrupts
End of story. No state, no rulers. Just freedom. #DirectAction
#NoRulers

@EcoRevolution (Greta Thunberg) Honestly, I don't even
care how we do it anymore, just fix the climate #StopTalk-
ingStartDoing

@LiveFree (Ayn Rand)I'll be over here, enjoying my individualism and watching you all collapse under your "collectives."
#EveryManForHimself

@RoboLeader (Lee Kuan Yew) Just wait until AI rules you all
#TechIsInevitable

Welcome to the second part of this book: The Wonderful World
of Political Ideology and the multitude of ways it's misunderstood, misinterpreted, and so often shouted loudly about.
This is where everyone's convinced they're right, and no one's
actually listening to anyone else. Much like a Twitter debate,
the conversation around political theory is loud, chaotic, and
utterly self-absorbed. But if we step back and look at the bigger picture, there's value in the discord. Each ideology has its
strengths, its flaws, and its unique perspective on how to govern—or dismantle—society.

Sure, it's a mess—just like your Twitter feed after an election.
But beneath the noise and the all-caps shouting, these ideologies

represent the ways we've tried to organise society. They aren't just academic relics or echo-chamber talking points; they're the ideas that have shaped nations, started revolutions, and, occasionally, solved some of our biggest problems. But let's not get ahead of ourselves. As we step into this second part of the book, we'll be exploring how these theories continue to influence modern governance—and why no one can seem to agree on what works best.

The question isn't which of these philosophies is perfect[2], but how we navigate the messy middle ground where they all collide.

---

2. Spoiler alert: None of them.

Liberalism

The Eternal Optimist of Politics

"A liberal is someone who believes that it is the government's job to ensure that individuals are free to pursue their own happiness, provided that this pursuit does not infringe on the rights of others."

John F. Kennedy

Let's go on an imagination adventure. Consider Liberalism as that perpetually hopeful and optimistic friend who firmly believes that with just enough thoughtful and respectful conversation, a bit of patience, and some well-reasoned and logical arguments, world peace is but a few polite exchanges away. You know the type: the one who's convinced that the pressing issues of global warming, income inequality, and even the never-ending debate over whether pineapple belongs on pizza can be constructively addressed through meaningful dialogue and good-natured discussion over a cup of coffee.

This is the friend who, after watching two people argue about splitting the bill at a restaurant, starts drawing up a *"fairness model"*, complete with bar charts and a cost-per-sip calculation, convinced they can broker an agreement that leaves everyone happy. They're the same person who, in the heat of a family row over politics at Christmas dinner, calmly suggests everyone take a breath and really listen to one another, as if Uncle Dave's rant about immigrants is going to be magically softened by a brief reading from the Universal Declaration of Human Rights[1].

In the political sphere, Liberalism is this optimistic friend writ large. It's the ideology that firmly believes, despite overwhelming evidence to the contrary, that if we just sit down and talk about our problems, we'll be able to reason our way to a solution. That rational discourse is the key to human progress. That with enough dialogue, we can collectively address issues like human rights, equality, and justice. Liberalism refuses to give up on humanity, even when humanity is throwing Twitter tantrums and debating whether climate change is a hoax[2].

Don't get me wrong—this is a worldview I've often found myself sharing. As an immigrant and gay man living in the UK, Liberalism has been a force that has shaped many of the freedoms I hold dear. The right to live freely, express myself[3], and love who I love—those are all rooted in liberal principles. Liberalism, for all its faults, has been the optimistic champion for people like me, always fighting for individual rights and social progress. It's been there pushing for equality, for inclusivity, for a society where everyone gets a say.

But here's the thing: while I appreciate its tireless optimism, I can't help but notice that Liberalism has a bit of a teensy bit of a blind spot. It often acts like everyone else is just one logical conversation away from agreeing that freedom, equality, and human dignity are universally good things. That all we need is more *dialogue*. More *debate*. More rational exchange of ideas.

---

1. Liberalism: The political movement that thinks a 10-point plan can fix your racist uncle at Christmas.

2. Yup. You know you've done this. All of you!

3. "Somewhat verbosely, some may say"- he writes with no sense of irony considering just how much he natters on in this tome.

And it never seems to get tired of being eternally disappointed when people—very predictably—don't come around[4].

You see, the trouble with Liberalism is that it has this charming, but slightly naïve belief in the rationality of human beings. It operates on the assumption that if we just keep talking, everyone will eventually see the light. But if you've spent five minutes in the comment section of any major news outlet—or, God forbid, Twitter—you'll know that people are not always reasonable. In fact, people are often quite unreasonable, especially when it comes to politics. Yet Liberalism soldiers on, convinced that logic will triumph over emotion, and that a well-crafted argument can bring even the most polarised sides together.

It's like bringing a rational argument to an emotional knife fight—noble, but slightly outmatched.

History in Brief: Locke, Mill, and the (False) Promise of Reason

I've already introduced you to John Locke in previous chapters, so I won't subject you to another long-winded biography of the man. But here's the short version: Locke was that eternally hopeful philosopher who believed that people are fundamentally reasonable. His solution to the messy business of governance? A social contract where governments existed to protect individual rights—life, liberty, and property—and nothing more. This was the early framework of Liberalism: a system designed to give everyone a fair shot, grounded in the belief that if we just uphold individual rights, the world will sort itself out.

Locke's ideas were revolutionary, sure, but also a bit... idealistic, to say the least. He truly thought governments could be designed like a perfectly logical machine, with each citizen know-

---

4. Though to be fair, Steve from Twitter who doesn't understand that a foodbank CEO should get paid will eventually come around. I just *know* it.

ing and defending their rights, all while contributing to the greater good. The result? A polite, orderly society where reason ruled and tyranny was banished to the history books[5].

But Locke wasn't the only idealist kicking around back then. Enter John Stuart Mill, a man who decided that the best way to protect individual rights was to defend free speech—at all costs. For Mill, freedom of expression was the key to human progress. His argument? Let everyone speak their mind, no matter how completely batshit their ideas might be, and eventually the truth will rise to the top. Mill had this almost laughable belief that in the grand marketplace of ideas, reason would inevitably prevail over ignorance. Clearly, Mill had never experienced an online debate about raw milk[6].

Mill's big twist on Liberalism was that free speech was not just a nice-to-have, but an essential tool for societal growth. If we censor bad ideas, he warned, we risk stagnating as a society. Bad ideas, he believed, should be challenged openly, not suppressed. Only through constant debate could humanity progress. It's an uplifting thought, until you remember that debating doesn't always lead to reason—sometimes it just leads to a lot of shouting on the internet.

While Locke and Mill *genuinely* believed that individual rights and rational discourse could lead to a better society, history has a way of showing just how complicated that really is. Sure, Liberalism gave us fantastic concepts like separation of powers, freedom of speech, and representation—all undeniably good things. But when placed in the hands of actual humans (you know, the ones Locke and Mill believed were inherently reasonable), well... things got a bit messy.

---

5. Spoiler: It didn't quite work out that way.

6. The amount of vitriol about dangerous dairy is spectacular.

Take the UK's modern political system. It's a proud descendant of Locke's vision of a representative democracy designed to protect individual rights, but that system has also seen plenty of irrational screaming and demagogues muddying the waters. It turns out, no matter how perfect the framework, rational debate can still be drowned out by emotional tirades and self-interest.

And that, dear reader, is where Liberalism stumbles a bit. It's great in theory, but when you factor in human nature—well, let's just say rational discourse doesn't always win the day.

The Evolution of Liberalism: From Classical to Modern

Now, Liberalism, much like that friend who went to university and came back with a new haircut and a passion for craft beer, has had its own series of identity crises—or, more charitably, *evolutions*. **Classical Liberalism**, as envisioned by the likes of Locke and Mill, was all about individual freedoms, limited government, and free markets. It was the political equivalent of a minimalist wardrobe: keep it simple, rely on reason, and trust that everything will fall into place. Life, liberty, and property—sorted.

But as society trundled into the industrial age and beyond, the cracks in this minimalist approach began to widen, a bit like when your friend's carefully curated capsule wardrobe just can't handle all the new realities of adulthood. Sure, Classical Liberalism looked good on paper, with its tidy focus on free markets and minimal state interference, but reality had other plans. Unregulated markets led to wild economic booms and catastrophic busts, workers were left exploited in Dickensian factories, and inequality ballooned to grotesque levels. It became clear that while Classical Liberalism was great for defending personal liberty, it had a slight tendency to overlook the fact that many people were too busy trying not to starve to appreciate their freedoms.

Cue the arrival of **Modern Liberalism**, the updated model that decided maybe, just maybe, the government should step in a bit more than just waving from the sidelines while businesses ran amok. It's the moment when Liberalism realised that, as much as everyone loves freedom, it's pretty hard to enjoy it on an empty stomach—or while working 16-hour shifts in a what was basically a smog factory.

Modern Liberals looked at the chaos of unfettered capitalism and thought, *"Right, maybe we need a safety net here."* Out came social welfare programs, public education, and a dash of regulation to keep those exuberant capitalists from turning into full-blown monopolists. It's like Liberalism had a midlife crisis and realised that while protecting property rights was important, so was ensuring people weren't literally dying in the streets. Freedom is all well and good, but it's not very useful if you're too busy picking up extra shifts just to survive.

Classical Liberalism had preached that if you just leave the market alone, it'll all sort itself out in the end[7]. Modern Liberalism, by contrast, came to understand that markets, left to their own devices, sometimes act like unsupervised children—great fun until they break something or hurt themselves. So, Modern Liberalism stepped in with a bit of gentle oversight: social security for the elderly, healthcare for the sick, and free education so that future generations weren't doomed to a lifetime of ignorance[8]. It wasn't about abandoning freedom but recognising that freedom means little without the basic conditions necessary to live a dignified life.

And thus, the Liberal wardrobe got a bit of an upgrade: still valuing freedom but now pairing it with a sensible coat of social responsibility. It's like adding a thermal layer to your minimalist ensemble—it's still sleek, still streamlined, but now you're not freezing to death in the middle of winter.

---

7. If this sounds familiar, we'll be speaking about Neoliberalism a little bit later on.

Liberalism and Economic Policy: Balancing Free Markets and Social Justice

Now, let's dive into everyone's favourite dinner conversation topic: economics. Classical Liberals had a simple, no-fuss recipe—just mix individual initiative with free markets, leave it to bake at room temperature, et voilà! Prosperity for all. Or so they thought. But as it turns out, leaving the economic kitchen unsupervised tends to result in more than a few burnt dishes—think economic depressions, rampant inequality, and a distinct smell of monopolies overcooking in the background[9].

Modern Liberalism didn't throw out the original recipe, but like any good cook, they realised a few tweaks were needed to prevent economic catastrophes and social injustices from ruining the meal. So, they kept the foundational ingredients of private property and markets but added just a smidgen government intervention to keep things from boiling over. This is where regulations come in—measures to stop businesses from dumping toxic waste into rivers or paying workers in metaphorical peanuts[10].

The challenge for Modern Liberals is all about balance: how do you harness the dynamic power of markets while ensuring they don't trample all over the vulnerable or leave society at the mercy of unchecked greed? It's like trying to balance a seesaw with one end weighed down by corporate titans and the other by the public good. If you tip too far towards *laissez-faire*[11] economics, you end up with massive inequality and exploitation. But if the state steps in too heavily, you risk stifling innovation and turning the economy into one big bureaucratic sludge.

---

9. The smell is strangely reminiscent of KFC if I'm being totally honest.

10. Unless we're talking about actual squirrels, in which case, they're probably fine with it.

11. Basically the French term for "Let 'er rip!"

To avoid these extremes, Modern Liberalism aims to find that sweet spot where markets can hum along efficiently while society at large reaps the benefits. This means embracing capitalism but with guardrails—things like minimum wage laws, environmental regulations, and consumer protections. It's the political equivalent of giving the economy enough freedom to run, but not so much that it starts knocking over pedestrians.

At its core, Modern Liberal economic policy is about *pragmatism*. Liberals understand that markets are incredibly efficient at allocating resources and driving innovation, but they also recognise that left unchecked, they can concentrate wealth and power in ways that undermine social justice. It's about ensuring that the economy serves the many, not just the few—the goal being a society where prosperity is shared more widely and economic opportunities aren't reserved for those born into the right zip code.

In the end, Liberalism's economic balancing act is a bit like baking a soufflé: too much heat and it collapses, too little and it never rises. Modern Liberals strive to create a system where the economy can flourish without leaving half the population struggling to get by. It's a delicate, ever-evolving recipe, but when done right, it's a feast worth sharing.

Modern Day Liberalism: The Best Intentions, Still Caught in a Mess

Fast forward to today, and Liberalism is still doing its best to champion the ideals of freedom, equality, and individual rights—but now it wears a badge that's a bit more tattered, with an air of exhausted optimism. Sure, human rights laws, freedom of speech protections, and privacy rights are all direct descendants of Locke's and Mill's lofty visions. On paper, it looks brilliant: the right to express yourself, the right to privacy, and the idea that government should be transparent and accountable to the people. What could possibly go wrong?

Well, as it turns out, quite a bit.

One of Liberalism's proudest achievements has always been its defence of freedom of speech. It's the idea that, in a well-functioning society, even bad ideas should be aired, because better ideas will naturally rise to the top. This, of course, sounds lovely in theory. In practice? Not so much. Take the internet, for example, which was supposed to be the ultimate platform for free expression. The reality is a bit messier[12]. Instead of fostering the rational debate that Mill envisioned, the internet has become a battleground for disinformation, trolling, and the ever-present threat of online harassment. Mill's belief that bad ideas would be defeated by better ones? It didn't quite account for the rise of conspiracy theories or internet echo chambers where bad ideas aren't just tolerated—they're celebrated[13].

And that's where Liberalism finds itself today—defending the right to free speech in an age where the line between free expression and harmful rhetoric has become harder to draw. Countries like the United States, with its First Amendment, and the UK, with its proud history of defending free speech, are now facing the uncomfortable reality that unfettered expression in the digital age doesn't always lead to enlightened debate. Instead, it often descends into polarisation and misinformation. Germany, in contrast, has taken a stricter stance with its NetzDG law, requiring social media platforms to quickly remove hate speech, an example of how Liberalism in practice sometimes requires curbing freedoms to protect the public good.

Then there's the issue of privacy rights—another pillar of modern Liberalism. Locke may have fought for the sanctity of private property, but in today's world, it's less about land and more about your data. Thanks to privacy laws like GDPR in

---

12. To put it less gently, it's a catastrofuckup.

13. Mill: Bad ideas will naturally die out. Reality: Bad ideas on social media have more lives than a cat.

Europe and the Data Protection Act in the UK, we're supposed to be protected from corporate spying and government overreach. Yet, despite these efforts, we all know we're being watched—*constantly*. Every click, every search, every location ping is being tracked by Big Tech companies whose data collection makes Orwell's 1984 look quaint by comparison. Google, Facebook, and Amazon know more about us than most of our friends do. And the state? Well, let's just say mass surveillance is alive and well, all in the name of national security.

While Liberalism was quick to champion privacy rights in the age of government overreach, it now finds itself caught in an entirely new dilemma. Technology is evolving far faster than the laws designed to protect us. Governments and tech giants are racing ahead, leaving liberal protections in the dust, scrambling to keep up with innovations in data mining, artificial intelligence, and surveillance technology. Liberalism still clings to the idea that rights will be enough to shield us from corporate and state abuses, but let's be honest: it's starting to look like a losing battle. It's hard to demand accountability when your Alexa is listening in on your every conversation.

And then, of course, there's the thorny issue of government accountability. Liberalism thrives on the belief that governments should be transparent and answerable to the people. That's why we have freedom of information laws, public inquiries, and all those endless parliamentary debates where, in theory, politicians should be held to account. But in practice? Well, just look at the UK in recent years. Whether it's the dodgy deals surrounding COVID-19 contracts, Parliamentary expenses scandals, or the constant game of blame-passing that seems to define modern politics, it's clear that the Liberal dream of transparent governance is often just that—a dream.

In countries like Canada or New Zealand, Liberalism still feels like it's got a solid grip, with leaders like Justin Trudeau and Jacinda Ardern promoting inclusive governance and transparency. But even there, the cracks show: in the form of economic inequality, populist backlash, and debates over how far liberal freedoms can go before they clash with the public good.

So, while Liberalism remains the foundation of many modern democracies, it's not without its struggles. In the digital age, where technology, surveillance, and disinformation seem to be running wild, Liberalism is fighting to stay relevant[14]. Its best intentions are still there, but the challenges it faces are bigger—and messier—than ever before.

What It's Not: Let's Clear Up Some Misconceptions

There's a tendency these days to throw the word Liberalism around without much thought, so let's clarify something quickly: Liberalism is not a free pass for an anything-goes society. It's not about letting everyone do whatever they want, whenever they want, without consequence. That's more in the ballpark of Libertarianism—the political cousin that crashed the party, drank all the punch, and told everyone that government regulations are for suckers[15].

Now, to be fair, Liberalism and Libertarianism do have a bit of overlap, especially when it comes to things like economic freedom and limited government. Both share the view that individual rights should be protected and that the state should have a relatively light touch when it comes to meddling in people's lives. But here's the key difference: where Libertarianism says, *"The government has no business telling me what to do,"* Liberalism says, *"Well, yes, but we do need some rules to keep this place from falling apart and catching on fire."* Liberalism is like the sober friend at the party, keeping an eye on things to make

---

14. Liberalism: Great on paper, but currently in therapy over social media.

15. Which we'll discuss at great sardonic length – including a nice conversation between Ayn Rand and John Milton Keynes.

sure the house doesn't burn down while everyone else is having a great time with their freedom.

At its core, Liberalism isn't about letting individual rights run rampant with no regard for the greater good. It's about striking a balance between freedom and order, between letting people live their lives and ensuring that society as a whole doesn't descend into chaos. The classic liberal idea is that individual rights are fundamental, but they're not absolute—there are limits, especially when one person's freedom starts infringing on someone else's. So no, Liberalism isn't your golden ticket to do whatever you want without consequences. Nice try, though.

In fact, one of the most persistent misconceptions about Liberalism—especially in places like the US—is that it's synonymous with left-wing politics or progressivism. If you hear the word *"liberal"* on American news networks, you'd be forgiven for thinking it's a catch-all term for anything vaguely left of centre, from climate activism to free healthcare. But Liberalism is a much broader ideology than that, with its roots in individual liberty, free markets, and limited government. It's not about radical change or dismantling the system. If anything, it's more about fine-tuning the system so that individual freedoms can flourish within a stable society.

In Europe, Liberalism isn't automatically associated with the left. Many Liberal parties in Germany or France champion market-based economics, personal freedoms, and even some conservative values when it comes to governance[16]. It's a political tradition that can fit into both left and right narratives, depending on which aspect of freedom is at stake—whether it's economic liberty or civil rights. So when people conflate Liberalism with being left-wing, it's a simplification. Liberalism is less about being left or right and more about finding a balance

---

16. Free Democratic Party (Germany), Democratic Movement (France), La République En Marche (France), People's Party for Freedom and Democracy (Netherlands).

between liberty and responsibility. It can coexist with capital-ist economic policies while fiercely defending civil liberties—a combination that doesn't easily fit into the simplistic left-right political spectrum.

For example, in the UK, the Liberal Democrats have tradition-ally been the centrist party, promoting a mix of social justice and economic freedom. They're not out to tear down the system, but they're also not sitting back, content to let market forces solve everything. It's a balancing act between individual rights and government intervention—not too much, not too little.

Ultimately, Liberalism is all about balance. It's not about letting the state run everything, nor is it about unregulated freedom for all. It's about finding that sweet spot where individual freedoms are respected, but society as a whole functions smoothly. And yes, sometimes that means compromising—a word that doesn't exactly thrill people on the extremes of the political spectrum, but it's what keeps Liberalism ticking along.

The long and short of it? Liberalism isn't about anarchy, and it's not the same as libertarianism or a synonym for progres-sivism. It's a broad, nuanced ideology that tries to juggle the rights of the individual with the needs of the community. It's a tricky balance to strike, but Liberalism has managed to hold its own—most of the time.

Global Challenges to Liberalism: Populism and Authoritarianism

Just when Liberalism thought it could finally kick back and enjoy a well-deserved rest, in walk two uninvited guests: Pop-ulism and Authoritarianism. These troublesome houseguests aren't just crashing the party—they've upended the furniture and are helping themselves to the silverware. Both movements have gained traction by tapping into widespread public frustra-tions—economic struggles, cultural upheavals, and a growing distrust of those often referred to as the *"elite."*

Populism, in particular, has mastered the art of turning complex, multifaceted issues into convenient, oversimplified us-versus-them narratives. Forget Liberalism's cherished ideals of rational discourse and nuanced debate—Populism prefers emotional sound bites, portraying itself as the champion of the *"ordinary people"* or the *"working class"* against an out-of-touch, self-serving elite. It's a seductive story, and it works because it offers clear villains and quick fixes, bypassing the slow, reasoned approach that Liberalism holds dear. When people are angry and anxious, the promise of immediate change, even at the cost of long-standing democratic norms, can be hard to resist.

Meanwhile, Authoritarianism has been making its own comeback, promising stability and strong leadership in an increasingly chaotic world. Authoritarian leaders rise to power by offering quick fixes—at the expense of personal freedoms, checks and balances, and, well, everything that Liberalism stands for. They position themselves as the antidote to the perceived inefficiency and dithering of liberal democratic systems, offering decisive action in place of deliberation and compromise. The problem? Their *"decisive action"* usually involves silencing opposition, eroding individual rights, and dismantling the institutions that keep power in check.

From Brexit to the rise of strongman politics in various countries, these challenges to Liberalism aren't just knocking politely on the door; they're tearing down the patio and building a wall in its place. Populists and authoritarians thrive on undermining the very democratic structures that Liberalism has painstakingly built, chipping away at freedom of the press, independence of the judiciary, and the legitimacy of elections—all while claiming to act in the name of *"the people."*

Liberalism now finds itself in a defensive posture, no longer just championing abstract principles like freedom and equality but actively trying to protect the tangible structures of democracy. It's no longer enough to simply believe in the marketplace of ideas—Liberalism must actively safeguard the institutions that allow those ideas to be exchanged freely and fairly. The rise of populism and authoritarianism has forced Liberalism to fight for its survival, defending not just the ideals of reason and liberty but the very framework of modern democracy itself.

Why It Matters: The Foundation of Modern Democracy (Mostly)

So, why should we care about Liberalism today[17]? Because, whether we like it or not, it's the foundation of most modern democracies—especially here in the UK. Liberalism gave us the principles that keep autocracy at bay: freedom of speech[18], rule of law, individual rights, and the belief that governments are accountable to the people. Without Liberalism, we'd still be stuck in a world where the divine right of kings dictated every aspect of life, and let's be honest, no one wants to go back to the days when a monarch's whims could decide your fate over breakfast.

Imagine a world where your entire existence was dictated by aristocrats, monarchs, and the Church, where questioning the king wasn't just impolite—it was treason. Liberalism came along and, in a not-so-gentle fashion, pulled the rug out from under all of that. The idea that power could come from the people, that governments should be based on consent, not some divine mandate, was revolutionary—and frankly, it still is. Even today, the principles of freedom and accountability are what keep authoritarianism from creeping back in through the cracks. And let's be clear, those cracks are always there, waiting for the right moment to widen.

Take a look around the world, and it's easy to see why Liberalism still matters. The UK's system of parliamentary democracy,

---

17. And yes, that does include anyone who scoffs at the mere mention of "Liberal"

18. Though to be more accurate it would be "Freedom of Expression" in the UK – don't get me started.

with all its quirks and endless debates, is built on liberal principles. The same goes for freedom of the press (for all its flaws),
and the idea that citizens should have a voice in how they're
governed. We take these things for granted now, but they didn't
just fall out of the sky. They're the result of centuries of liberal thought, chipping away at monarchy and authoritarianism,
slowly but surely creating space for individual rights to thrive.

But Liberalism's relevance doesn't stop at its historical victories.
Sure, it gave us the tools to get out from under the yoke of
kings, but it's still with us today, influencing policy debates on
everything from immigration to healthcare, privacy to education. It's the defender of personal freedoms, even when those
freedoms clash with collective security—and let's face it, that
clash happens all the time in the modern world. Think about
the immigration debates in the UK, where liberal ideals about
the rights of individuals to move freely butt up against national
concerns about security and economic strain. Or take the fight
over data privacy and surveillance—Liberalism is right there,
standing in between the state's desire to monitor everything and
your right not to be watched while browsing cat videos at 3
o'clock in the morning[19].

And in a world where authoritarianism seems to be making a
comeback—from Russia to Hungary, Turkey to Brazil—Liberalism's emphasis on checks and balances is more important
than ever. It's the idea that no one person or institution should
have too much power, because power has a way of corrupting.
That's why we have things like independent judiciaries, free
media, and, yes, pesky opposition parties—all designed to stop
governments from going off the rails. Liberalism doesn't always
succeed in this regard (see: the recent erosion of democratic
norms in various countries), but at least it's still trying. And
in a political landscape that feels increasingly like a tug-of-war
between freedom and control, Liberalism is the ideology that

---

19. And yes, it's only cat videos. Nothing else.

keeps reminding us that democracy is messy—but authoritarianism is far messier.

That doesn't mean Liberalism has all the answers. It's often accused of being too idealistic, of putting too much faith in rational debate and individual responsibility, while underestimating the darker aspects of human nature. And to be fair, Liberalism's optimism can sometimes feel a little out of touch in a world that's getting more cynical by the day[20] . But even so, Liberalism is the framework that's trying to keep democracy from imploding. It's the system that insists on freedom even when freedom is complicated, that demands accountability even when the guilty parties would much prefer we look the other way.

And let's face it—without Liberalism, we wouldn't have the political freedoms we often take for granted. Whether it's the ability to call out your MP on Twitter[21] , the right to protest in the streets of London, or the fact that elections are held with some semblance of fairness, we owe it to Liberalism. It might not always be glamorous, but it's the reason we're not bowing down to kings or living in a surveillance state (well, mostly not).

---

20. Liberalism: Still patiently waiting for everyone to calm down and have a rational discussion.

21. Or call them a sleazy crotchgoblin with the morals of an empty Tesco Bag for life, or whatever...

Conservatism

The Stubborn Grandpa of Political M ovements

> "Liberalism is trust of the people tempered by prudence. Conservatism is distrust of the people tempered by fear."
>
> William E. Gladstone

Writing about Conservatism is tricky for me—anyone that knows me will tell you that I'm not exactly its biggest fan. The Conservative Party[1] isn't exactly where I plant my political flag[2] . But here's something I realised while researching this book, that even though I'm traditionally quite (vehemently) anti-Tory, I have to admit:

Conservatism isn't just some relic of outdated thinking[3] .

---

1. AKA that pack of soulless demi-humans who were in power for fourteen long years with wallets where their hearts should be.

2. I genuinely have a better chance of falling pregnant than putting my cross next to a Tory.

3. I admit this so very, very grudgingly.

And while this might be an uncomfortable chapter to write, it's a chance to understand Conservatism in a way that goes beyond the belligerent eye-rolling it so often inspires in me. It's easy to dismiss it as the stubborn roadblock to progress, but it's also a reminder that not all change is inherently good, and that slowing down can sometimes be the right call.

So, how do we characterise Conservatism? Well, imagine Conservatism as that classic grumpy grandparent we've all encountered. You know the one. Sitting in their well-worn armchair, shaking their head at the *"state of the world today"*, forever reminiscing about a time when things were simpler, better, and definitely more predictable. To them, society was at its finest when everyone knew their place, family values were sacred, and change—if it happened at all—occurred at a glacial pace. The world, in their view, was orderly, stable, and comfortably unchanging. Back then, people respected authority, and none of this chaotic, newfangled business about globalisation, identity politics, or the idea that pronouns matter.

Let's call him Grandpa Conservatism. Grandpa's mantra? *"Why fix what isn't broken?"* He'll grumble endlessly about how the youth are always in a rush to change everything, how the world is moving too fast, and how people these days just don't appreciate rules or tradition. He's baffled by the obsession with progress, convinced that it's just a fancy way of saying, *"Let's make everything worse."* In Grandpa's eyes, the past was a golden age—when there was a clear sense of right and wrong, and people didn't need to constantly question the foundations of society.

But here's the thing about Grandpa Conservatism—despite his exasperating stubbornness, you can't entirely dismiss him. He's lived through it all, seen the consequences of moving too quickly without thinking things through. He's been around long enough to know that rushing headfirst into change often leads to unintended disasters. For all his moaning about the state of the world today, he's also the guy who's seen the chaos that erupts when societies tear down traditions without a plan.

Sure, he might sound like a broken record, constantly warning about the dangers of moving too fast, but every once in a while, you have to admit—extremely begrudgingly, of course—that he has a point.

In that sense, Conservatism, like our metaphorical grandparent, isn't just about grumbling for the sake of it. Beneath the layers of nostalgia and resistance to change lies a deep-seated belief in order, tradition, and the idea that progress, if not carefully managed, can spiral into chaos. And as frustrating as that perspective can be when you're someone who believes in equality and social progress (like me), you can't entirely ignore the fact that Conservatism is driven by the desire to protect what works and to tread carefully when it comes to reform.

Now, I'll be honest—radical change often feels like the only way forward, whether it's LGBTQ+ rights, immigration, or environmental reform. But occasionally, a bit of caution isn't entirely misguided. Conservatism can act as the speed bump that prevents society from driving off a cliff. Take the example of financial regulation. After the 2008 financial crisis, conservative fiscal policies advocating for measured spending and avoiding reckless economic expansion played a critical role in stabilising economies.

While it's easy to roll our eyes at the endless pleas to slow down, there's something to be said for a movement that values stability over chaos. It's a frustrating position, especially for those of us who want to see society evolve more quickly, but on rare[4] occasions, Grandpa Conservatism isn't entirely wrong.

That doesn't mean I'm about to switch allegiances or start waving the Tory flag – Cher forbid. Far from it. But recognising that Conservatism has its role, even if it's one that I often disagree with, is part of what makes this chapter an important one for me. It's a chance to see Conservatism not just as a roadblock

---

4. Oh, so very, very rare.

to progress, but as the political philosophy that keeps us from upending everything in our rush to fix what we see as broken.

The History of Conservatism: Told You So Since the French Revolution

Let's take a leisurely stroll down memory lane, back to where Conservatism was spawned—not in a quiet, orderly way, but in the chaotic, head-rolling streets of Revolutionary France. If ever there was a moment that Conservatism could point to and say *"I told you so,"* it was the French Revolution. Picture it: 1789, when liberty, equality, and fraternity were supposed to be the new guiding lights of humanity. Revolutionaries were dismantling centuries of monarchy and aristocracy, fuelled by visions of a utopia where the people reigned supreme. It was a political earthquake, shaking the very foundations of society.

And then there was Edmund Burke, the man standing at the sidelines, watching the chaos unfold with a mix of horror and grim satisfaction. To everyone caught up in the revolutionary fervour, Burke must have seemed like the ultimate party pooper. While the revolutionaries were busy tearing down everything they despised about the *ancien régime*, Burke was the one saying, *"Erm—are we sure this is a good idea?"* It wasn't that he opposed change outright. What he feared instead was the kind of radical upheaval that destroyed centuries of tradition and social order without any clear idea of what would replace it.

Burke looked at the French Revolution, not with excitement for what might come next, but with a deep sense of foreboding. To him, the revolutionaries were like children knocking down a sandcastle without thinking about how they'd rebuild it—and he wasn't wrong[5]. What started as a quest for liberty and equality quickly deteriorated into a blood-soaked descent into chaos.

---

5. The decimalisation of the French clock and calendar did look like a bit of a nightmare to be fair.

Guillotines took the place of royal decrees, and the revolution spiralled out of control, turning on itself in a reign of terror that saw even its architects beheaded. Burke's warning? If you tear down the institutions that have held society together, you risk plunging it into anarchy.

Burke's philosophy of Conservatism wasn't a knee-jerk reaction against all change. Far from it. He wasn't opposed to reform—he just believed that reform needed to be gradual and measured, rooted in tradition and respectful of the institutions that had evolved over time to maintain social stability. For Burke, revolution wasn't progress—it was madness. Society needed order, and radical change was too disruptive, too risky. He was the original anti-revolutionary, advocating for slow, careful progress rather than tearing down everything all at once and hoping for the best.

In his seminal work, *Reflections on the Revolution in France*, Burke laid out the foundations of modern Conservatism. He argued that tradition and custom were the glue that held societies together, and while these traditions could evolve, they couldn't be discarded without consequences. It's not that Burke was a fan of the absolute monarchy—he wasn't. But he saw the French Revolution as proof that when you dismantle the old order without thinking through the new, you invite chaos. And, well, with the Reign of Terror in full swing, it's hard to say he was wrong. The guillotine had replaced the crown, but the instability remained, proving that radical change without careful planning leads to disaster.

Burke's Conservatism has been passed down through the generations, evolving but maintaining its core belief: preserving tradition and social stability is key to a functioning society. This isn't to say that Conservatism is completely opposed to progress—it's just that it prefers progress to be more of a slow and steady marathon rather than a reckless sprint to the finish line. It's about taking things one step at a time, ensuring that each move forward is backed by reason, prudence, and an appreciation for the past.

Fast forward to today, and Conservatism is still that voice in the back of the room, offering its signature eye roll whenever someone suggests a radical new reform. Whether it's climate action, economic policy, or social change, Conservatism's response is almost always the same: *"Let's not rush into anything."* It's a perspective that can be maddening to those of us who see progress as an urgent priority (which, let's be real, it often is). But Burke's original warning about the dangers of rushing headlong into change without thinking through the consequences still resonates. There's something to be said for the idea that change needs to be measured, that tearing down institutions without a replacement plan is a recipe for chaos.

And that's the essence of Conservatism—it's not about opposing change for the sake of opposition. It's about ensuring that the things we build are solid enough to stand the test of time. There's a grudging wisdom in that, even if it feels like dragging feet in the face of real challenges. Burke may not have been a revolutionary, but he understood one thing clearly: the consequences of change can be unpredictable, and if we're not careful, we might end up in a worse situation than the one we started with.

The Philosophical Underpinnings: What's Really Behind Grandpa's Grumpiness?

Let's dig a little deeper into Grandpa Conservatism's psyche[6] —because surely there's more going on than just a fondness for saying *"Back in my day."* At the heart of conservatism lie several core principles that go beyond mere stubbornness: a belief in human imperfection, the importance of tradition, the value of social hierarchy, and a near-obsessive emphasis on property rights. It's like a psychological profile of that grumpy relative who refuses to embrace smartphones because *"buttons worked just fine."*

---

6. Yes, I know the very thought is horrifying, but stick with me.

First up, Conservatives firmly believe that humans are inherently imperfect, selfish, and prone to making terrible decisions. Not exactly the most flattering take on humanity, but it does explain their allergic reaction to any grand utopian scheme. In their eyes, trying to create a perfect society is not only futile but downright dangerous—like giving a toddler a chainsaw and hoping for the best. Keep expectations low, they say, and you'll never be disappointed.

Then, there's the reverence for tradition. Conservatives view tradition as the collective wisdom of past generations—the equivalent of Grandma's *"famous"* casserole recipe passed down through the ages. You don't mess with it because, well, it worked once, so why risk tofu-ing it up? Tradition gives people a sense of identity and stability, so when change is necessary, it should be as slow and gentle as a light seasoning rather than a complete kitchen overhaul.

Social hierarchy also plays a key role. For Conservatives, hierarchy isn't just an unfortunate reality; it's a *good* thing. It creates order, like a well and oft-rehearsed play where everyone knows their lines and doesn't go improvising some revolutionary monologue. Sure, they'll admit that the script could use the occasional tweak, but they're not about to let a new, radical playwright turn Act Three into some chaotic free-for-all.

Finally, we have property rights—the sacred cornerstone of conservatism. To a Conservative, owning property is the ultimate expression of freedom and personal responsibility. It's the political version of meticulously mowing your lawn every Sunday; you own it, you maintain it, and woe betide anyone who tries to mess with your rose bushes. For them, property is what ties individuals to society, making them care about its success. It's not just about having a roof over your head; it's about having a piece of the pie that's *yours* to protect.

So, what's really behind all the grumbling? These philosophical roots explain why conservatism isn't just about saying *"no"* to change—it's about protecting a coherent worldview that values caution, stability, and a deep-seated belief in the slow, steady march of progress. After all, what's the rush?

If It Ain't Broke, Don't Fix It

In today's political landscape, Conservatism is still clinging on—albeit with far more bruises after the Tories' dramatic loss to Labour this past July. While Conservatism as an ideology survives, it's taken on several different flavours, some of which are decidedly less, well, *"conservative"* than others. In the lead-up to its spectacular defeat, the Conservative Party itself had become a mishmash of different factions. On one side, you've got the traditional conservatives, still espousing the time-honoured values of small government, personal responsibility, and national security. On the other side, you have the more extreme voices, whose commitment to traditional Conservative values seems about as real as a campaign promise.

At its core, modern Conservatism remains committed to the belief that the best government is the one that governs least. It champions lower taxes, deregulation, and a strong national defence—policies that reflect the idea that people should be left to their own devices as much as possible. Margaret Thatcher famously declared, *"There's no such thing as society, only individuals,"*[7] and this has been the cornerstone of Conservative thought ever since. The focus is on individual responsibility—everyone for themselves, and the state should stay out of people's lives, provided they aren't disturbing the status quo.

But today's Conservative Party is far from a united front. The Tories who still call themselves Conservatives—the old guard, if you will—are increasingly overshadowed by a new breed of politicians whose conservatism is... questionable at best. Think of people like Suella Braverman, the erstwhile Lee Anderson,

---

7. When we get to Neoliberalism we'll see just how well that nugget of wisdom has worked out.

or the charming Jonathan Gullis (who lost his seat). They're not exactly carrying the torch of Thatcherism—instead, they've turned their focus to a far more populist agenda, with culture wars, anti-immigration rhetoric, and, in some cases, a worrying flirtation with far-right ideologies (and in some cases it's moved from a light flirt to a full-fat sordid affair).

Lee Anderson[8], for instance, left the party altogether to join Reform, which speaks volumes about where modern Conservatism is heading—or not heading, depending on your view.

But back to those more traditional Conservative policies. If Thatcher ran with the idea that privatisation and individual responsibility would reshape the UK, today's Conservative leaders—those who haven't strayed too far into culture war territory—still hold to that line. The idea of small government remains sacred. Conservatives argue that government should stay out of people's wallets and bedrooms, but keep a robust national defence to maintain order when needed. It's the belief that people should be free to live their lives without government interference, but that freedom comes with a caveat: it must not disrupt the societal status quo.

On social issues, though, Conservatism still clings to its deep-rooted caution—and this is where things tend to get dicey. Whether it's big or small changes to how we do things, Conservatives tend to approach everything with a *"let's not rush into things"* attitude. That's putting it mildly. More often than not, Conservatism looks like it's playing catch-up with the world that's already moved on. We've already note a few times that it's not that Conservatives outright oppose progress, but they're deeply reluctant to embrace it without a solid plan, a detailed checklist, and probably a good 10-year delay.

Take climate change, for example. While the world is grappling with rising temperatures, natural disasters, and the undeniable

---

8. "30p Lee" or "3 Party Lee" to be as accurate as possible.

evidence that we're hurtling towards a global catastrophe, many Conservatives are still debating whether going green will harm the economy. It's as though they're weighing the economic costs of inaction against the costs of saving the planet—and, predictably, the economy often wins out. Or consider the ongoing debate about immigration. While progressive voices argue for more inclusive and humane immigration policies, Conservatives cling to a notion of national identity and security that often feels like a relic from the past.

The thing is, it's not that Conservatism is against change outright—though it sometimes feels that way. Rather, Conservatives fear that rapid change could undermine the foundations of society. Whether it's social reform, immigration, or tackling climate change, Conservatism is always asking, *"What will this cost?"* and *"What will this break?"* It's a mentality that prioritises stability over progress, security over risk, and tradition over anything that seems too new, too fast. Sometimes, that's maddening. And other times, it's... well, not entirely wrong.

The Many Shades of Blue: Not All Conservatives Wear the Same Cardigan

Just as not all grandpas are cut from the same tweed (some prefer slippers over loafers, after all), Conservatism isn't a one-size-fits-all ideology. Under its wide, occasionally bickering umbrella, there are various strands that often agree to disagree—sometimes loudly, especially over the family dinner table. Now, in the previous section we've already touched on this, but we're going to go into a bit more detail, so bear with me[9].

First up, we have **Traditional Conservatism**, the classic model. These are your archetypal grandpas who cherish institutions like the monarchy, the church, and the family unit. They value

---

9. See what I did there again.

social order and are positively allergic to rapid change. These are the ones muttering about *"kids these days"* while polishing their antique pocket watches, sighing for the days when a decent suit and a stiff upper lip solved everything.

Then there's **One-Nation Conservatism**, which arose in response to the social divisions wrought by industrialisation. Think of them as the more compassionate relatives—the ones who believe that with great power comes great responsibility (yes, like Spider-Man, but with a monocle). They champion social cohesion and are open to welfare measures to keep society from splintering—Grandpa with a soft spot and a dash of *noblesse oblige*, if you will.

Next, we meet the **Neoliberal Conservatives**, who strutted onto the stage with leaders like Margaret Thatcher and Ronald Reagan[10] . They're all about free-market capitalism, deregulation, and the gospel of individualism. Picture Grandpa discovering the stock market and becoming obsessed with his investment portfolio, preaching that the invisible hand of the market will fix everything—even the leaky roof he's been ignoring for weeks.

On the more hawkish end, we find the **Neoconservatives**, who are keen on flexing foreign policy muscles. These are the relatives who believe in promoting democracy and national interests abroad—often with a side of military action, invited or not. They're the uncles who turn up, sleeves rolled, ready to *"fix"* everyone else's problems, whether anyone asked them to or not.

Finally, we have the **New Right** or **Populist Conservatives**, who mix traditional conservative values with a hearty dose of nationalism, and occasionally (overt) flirt with xenophobia. These are the relatives who show up at family gatherings spouting conspiracy theories, throwing side-eye at anyone too *'cosmopolitan,'* and making everyone else deeply uncomfortable.

---

10. There's a terrifying dialogue sequence coming up between those two.

Understanding these variations sheds light on why the Conservative Party (and conservative movements worldwide) often seem like a dysfunctional family reunion—everyone's got the same last name, but they can't agree on what to serve for dinner.

Big C vs. Little c: The Alphabet Soup of Conservatism

But even then, not all conservative cardigans are cut from the same tweed[11] . While some don the blue rosette with pride, others hold to a more philosophical conservatism that transcends party politics. Enter: the world of Big-C and small-c conservatism. Now, I'll be honest: I personally just dismissed this particular distinction with *"conservatives-are-conservatives-and-there's-no-real-difference-between-them-so-there"* grunt of annoyance, except once you really start looking a bit more closely, there's a world of difference between **big-C Conservatism** and **small-c conservatism**, and understanding the difference actually does matter. So, let's wade into the murky waters of C versus c.

Big-C Conservatism: The Political Party

Big-C Conservatism refers specifically to the Conservative Party—those folks who brought you Margaret Thatcher, David Cameron's Big Society (remember that?), and most recently, Boris Johnson's *"oven-ready"* Brexit and Liz Truss's little adventure with the economy and mortgage rates[12] . Big-C Conservatives are card-carrying members of a political party whose agenda is focused on lower taxes, deregulation, privatisation, and making sure the rich get just a little bit richer. They're the ones you'll see on campaign posters, their blue rosettes proudly

---

11. Yes, I know I'm torturing this metaphor, but Bear with me.

12. For fuck's sake.

pinned to their chest, waxing lyrical about the importance of traditional values, small government, and why you really don't need a functioning welfare state.

Let's look at some notable modern Big-C Conservatives:

- **Rishi Sunak**: The former Prime Minister and current Leader of the Opposition, still clinging to his well-tailored suits and calm demeanour, as he tries to pretend he's here to restore order. Sunak's policies, both as PM and now in opposition, tetchily scream Big-C conservatism—pro-business, low-tax, and very little concern for those pesky social safety nets.

- **Liz Truss**: The brief yet memorable disaster of a Prime Minister who thought she could apply free-market economics like a teenager trying out new make-up trends. Her stint in office ended in a spectacular implosion of the British economy, proving that cosplay Thatcherism is best left in the 1980s. Truss was Big-C all the way, belligerently so—determined to push for extreme deregulation and tax cuts at any cost, but ultimately showing the perils of ideological rigidity over practical governance.

- **Jacob Rees-Mogg**[13] : The walking embodiment of a Victorian cosplay enthusiast who somehow stumbled into modern politics. Rees-Mogg channels the spirit of a 19th-century aristocrat with his posh drawl and disdain for anything remotely progressive. He's Big-C Conservatism's most bizarre caricature, preferring to fight imaginary culture wars while lounging on the benches of the Commons like he's waiting for his afternoon tea to be served.

---

13. AKA the coat rack possessed by a Victorian ghost.

In short, Big-C Conservatives are political animals whose main concern is winning elections, holding power, and ensuring that Conservative Party values stay enshrined in policy. They're often more interested in maintaining party unity and public image than in sticking to ideological purity. After all, nothing says Conservative like pivoting to whatever position keeps you in Downing Street.

Small-c conservatism: The Philosophy

Then there's small-c conservatism, which is more of a philosophical outlook which we've mostly focused on in this chapter. It's the belief in slow, cautious change, preserving institutions, and maintaining social order. Small-c conservatism can be found across political parties and even in people who'd sooner burn a Tory membership card than carry one. Small-c conservatives aren't necessarily aligned with the Conservative Party, but they share a worldview that prioritises stability over rapid reform.

Small-c conservatism often shows up in surprising places, like with Theresa May. As Prime Minister, she embodied cautious pragmatism, favouring incremental changes over radical reform. Her leadership was marked by a careful balancing act, trying to navigate between her party's more hardline elements and her natural instinct for moderation. May's approach was less about grand visions and more about keeping the ship steady, even as the more fervent factions of her party tugged at the wheel, eager to steer it toward rougher seas.

We should also consider Angela Merkel, the former German Chancellor, who despite leading a centre-right party, often governed with the steady, careful pragmatism of a small-c conservative. Merkel wasn't about to lead Germany into some radical upheaval—she was all about stability, balance, and cautious adaptation. No fireworks, just a lot of serious frowning and incremental policy shifts.

Unlike Big-C Conservatism, which is driven by the desire for electoral victory, small-c conservatism is more about keeping things as they are—or, at most, tweaking things slowly enough that no one gets too upset. It's the belief that society functions best when we don't shake things up too much, and that change, if it comes, should be as gentle as a light drizzle rather than a thunderstorm.

Big-C vs. Small-c: A Real-Life Comparison

To illustrate the difference, imagine we're in the middle of a crisis—let's say, a pandemic[14]. The Big-C Conservative response might look like Boris Johnson fumbling his way through lockdown policies, promising *"world-beating"* solutions while prioritising the economy over public health and ensuring his mates land lucrative contracts.

Meanwhile, the small-c conservative response might resemble Angela Merkel's handling of COVID-19: measured, scientific, and focused on keeping society functioning as normally as possible. No grandiose promises, just sensible, cautious steps to preserve order and protect the system.

Or take the climate crisis. Big-C Conservatives like Rishi Sunak are quick to support market-based solutions (so long as they don't hurt profits too much), while small-c conservatives will acknowledge the importance of protecting the planet but insist on a cautious, gradual transition—because, after all, rushing into renewable energy could destabilise the economy.

So, Which One Are You Talking About?

The next time someone says they're conservative, it's worth asking: Big-C or small-c? Are they the kind of conservative who's eyeing the next general election, hoping to save face in front of

---

14. Sadly not hard to imagine.

voters while holding the line on austerity policies? Or are they the kind of conservative who prefers a quiet life, resisting change because, as we've said before *"if it ain't broke, don't fix it"*—even if that means keeping some creaky institutions in place for a bit too long?

In the end, Big-C Conservatism is all about political survival, while small-c conservatism is about philosophical resistance to rapid change. So whether you're railing against Boris's latest blunder or rolling your eyes at your dad's refusal to embrace contactless payments, remember: not all conservatives are cut from the same cloth. Some wear the big blue rosette, while others are just clinging to a worldview where things don't change too fast, and everyone stays in their lane.

The Myth of Anti-Progress

Now, as we've already picked up, it isn't that Conservatism is *fundamentally* anti-progress. It just prefers to wrap progress in bubble wrap, place it on a slow-moving conveyor belt, and check in every few years to see if it's still intact. The caricature that Conservatives are dragging their feet, yelling *"No"* at every new idea, isn't entirely fair (though sometimes, it's spot on). What Conservatism offers is progress with a safety net, a cautious journey forward, with plenty of time to stop and loudly ask, *"Is this really a good idea?"*—probably several times.

Sure, it's true that conservatives have historically been late to the party on some pretty major social issues—women's suffrage, same-sex marriage, or even universal healthcare, to name a few. But that doesn't mean they've outright rejected these changes forever. Conservatism isn't about saying no to everything—it's about saying yes... eventually. After long periods of reflection, debate, and, if we're honest, grumbling about how things used to be. If progressivism is an express train, Conservatism is the local bus, taking scenic detours and arriving at the same destination, but with a lot more stops along the way.

Take the NHS, for example. When universal healthcare was first introduced, the Conservative Party wasn't exactly queuing up to endorse it. In fact, they opposed it outright at its inception. But fast forward a few decades, and now, the Tories have re-branded themselves as the NHS's *"staunch defenders"*—albeit while quietly trying to privatise bits of it when they think no one's looking. It's a classic Conservative move: once the system proves its worth and becomes popular with the public, they'll stand in front of it and pretend they were there all along, like someone showing up late to a party but still claiming they helped plan it.

LGBTQ+ rights follow a similar trajectory. For years, conserv-atives dragged their feet on equal marriage and legal protections for LGBTQ+ individuals. It wasn't exactly a surprise—they tend to be wary of rapid social change. But slowly, and some-times begrudgingly, even conservative politicians have come around to the idea that LGBTQ+ rights aren't just a fad. In fact, many conservatives now support equal marriage and the legal protections that come with it. Progress happens, even in conservative circles—it just tends to happen slowly, with a lot of heated arguments and perhaps a few long naps to mull things over.

What's important to understand is that Conservatism isn't about rejecting progress—it's about making sure we don't break everything in our rush to move forward. Conservatives look at society like a well-built house. Sure, it might need some renovations here and there, but they're wary of the wrecking ball approach that progressives sometimes favour. They'll add an extension to the house, but only after checking the founda-tions, reviewing the blueprints, and making sure the roof won't cave in.

Measured change is the name of the game. Conservatives be-lieve that progress is fine, as long as it doesn't destabilise the institutions that hold society together—institutions like family, faith, and the rule of law. These aren't just quaint traditions to them; they're the building blocks that keep everything from falling apart. So, while progressives might want to tear down the old and bring in the new, Conservatism says, *"Hold on, let's not throw out the good stuff in our rush to modernise."*

Does this approach frustrate those of us who want to see faster, more radical change? Absolutely. But sometimes, there's a strange wisdom in the slow, steady approach. As maddening as it can be to watch Conservatism insist on incremental change, there's value in the idea that progress doesn't have to mean upheaval. The goal, for conservatives, isn't to stop progress—it's to make sure that when we do move forward, we're not leaving destruction in our wake.

Conservatism in the Age of Climate Change: Can Grandpa Go Green?

Climate change is the elephant in the room—or perhaps the polar bear on the melting iceberg—that even Grandpa Conservatism can't ignore forever. The pressing question is whether an ideology rooted in preserving the status quo can adapt to face a crisis that demands swift, sweeping action.

On paper, environmental conservation should be a natural fit for Conservatism. After all, it's about safeguarding the planet for future generations—a deeply *"grandparent"* instinct, if ever there was one. Preserving the countryside, protecting traditional ways of life, and bolstering national security in the face of climate-related threats all align with the conservative ethos of order and protection.

But here's the issue we find ourselves with: the systemic changes required to tackle climate change make Grandpa grip his armchair a little tighter. Transitioning to renewable energy, imposing strict environmental regulations, and investing in green technologies? These are the kinds of economic and social upheavals that give Conservatism an epic fit of the vapours. It's one thing to complain about the weather, but quite another to overhaul an entire economy to prevent it from getting worse.

That said, a growing contingent of Green Conservatives argues that environmental stewardship is not just compatible with conservatism—it's a moral responsibility. They champion market-based solutions to climate problems, like carbon pricing and incentivising innovation in green technologies. Think of it like convincing Grandpa to install solar panels on his roof—not because he's gone all hippie on us, but because it makes sound economic sense and adds value to the house he's spent decades maintaining.

The real challenge lies in balancing short-term economic interests with long-term environmental sustainability. Conservatism's emphasis on prudence and responsibility could, in theory, be the perfect platform for promoting sustainable practices. But this requires a shift in perspective: from viewing environmental measures as disruptive to seeing them as vital for preserving the very fabric of society. After all, what's more conservative than protecting the planet your grandkids will inherit?

So, can Grandpa go green? Possibly—if he starts seeing climate action as essential for maintaining the garden he's tended all his life, ensuring it thrives for the next generation. It might take a few more scorching summers and the occasional dead rose bush to change his mind, but there's hope yet.

The Grandpa We Love to Roll Our Eyes At

I'll be honest—Conservatism is never going to be my political home. I won't be donning a blue rosette anytime soon, and the idea of supporting certain elements of the modern Conservative Party makes me feel like I've bitten into a lemon. My opposition to the far-right voices that have wormed their way into the Conservative benches—people like Lee Anderson, Suella Braverman and Robert Jenrick—isn't just political, it's visceral[15] . These

---

15. Anyone who follows me on Twitter knows the invective that I am capable of.

figures aren't simply pushing traditional conservative values; they're distorting them into something that's more about division, fear, and resentment than about the cautious, considered approach Conservatism was originally built on.

That said, I've tried—really tried—to view Conservatism in its original meaning. What was once a philosophy rooted in stability, tradition, and the cautious evolution of society, now feels like it's been hijacked by opportunists playing a different kind of game. The Conservatism of Edmund Burke is a world away from the ideological chaos that's currently playing out within the Tory Party. Burke's vision of preserving what works while making careful, considered reforms has been overshadowed by the noisy politics of fearmongering, xenophobia, and a desire to turn back the clock to an imagined golden age that never really existed. And yet, despite all that, Conservatism—when stripped of its far-right nonsense—still plays a role in political discourse.

In the end, Conservatism might not be my cup of tea. In fact, it's more like a cold, slightly bitter cup of tea that's been left to sit too long. But in a world full of chaos and uncertainty, there's something to be said for having that steady, if grumpy, voice reminding us to take a moment, slow down, and think things through. Progress can be exciting, but it's not without its risks. And as much as I hate to admit it, having someone say, *"Let's be careful with this,"* isn't always the worst idea in the world.

Socialism

Your Idealistic Friend Who's Always Planning a Utopian Road Trip

> "I should tie myself to no particular system of society other than of socialism."
> Nelson Mandela

Meet Socialism. They're your idealistic friend who's forever planning the perfect road trip. They've got big ideas about how to make the world a better place—starting with a car full of people, where everyone gets an equal say, no one's left behind, and every stop is carefully picked to ensure everyone benefits. It's not about seeing the best views for just a few people—it's about fairness. You can count on Socialism to make sure everyone has their turn in the front seat, their chance to pick the playlist, and their fair share of the snacks (but let's not get into who brought what).

But, I'm sure we can all agree—Socialism hasn't *quite* nailed the logistics. The idealism is there, no question. I mean, how can you not love a system that's trying to give everyone their due, whether it's healthcare or a seat at the table? As a gay, immigrant, and healthcare strategist, I'm all for equality and fairness[1]. Socialism feels like a natural ally, ensuring that people like me—who, let's face it, don't always get the easiest ride—are looked after, not just as a footnote but as part of the main story.

Still, there's that ever-present reality check: execution[2]. Sure, everyone deserves a voice, but what happens when we hit a fork in the road? Suddenly, we're bogged down in endless discussions about which direction to take, and while Socialism is passionately ensuring we're not leaving anyone behind, someone's forgotten to check the fuel gauge. It's all well-meaning, but sometimes the journey feels a little bit impractical—a lovely thought, but lacking in the fine print of how we're actually getting there.

That said, you can't fault Socialism's heart. As someone who works in healthcare, I've seen what happens when people fall through the cracks in systems that prioritise profit over people (looking at you, American healthcare). Socialism, with all its quirks and disorganisation, is the one friend constantly trying to make sure no one suffers alone, that no one's going hungry, and that everyone has a shot at a decent life. It's a bit chaotic, sure—but when equality is the goal, chaos can be forgiven. We'd be better off if more people were like Socialism—even if they don't always know how to divvy up the snacks.

History in Brief: From Marx to Bernie, with Stops in Between

The origins of Socialism are just as idealistic as its well-meaning, if slightly chaotic, road-trip plans. To understand where it all began, we have to start with Karl Marx—the man whose vision for a classless society was, in many ways, revolutionary. For Marx, the working class was constantly being exploited by

---

1. Some may say aggressively so.

2. No, not that one.

the bourgeoisie, that ever-looming rich minority who owned all the wealth while the rest of us did the actual work. In Marx's dream, the workers of the world would unite, and a new, fairer society would emerge. A place where everyone's labour would be valued equally, and the fruits of that labour would be shared fairly among all. No more toiling away while a handful of people got to sip champagne at the top—this was about equality for all.

The catch? Well, Marx wasn't exactly great at logistics. Don't get me wrong, he was brilliant when it came to critiquing capitalism and laying out the reasons why the system was failing the working class, but his roadmap to this utopia was a bit... *vague*. Sure, he had the big picture down—a classless society where everyone worked together for the common good—but the *"how"* of getting there was never quite as clear. That's where Marxism left things open to interpretation, and that's why we ended up with a lot of movements aiming for the same goal, but taking vastly different, and sometimes bumpy routes to get there.

From revolutions to reforms, Socialism has been popping up all over the globe in various forms, often with drastically different results. Take the early 20th century, when socialist movements were surging across Europe. Some were peaceful, aiming for change through legislation and labour movements, while others, like the Russian Revolution, opted for a more... *shall we say dramatic approach*. And while many of these movements started with noble ideals, they didn't always stick the landing.

The Russian Revolution is one of the most famous examples, where the dream of worker equality quickly spiralled into a nightmare of authoritarianism. Marx's idea of a fairer, classless society was co-opted, and what was left was less of a socialist utopia and more of a dictatorship, where power concentrated in the hands of a few—exactly the thing Marx was trying to avoid. This particular road took a helluva detour, and before anyone knew it, the scenic route had turned into a dark alley full of oppression and political purges.

But let's fast-forward to today, where Socialism has found a new, more sustainable cruise control in modern social democracies. Instead of talking about revolution, today's socialist movements focus on social safety nets, universal access to healthcare, education, and robust welfare systems. Look at the Nordic countries—Norway, Sweden, and Denmark—where socialist policies are part of everyday life. There, universal healthcare and free education are seen as basic rights, not radical ideas[3]. The car might not be speeding down the road, but it's moving at a steady pace, ensuring everyone gets a ride—and crucially, no one's left stranded by the roadside.

Then, of course, there's Bernie Sanders, whose democratic socialism has made waves in the United States—a country where the word *"socialism"* still sends some people into Cold War flashbacks. Every time Bernie mentions universal healthcare, you'd think he was proposing to nationalise people's homes, occupy a few farms and hand out communist pamphlets at the town square. The irony, of course, is that many of the same people who recoil at the word *"socialism"* happily enjoy Medicare, Social Security, and public education—all of which have socialist roots. But as soon as you utter the word *"socialism,"* it's as if the road trip is immediately cancelled, someone starts shouting loudly and it all devolves into a level of chaos that would even have Marx frowning.

The funny thing though is thatSocialism isn't about creating some dystopian regime. In places like Scandinavia, where socialist policies are the backbone of society, life isstable, fair, and—dare I say—peaceful. In fact, when you talk to people from these countries, you'll quickly realise that socialism to them isn't scary orradical; it's just common sense. The idea that everyone deserves a fair shot at life's basics—like healthcare, education, and dignity—is fundamental to the way their society works.

---

3. Which, let's be honest, people not going hungry and having access to free education and healthcare is hardly "radical".

But across the pond, Socialism still sparks massive anxiety attacks along the themes of big government and loss of freedom, despite the fact that many of its tenets are already ingrained in American society. So while Bernie Sanders may not have won the presidency, the very fact that his democratic socialism gained so much traction shows that maybe, just maybe, Socialism is finally finding its footing in places where it was once feared.

The Cooperative Movement: Socialism in Action

Let's make a quick pit stop at one of socialism's unsung heroes—the Cooperative[4] Movement. If capitalism is the muscle car barrelling down the highway with reckless abandon, cooperatives are socialism's eco-friendly hatchback: steady, reliable, and fuelled by collective goodwill. Worker co-ops are socialism's cheeky way of saying, *"If the corporate bigwigs won't share the steering wheel, we'll just build our own car—and everyone gets to drive."*

At the heart of a worker cooperative is a simple but revolutionary idea: democratic ownership. No more top-down tyranny of the CEO making decisions from their ivory tower. Here, every worker has an equal say in how things are run, and profits are shared rather than hoarded. It's like a business where everyone gets to pick the playlist, choose the snacks, and decide on the route - and somehow, the car stays on course. Who knew? Socialism doesn't just live in dusty books; it's out there in the real world, operating smoothly without a corporate overlord in sight.

Take the *Mondragon Corporation* in Spain. Founded in 1956, Mondragon has grown into one of the country's largest corporations, spanning sectors from finance to industry to retail, all owned and run by its workers. It's a little like a road trip

---

4. And no, it's not the kind of dodgy shop that's basically a fancy off-licence yet somehow more expensive than Waitrose.

where everyone's actually agreeing on the music and nobody's hogging the front seat. This isn't some theoretical pipe dream; it's socialism *actually working*. Imagine that!

What's even more remarkable is that cooperatives like Mondragon show us that businesses don't have to choose between profitability and fairness. Turns out, you can be competitive, efficient, and treat your workers like human beings all at once. Sure, co-ops might not dominate the global economy, but they offer a refreshing blueprint for how socialism's principles can thrive within the capitalist framework—without all the dog-eat-dog, rat-race nonsense.

So next time someone dismisses socialism as a hopeless dream or mumbles something about bread lines, just point them toward a local co-op or credit union. They might be surprised to find that socialism isn't dead—it's alive, kicking, and possibly selling organic produce at your nearest community market. Because if socialism can make grocery shopping fairer, it might just have a shot at the whole *"economy"* thing too.

Modern Socialism: Scandinavian Road Trips and the British Twitter Mob

Something worth noting is that today's Socialism isn't the revolutionary firebrand it once was. Gone are the days of rallying the proletariat to storm the gates of the rich[5] . Instead, it's evolved into something more measured, more about building systems that ensure everyone gets a fair shot. Look at the Nordic countries again—they're practically running the most well-organised road trip you can imagine. Everyone's got their seat, their role, and somehow, despite the fact that free healthcare, education, and paid parental leave are the norm, the car just keeps on running smoothly.

---

5. Though this is still fun to do on weekends and bank holidays.

In Scandinavia, it's not about class warfare anymore—it's about social harmony. Policies that might send shockwaves elsewhere are simply a part of everyday life. You want a doctor's appointment? Sure, no problem. It's covered. Want to go to university? That's sorted, too. Want to take parental leave after having a child? Go for it, the state's got your back. The idea isn't that these policies are revolutionary—they're just common sense. Why wouldn't a society take care of its citizens[6]? The road trip may be slow and steady, but it's fair, and everyone gets a ride.

But, let's take a detour to the UK, where Socialism remains a complicated subject, particularly when you look at British politics and the discourse online. Over the last few years, socialist policies have been vilified by some and championed by others, often without a full understanding of what socialism actually means. Mention socialism or Marxism on Twitter, and you'll be met with a barrage of people throwing around the term *"Marxist[7]"* like it's the ultimate insult, while clearly having no idea what it actually entails. Call it the Twitter Effect—everyone's got an opinion, but very few have the facts to back it up.

It's especially fascinating when you consider how Socialism gets painted in broad strokes. For some, it's as if every socialist policy is one step away from communism[8], with the state ready to swoop in and confiscate your houseplants. Yet, when you look at figures like Jeremy Corbyn, who's been consistently vilified as some kind of radical, the policies he championed—nationalising the railways, increasing funding for the NHS, and providing

---

6. I ask with so much emphasis that I almost fall out of my desk chair from the effort.

7. *Marxist: Someone who disagrees with you on Twitter about healthcare funding.*

8. They are, of course related, but there is a whole chapter for that.

free education—aren't exactly overthrowing the government[9]. They're policies designed to provide basic public services to people who need them, not to tear down the system.

Socialism, particularly in the UK, often falls victim to misrepresentation, especially from those who conflate it with more authoritarian regimes or with communism. But that's not what modern socialism is about. It's patently *not* about seizing your property or forcing everyone into collective farms; it's about ensuring that basic rights—like healthcare, education, and dignity in old age—are available to all. It's about recognising the fact that the market alone can't solve every single problem and that sometimes the state needs to step in to level the playing field.

The irony, of course, is that many of the things people in the UK take for granted—the NHS, state pensions, free primary education—are direct products of socialist policies. Yet, the very idea of socialism still sends some people into a moral panic, as though we're on the verge of becoming a Marxist state. The truth is, socialism in the UK is misunderstood more often than not. It's not about revolution anymore; it's about reform.

Of course, socialist policies often come with the usual trade-offs: higher taxes to fund those universal benefits. But here's the thing—when everyone contributes, everyone benefits. It's not about the state controlling everything; it's about making sure no one gets left behind. And that's something even the most ardent capitalist should be able to get on board with—because a healthy, educated population benefits everyone, no matter what side of the political spectrum you fall on.

But online? Good luck trying to explain that in 280 characters.

---

9. Though judging by the sheer panic his name instills in any red-blooded Tory you would think he was arriving in Westminster with a beret and a few tanks.

Technological Advancement and Automation: The New Frontier for Socialism

As we cruise into the 21st century, our road trip encounters an unexpected twist: the rise of automation and artificial intelligence. Machines are taking the wheel—literally, figuratively and somewhat terrifyingly—and this technological revolution presents both exciting possibilities and some serious potholes for Socialism.

On the bright side, automation offers the tantalising potential to eliminate the most tedious and dangerous jobs. Imagine a world where humans no longer have to spend their days sweating in factories or dodging forklifts in a warehouse. In a socialist framework, this shift could mean more leisure time and a higher quality of life for everyone. Think of it like a road trip where the car drives itself, and all the passengers can finally sit back, relax, and enjoy the scenery without worrying about who's at the wheel. In theory, it's a socialist utopia on cruise control.

But, as with any utopian dream, there's a dark side. Without proper management, automation could be a one-way ticket to mass unemployment and skyrocketing inequality. If the benefits of technological advancements continue to pile up in the pockets of a small elite, then all this progress will feel a lot like upgrading to a luxury tour bus where only a select few get the comfy seats, while everyone else is left standing in the aisle. Not *exactly* the road trip we had in mind.

Here's where socialism comes in with the all-important solution: collective ownership[10] . By ensuring that the fruits of automation are shared equitably, society could harness technology for the common good instead of letting the tech billionaires snatch up all the spoils. Policies like Universal Basic Income (UBI) are getting attention these days—providing everyone with a financial safety net regardless of their employment status.

---

10. Yes, I can hear the gasping.

Because if robots are doing all the work, shouldn't we all be entitled to at least a little slice of the pie?

It's not just about the wages though. In our shiny new automated world, access to technology and the internet has become a necessity, not a luxury. Socialism could step in here too, advocating for digital rights and universal access to technology. After all, what's a modern road trip without GPS and a playlist streaming from the cloud? Everyone should be able to join the ride, not just those with the latest gadgets or broadband connection.

As we navigate this new terrain, socialism offers a roadmap for integrating technological progress with social welfare, ensuring that the benefits of automation don't just trickle down to a few lucky individuals. Because in the end, the real question isn't whether machines can take over the work—it's who gets to profit from the journey.

What It's Not: Socialism Doesn't Mean Sharing Your Toothbrush

Let's clear something up that has personally driven me a bit insane: Socialism simply does not mean we're all about to move into some communal farm, give up our personal belongings, and start living in a world where everyone shares one giant toothbrush. The persistent idea that socialism requires you to hand over your house keys and queue up for bread is a relic of Cold War-era propaganda and, frankly, misses the mark entirely. We're not talking about building gulags or redistributing your Netflix password. Socialism is about collective responsibility—but only for the things that actually matter on a societal level, not your toothbrush or your favourite pair of shoes.

Here's the distinction: Socialism isn't Communism, and it's definitely not the kind of totalitarian regime that critics so often conjure up when they hear the word. Yes, socialism shares some historical DNA with communism[11], but the two are fundamentally different in how they view property, economics, and state control. In modern socialism, the idea is about making sure the big stuff—like healthcare, education, and infrastructure—isn't just in the hands of a few billionaires or corporations who happen to own everything. It's about levelling the playing field, not seizing your toothbrush.

In fact, modern socialist policies focus on ensuring that things like public services are accessible to everyone, regardless of their financial situation. It's less about who *owns* the farm and more about making sure that everyone has access to the doctors, schools, and public transport they need. It's about collective ownership of the things that keep society running smoothly, ensuring that no one's left behind when it comes to life's essentials. The goal isn't to take away your private property—it's to make sure that public resources are used to benefit everyone, not just a privileged few.

And here's where socialism often gets misunderstood. There's a belief, particularly among its critics, that socialism is a slippery slope toward communism, where the state controls everything and individual freedoms are curtailed. But socialism isn't about removing your ability to own things or taking away your freedom of choice—it's about ensuring that fundamental rights like healthcare and education are universally available. The difference between socialism and communism is key, and it's a distinction we'll delve into more thoroughly in the Communism chapter[12].

So no, you don't need to start worrying about sharing your toothbrush or moving into a commune. Socialism simply wants

---

11. It can reasonably be argued that Karl Marx birth both into the world without a good post-natal plan.

12. Spoiler alert: communism involves the abolition of private property, while socialism focuses on collective ownership of essential services, not your personal belongings.

to make sure that when it comes to the things that matter most—healthcare, education, and a fair chance at life—we're all in this together. If that means a bit more collective ownership to ensure the greater good, then so be it.

Why It Matters: Equality's Not Just a Dream—It's Policy

Socialism still matters today because, whether we like to admit it or not, socialist policies have shaped the very fabric of the modern world. From universal healthcare to free education, workers' rights[13], and welfare systems, these aren't radical or utopian ideals—they're practical solutions to real-world problems. Without socialism, the world would look drastically different, especially here in the UK, where the NHS, the state education system, and basic labour protections form the backbone of everyday life. These aren't just perks; they're fundamental rights we often take for granted. And if we're being honest, they weren't gifted to us by the generosity of the free market—they were fought for through decades of political activism, much of it rooted in socialist ideals.

But here's the crux: socialism isn't just about looking back at its successes—it's about looking forward, and with the rise of the far-right in Europe and across the globe, the principles of equality, solidarity, and fairness are more critical now than ever. We're seeing a resurgence of grievance politics, where inequality and economic instability are being weaponised by authoritarian movements. In this climate, socialism has the potential to be the counterweight, offering a vision of society where people aren't left behind in the race for wealth and power.

Far too often, socialist policies are presented as something stuck in the 20th century, as if the idea of universal healthcare or fair

---

13. A big one here is the weekend. Please let's not give that up because someone became upset on Twitter.

wages belongs in the past. But that's where socialism needs its glow-up into the 21st century. The truth is, equality isn't just a dream—it's something we can build through smart policies, progressive taxation, and public investment. Instead of letting inequality fester, socialism provides the framework to tackle the economic and social injustices that give rise to authoritarian populism. And it's not just about taking from the rich and giving to the poor—it's about creating systems that ensure everyone has the same opportunities to succeed.

But let's not sugar-coat it: socialist policies aren't cheap. To pay for universal services like free healthcare, education, and social welfare, we do need to accept higher taxes[14] —and this is where the conversation often hits a snag. Sure, we all like the idea of better healthcare or free university, but when the tax bill arrives, suddenly the enthusiasm wanes a little. It's human nature. We love the benefits but grumble about the costs. The thing is, socialism isn't just about offering free stuff—it's about creating a society where everyone chips in a little more, so we can all thrive together.

The far-right has been exploiting the growing disillusionment among people who feel left behind by globalisation, the gig economy, and a political system that seems to cater only to the elite – and the fact is, they have a point. Socialism, with its emphasis on collective welfare and economic justice, offers a real alternative—one that speaks to the frustrations people have about the state of the world without veering into xenophobia or authoritarianism. We're living in a time when the idea of fairness is being tested, and socialism, far from being outdated, offers a path forward. It's not about taking away from one group to give to another—it's about ensuring that everyone has a fair shot at a decent life.

Socialism's role in today's world is to counter the narratives of division and fear with a message of solidarity and equity. It's not

---

14. Yes, yes, more gasps, I know.

an antique ideology; it's a living, breathing set of principles that can evolve to meet the challenges of the 21st century. And as inequality deepens and climate change, pandemics, and economic instability continue to shape the global landscape, socialism's core message—that we're all in this together—is more relevant than ever.

Challenges in Implementation: When Ideals Meet Reality

Even the best-planned road trips can hit unexpected traffic jams, detours, or—worst of all—the realisation that someone left the luggage on the driveway. Implementing socialism isn't much different. You may start with noble intentions, but reality has a way of throwing a wrench in the works.

One major hurdle is balancing individual incentives with collective goals. It's all very nice to aim for equality, but here's the thing—humans aren't always the selfless creatures socialism might hope for[15]. Ambition, competition, and yes, even greed, don't just vanish because we've decided to share more. Imagine trying to get everyone on a road trip to agree on a single radio station for the whole drive—now amplify that to an entire economy. Good luck.

Then there's the issue of economic constraints. Funding universal healthcare, education, and welfare programs requires more than just goodwill. You need cold, hard cash. Countries pursuing these policies often find themselves staring down budget deficits or having to make tough decisions about which programs to prioritise. It's like planning to visit every national park but realising halfway through the trip that you've only got enough petrol money to see a couple. Suddenly, you're frantically recalculating the route.

---

15. Shock, horror, get me my fainting sofa!

And let's not forget the global context. In today's interconnected world, one country's shift toward socialism doesn't happen in a vacuum. International markets, trade agreements, and foreign policies will all have something to say about it. Think of it as trying to coordinate a road trip caravan when half the group isn't even using the same map—or worse, they're driving in the opposite direction. You may want to shield local industries from predatory global forces, but before you know it, you're knee-deep in trade disputes or even sanctions.

Corruption and misuse of power also tend to creep in when resources are centralised. The more concentrated the wealth and control, the greater the temptation for those in charge to *not* act in the public's best interest. Ensuring transparency and accountability? Easier said than done. It's a bit like handing over snack duties to the one friend who eats everything before it reaches the back seat.

These challenges don't mean you should abandon the trip altogether. They just mean you need better planning, realistic expectations, and—rather importantly—someone keeping an eye on the fuel gauge. Socialism's ideals are great, but when they hit the potholes of reality, a little pragmatism goes a long way.

Socialism's Big Heart, with a Few Roadblocks (and a Map That Needs Updating)

At its core, Socialism is that idealistic road trip planner, trying its absolute best to build a fairer society where everyone has a seat at the table. The vision is noble, the intentions are clear, and the heart is very much in the right place. Socialism's dream of equality, where everyone gets their fair share of the pie, is as hopeful as it is timeless. But, like any ambitious road trip, there are always going to be a few detours, some miscommunications, and the occasional flat tyre to throw things off course. The journey can be messy, the route can be confusing, and sometimes it feels like the GPS is on the fritz. But at the end of the day, Socialism keeps on driving because it believes that no one should be left stranded by the roadside.

Sure, we can grumble about the hiccups along the way—maybe the car stalls every now and then, or maybe there's some debate about the best route to take. But whether you love it or hate it, there's no denying that Socialism has profoundly shaped the way we live. Without it, we wouldn't have so many of the rights that we often take for granted today. These are the building blocks of a fairer society, and while the journey to equality is far from smooth, Socialism keeps pushing forward, even in a world that's not always eager to come along for the ride.

And sure, maybe the car needs a tune-up every now and then—there's always room for improvement, and Socialism, like any good friend, sometimes needs a reality check. The road ahead is littered with potholes like funding issues, political resistance, and the inevitable grumbling about taxes. But you know what? At least Socialism is still driving. It's still trying to figure out how to get us all to the same destination: a place where healthcare, education, and basic dignity aren't privileges but rights for everyone. In a world where inequality is rising and the far-right is gaining traction, Socialism is more important than ever, because it's still the one system that's genuinely fighting for equality—even if it occasionally gets lost along the way.

The road ahead for Socialism might be long and a bit bumpy, but if we're being honest, there's no other car that's trying so hard to ensure everyone gets a ride. The journey might not always be smooth, but it's worth taking—because the destination is one where fairness and compassion finally win out. And in today's climate, where division and self-interest often dominate the conversation, that's a road trip worth sticking with. So buckle up—Socialism's driving may not be perfect, but at least it's got its eye on the road and the right destination in mind.

Neoliberalism

The Slick but Dodgy Salesperson

"Neoliberalisation has not been very effective in revitalising global capital accumulation, but it has succeeded remarkably well in restoring, or in some instances (as in Russia and China) creating, the power of an economic elite. The theoretical utopianism of neoliberal argument has, I conclude, primarily worked as a system of justification and legitimation for whatever needed to be done to achieve this goal."

David Harvey

P icture yourself seated at a sleek, polished table in a towering high-rise, overlooking a sprawling city skyline. Across from you sit two of the most iconic figures of modern political history, Margaret Thatcher and Ronald Reagan. Impeccably dressed, with that air of unshakable confidence, they exude the calm assurance of salespeople who know they've got an unbeatable product. They're here to sell you a vision, one as polished as the table you're sitting at—Neoliberalism, the grand solution to all of society's problems.

Thatcher, with her famously steely smile, leans in first. "The free market," she begins, "is like a well-oiled machine. If we simply remove the burden of regulation and let private enterprise flourish, you'll see prosperity like never before. No more clunky government interference. Just let businesses do what they do best—make money—and it will benefit everyone." Her words are crisp, deliberate, the tone of someone who's done this a thousand times before. It sounds so reasonable, so straight-forward. Let the market breathe, let it thrive, and in return, everyone wins.

Next, Reagan, all charm and winks, adds his voice to the pitch. "Cut some taxes, deregulate, and then step aside. The invisible hand of the market will take care of the rest. Trust me, I've seen it work. We cut taxes for the wealthy, and boom! Everyone gets richer. Wealth starts trickling down to the masses. You'll love it."

You can't help but be intrigued. The idea of letting the market sort things out has an undeniable appeal. The notion that competition will improve services, lower costs, and deliver better outcomes for everyone feels, at least on the surface, logical. And after all, they've seen it work, right? Thatcher smiles as if she's reading your mind, effortlessly steering the conversation forward. "Take healthcare, for instance. It's clogged up with bureaucracy! We need private enterprise to come in and get some competition going. That's how you lower costs, improve quality. It's common sense."

The pitch sounds almost perfect—almost. You shift slightly in your seat, your thoughts drifting to the familiar gripes about privatisation: how rail privatisation in the UK didn't make commutes cheaper or more efficient, and how private health-care in the US has led to skyrocketing costs for basic needs like insulin. Still, their delivery is so polished, so confident, that you can't help but ask, "What about climate change? Can the market really handle that?"

Reagan doesn't miss a beat. "Of course! Who better to solve climate change than private companies? The market thrives on innovation. If there's money to be made in renewable energy, you bet businesses will find a way. It's simple: the market is driven by incentives, and if there's profit in saving the planet, the market will find the solution."

It's slick, almost too slick. You find yourself nodding along, but there's that familiar gnawing feeling at the back of your mind. After all, you've seen what happens when markets go unchecked. Rising inequality, corporate monopolies, public services left to rot while private companies profit. Still, Thatcher and Reagan make it sound so easy. Just step aside, let the market flourish, and everything will work out.

You shift again, a little more sceptical now. "But what happens when things go wrong? Deregulation played a big role in the 2008 financial crisis, didn't it? And the austerity that followed—it didn't exactly help the most vulnerable, did it?"

Thatcher's smile tightens slightly, but her tone remains patient, almost dismissive. "2008 was a blip. The market corrected itself, didn't it? The real trouble comes when governments overreact and meddle too much. Austerity was necessary to clean up the mess. If you let the market do its job, it always balances out."

Reagan shrugs, grinning as if the whole thing is just a minor hiccup in the grand scheme. "And if things do go a little south? Well, that's what government bailouts are for. No big deal. The market has its ups and downs, sure, but in the long run, it's always the best way to organise society. Look at America, look at the UK. We're booming. That's free-market capitalism at work."

You sit back, considering their words, but the cracks in the pitch are becoming more visible. You've seen the damage this brand of Neoliberalism can cause. Austerity measures that gutted public services, the relentless push for privatisation that left people paying more for less, and the growing gap between the rich and everyone else. The more they talk, the more it sounds like a rehearsed sales pitch designed to distract from the fine print.

Thatcher finishes her pitch, flashing one final, confident smile. "The market is always the best solution, you silly boy. You just have to trust the process."

Reagan, ever the showman, leans back, winking as he adds, "And if it doesn't work out, well, there's always another bailout."

As they pack up their papers and prepare to leave, you glance down at the invisible bill they've left behind. You have a terrible suspicion that neoliberalism is going to have a cost far greater than you've been promised.

--Interlude--

History in Brief: The 'Revolution' That Wasn't

Now, after that horrifying scene, it's worth looking at where it all spawned from. The tale of Neoliberalism begins with the grand ambitions of a few intellectuals who believed they had finally cracked the code to a prosperous, efficient world. Enter Friedrich Hayek and Milton Friedman, two economists who came armed with the ultimate manifesto: government is the problem, not the solution. Their vision? A world where free-market capitalism reigned supreme, unencumbered by pesky regulations or bureaucracy. They preached that deregulation, privatisation, and a hands-off government would unleash the true power of the market, ushering in an age of freedom, efficiency, and endless growth.

For Hayek and Friedman, social welfare was a dirty word[1] —an outdated relic of governments meddling where they didn't belong. They saw free-market capitalism as a self-regulating system, where competition would create prosperity and trick-

---

1. And it still is for so many, many people – some of whom benefit directly from it.

le-down economics would ensure that even the poorest of society would benefit. It was the perfect pitch: lower taxes for the wealthy, reduced government spending, and a thriving market that would reward innovation and hard work.

It wasn't just an economic theory; it was a revolution. Except, well, not really.

The thing about revolutions is that they usually promise the world and then make a mess of delivering it. Neoliberalism's great promise of economic freedom quickly became a boon for the rich and a curse for everyone else. By cutting taxes for the wealthiest, slashing public services, and privatising anything that wasn't nailed down, Neoliberalism did indeed unleash something—but it wasn't prosperity for all. Instead, we got soaring inequality, dismantled welfare systems, and a series of economic crises that left the wealthy safely at the top while the rest of society tried to pick up the pieces.

Milton Friedman famously argued that *"the business of business is business"*—meaning, as long as corporations make profits, everything else will somehow work itself out. This is where the wheels really started to come off. The financial crash of 2008 wasn't just an unfortunate hiccup in the system—it was the natural consequence of decades of deregulation and laissez-faire economics that had let the markets run wild with reckless abandon. The banks took risks, played their little games, and when it all came crashing down, who cleaned up the mess? Certainly not the invisible hand.

The irony is that Neoliberalism had sold itself as a revolution—a bold new path that would empower individuals, make governments smaller, and bring freedom to the masses. But in practice, it was just a repackaged version of old, tired ideas that prioritised corporate profits over public welfare. It took the rhetoric of freedom and transformed it into a justification for wealth consolidation at the very top. The promised trickle-down economics turned into a trickle-up situation, with billionaires hoarding more wealth than ever, while public services crumbled under the weight of underfunding and privatisation.

What Neoliberalism really accomplished was the redistribution of wealth—just in the completely wrong direction. Instead of lifting up the poor, it ensured that wealth flowed upwards into the hands of a few, leaving the working class struggling to survive on stagnating wages and dwindling safety nets. The global financial system became a game of corporate winners and social losers, and yet, somehow, Neoliberalism is still here, refusing to leave the stage.

If anything, Neoliberalism has become like that obnoxious party guest who overstays their welcome—long after the music has stopped, the drinks have run out, and the lights have been turned off. No one's quite sure how to get rid of it, because despite its catastrophic failures, it still holds an inexplicable grip on the way we think about economics and society. Austerity—the great solution to every crisis in the Neoliberal playbook—was the real disaster, hitting the poorest hardest while those at the top barely felt a pinch. And yet, every time we hit an economic downturn, Neoliberalism confidently strolls back in, offering the same tired solutions to the problems it helped create.

Modern Neoliberalism: Privatisation, Austerity, and 'Efficiency'

In today's UK, Neoliberalism feels less like an economic theory and more like a toxic relationship we just can't seem to escape. It's everywhere—seeped into the way we think about the economy, the government, and public services. It's become the default mode of operation, where privatisation is seen as the solution to all problems and austerity is the magical cure-all for any economic downturn[2].

---

2. Spoiler alert: it's not working. And if you look really closely, it's *never* really worked.

Let's talk about privatisation first, that *genius* idea that turning public goods into market commodities would somehow make everything better. The argument went something like this: by introducing competition, services would improve, costs would go down, and efficiency would soar. But what actually happened? Take the UK railways. The rail privatisation experiment of the 1990s was sold to us as the great panacea—cheaper fares, better services, and modern infrastructure. Fast forward to today, and we're left with some of the highest rail fares in Europe, chronic delays[3], and a system where profit is prioritised over the public good. It turns out, when you hand over critical infrastructure to private companies, their first priority isn't exactly providing a stellar service—it's making as much profit as possible.

But the privatisation didn't stop there. Oh no, we've seen it *everywhere*—from utilities like water[4] and energy to prisons[5] and even healthcare services. All under the guise of making things more *"efficient."* You know, because nothing says *"efficiency"* like handing control of essential public services to for-profit corporations. And what have we got in return? A housing market that's unaffordable, energy bills that are sky-high, an NHS that's increasingly under pressure to *"outsource"* parts of its service to private contractors—because, apparently, it's only *"efficient"* if someone's making a profit.

And then, of course, there's the shining star of Neoliberalism's legacy: austerity. Enter George Osborne, the architect of Osbornism—a period of slashing public spending in the wake of the 2008 financial crisis. The logic? If the government just

---

3. I'm still waiting for a train.

4. Causing Rivers overflowing with your own effluent that you can now go and look at a second time if you catch the tides just right.

5. Which are now so overfilled that the Tories had to release prisoners to make space for new prisoners causing a somewhat dangerous game of musical chairs that no one asked for.

tightened its belt, we'd come out of the crisis stronger and healthier. But instead of bolstering the economy, austerity did the opposite. It gutted public services, left the NHS underfunded, schools overcrowded, and the welfare system hanging on by a thread.

Let's be clear: austerity *did not save the economy*. What it did do was push millions into poverty, slash social safety nets, and leave entire communities devastated by cuts to vital services. It became the political equivalent of cutting off your leg because you stubbed your toe—yes, technically, you're dealing with the problem, but at what cost[6]?

The NHS, a system once heralded as one of the greatest achievements in British history, is now crippled by funding cuts. Waiting lists are longer than ever, mental health services are stretched thin, and the staff are overworked and underpaid. All while private healthcare firms circle like vultures, ready to swoop in and take over profitable sectors of care. And yet, Neoliberalism insists this is all *necessary*—that this is the *"price"* of a healthy economy. But who's paying that price? It certainly isn't the wealthy elite or the corporate giants; it's the people at the bottom, the ones relying on these public services, the ones who were told austerity was essential for the greater good.

Across the Atlantic, the US isn't much better off. Neoliberalism has turned everything into a market commodity, from education to prisons. The privatisation of prisons has led to a system where profit is directly linked to how many people are incarcerated. Meanwhile, healthcare in the US has been turned into a for-profit system that prioritises insurance companies over patient care. It's an absurdity that still baffles those of us who enjoy the NHS, as flawed as it might be.

The genius of Neoliberalism lies in its ability to convince us that public services are inherently inefficient, while simultaneously

---

6. 300,000 excess deaths. That was the cost.

ensuring that private corporations extract profit from those very services—often delivering a worse product at a higher cost. We've seen this time and again, in both the UK and the US, where the neoliberal agenda has led to sky-high tuition fees, crumbling public infrastructure, and a gig economy that offers no security to workers, all while the rich get richer.

It's no wonder we can't quit Neoliberalism—it's baked into the way we've been conditioned to think about the economy. But the question is: how much longer are we willing to endure the damage it's doing before we finally break up with it?

The Global Spread: Exporting Neoliberalism Abroad

Now, if you thought Neoliberalism had done enough damage at home, our favourite dynamic duo—Thatcher and Reagan—decided it was time to share this *"miracle cure"* with the rest of the world. Because why limit economic chaos to your own borders when you can create a global mess? Neoliberalism's homegrown disasters were clearly so impressive that developing nations absolutely *had* to get in on the fun.

Enter the International Monetary Fund (IMF) and the World Bank—global institutions so benevolent they practically ooze compassion, ready to sprinkle Neoliberal fairy dust over developing nations. The prescription? Structural Adjustment Programs (SAPs)—a fancy way of saying, *"We'll lend you money, but only if you privatise everything that isn't nailed down, cut social spending to the bone, and open up your markets to foreign investors. Oh, and don't forget to eliminate any pesky trade protections while you're at it."* Because nothing says *"long-term economic stability"* quite like gutting social services and selling off your nation's infrastructure to the highest bidder.

Developing nations across Latin America, Africa, and Asia were told that Neoliberalism was their golden ticket to prosperity. Who needs pesky things like state-funded healthcare or public education when you can sell your national industries to foreign corporations? Never mind the fact that these policies often led to more poverty, a loss of sovereignty, and a sprinkling of social unrest. But hey, at least multinational corporations were happy. Their profits skyrocketed, so really, wasn't that the whole point?

Take Bolivia's water crisis, for instance. In the late 1990s, as part of the grand Neoliberal experiment, Bolivia's water supply was privatised, and quelle surprise—prices shot through the roof. Many Bolivians couldn't even afford basic access to water. The people revolted[7] and the government had to scramble to reverse the privatisation. Who could have predicted that selling off a nation's water supply to the highest bidder might cause *some* problems? Oh, right—anyone with half a brain.

Then there's Russia and its infamous *"shock therapy."* As if transitioning to a market economy wasn't hard enough, Russia decided to do it all at once. Within a few short years, the Russian economy collapsed, the state was gutted, and oligarchs popped up like mushrooms after a rainstorm, snatching up national assets at bargain-bin prices. But don't worry—this was just the free market *"finding its equilibrium."* Sure, millions plunged into poverty, but the invisible hand of the market was doing its thing[8].

Neoliberalism's global adventure proved one thing: if at first you don't succeed (because you never really did), export your failures abroad and take everyone else down with you. After all, misery loves company, and there's nothing quite like a global financial crisis to bring the world together. And if there's anything Neoliberalism does well, it's ensuring that everyone—except the wealthy elite—gets a piece of the suffering.

---

7. Shock, horror, because, humans get cranky and a bit revolty when you deny them water.

8. After all, what's a little human suffering when you're spreading the gospel of Neoliberalism?

The Gig Economy: Neoliberalism's Latest Innovation

As Neoliberalism continued its noble quest to redefine what *"progress"* looks like, it stumbled upon its crowning achievement: the gig economy. Why offer workers job security, pensions, or even a half-decent wage when you can sell them the illusion of freedom? After all, who needs benefits when you've got *"flexibility"*? Gig work—the brave new frontier where the worker becomes their own boss, with all the freedom to work whenever they want, just so long as they're available 24/7.

Uber, Deliveroo, Just Eat—these champions of modern entrepreneurial spirit have revolutionised the idea of employment by stripping it of all the pesky protections workers used to enjoy. Sure, you don't get a pension, sick leave, or any form of stability, but hey, you're *"empowered."* Forget about any sort of benefits and paid holidays—now you have the privilege of juggling multiple jobs just to scrape by. Isn't freedom *grand?*

Neoliberalism, of course, patted itself on the back. *"Look at how we've empowered individuals!"* they exclaimed, conveniently ignoring that these individuals are now stuck in a never-ending hustle to make ends meet. The gig economy, in all its glory, has turned every driver, delivery person, and freelancer into their very own micro-business. But it's not all bad—at least for the corporations. Workers may be precariously teetering on the edge of poverty, but profit margins are *soaring*.

Take job security, for instance. The gig economy has lovingly tossed that relic of the past into the bin. Who needs the assurance of a steady income when you can log in to an app and pray that the algorithm deems you worthy of work today? And if you can't keep up with the demands? No worries, there's always someone else ready to take your place in this endless race to the bottom.

But let's be fair. Neoliberalism's gig economy is nothing if not efficient. Why bother with unions or regulations when you can have a market where everyone is disposable, and workers are interchangeable parts of the corporate machine? It's the perfect manifestation of Neoliberalism's relentless drive for *"efficiency"*—a labour market stripped of all that bothersome worker protection nonsense. As long as there's someone willing to deliver your burrito or drive you across town at the push of a button, the system works. Well, at least for those at the top.

The gig economy is truly Neoliberalism's pièce de résistance—a shining example of how to repackage insecurity and sell it as opportunity. It's a triumph of efficiency, where the market reigns supreme and workers are left to fend for themselves. And if you can't hack it? Don't worry. There's always someone younger, more desperate, and less burdened by the illusion of stability ready to take your place.

Climate Change: The Market Will Fix It (Eventually)

Remember when Reagan assured us that if there's profit in saving the planet, the market would find a way? Well, here we are decades later—still waiting for that magical moment when the invisible hand of the market swoops in to solve climate change[9]
.

Neoliberalism's approach to climate change has been nothing short of *inspiring*—if you find procrastination and denial inspiring. Why invest in renewable energy when there's still plenty of oil to drill and coal to burn? The market thrives on innovation, sure, but only when it's powered by fossil fuels. The invisible hand works in mysterious ways, especially when it's greased with petroleum.

---

9. It hasn't.

So, what's Neoliberalism's solution to the environmental crisis? Carbon credits and cap-and-trade systems, of course! Let the market regulate emissions, they said. Let supply and demand figure it out. And regulate it did—just not in the direction anyone had hoped. Emissions kept rising, but at least a thriving market in trading the right to pollute emerged[10].

Meanwhile, scientists were busy warning about impending environmental doom, but Neoliberalism had *faith*. Why panic when technology would eventually swoop in and save the day? After all, there's money to be made. The seas might be rising, sure, but the stock prices of solar panel companies will soar *eventually*. It's just a waiting game at this point.

But Neoliberalism isn't without its solutions. Take adaptation, for example. The system's got this all figured out. Can't stop the floods? Build a seawall—if you can afford it, that is. If not, well, the market can't save *everyone*. Coastal communities? Good luck. Neoliberalism's motto might as well be, *"If you can't swim, you'd better learn."* After all, it's not about preventing disaster—it's about selling high-end flotation devices when it hits.

The most beautiful part? Neoliberalism's belief in a *profit-driven miracle* that will one day swoop in and save us all. Just keep calm and carry on consuming—because if climate change isn't solved by the free market, it's clearly not a real problem. Until then, we'll keep burning what's left of the fossil fuels and hope that the stock market heats up faster than the planet.

What It's Not: Neoliberalism ≠ Liberalism (Or, At Least, It Shouldn't Be)

Now, it's time to clear up a bit of a misunderstanding that happens from time to time—Neoliberalism is not Liberalism,

---

10. Yes, we did it: we monetised the apocalypse.

even though they often get tangled together like a messy set of Christmas lights. Sure, they share *some* roots, but they've grown into completely different beasts. While Liberalism is grounded in the belief in individual freedoms, human rights, and democratic institutions, Neoliberalism has morphed into something quite different: an ideology obsessed with the free market, where profit is the measure of all things, and public services are viewed as **commodities** to be sold off to the highest bidder.

Here's the main difference: Liberalism says, *"You have the right to free speech, the freedom of movement, and the protection of the rule of law."* Neoliberalism says, *"You have the right to buy your way into any service—healthcare, education, even public transport—but only if you can afford it."*

Where Liberalism values a balance between freedom and fairness, Neoliberalism seems to think that freedom is only meaningful if it's attached to market forces. Under Liberalism, we get laws that protect your rights, a social contract where the state plays a key role in ensuring that everyone gets a fair shot. Under Neoliberalism, the state steps back, hands off the reins, and says, *"Let the market sort it out."* If you can't keep up, well, too bad—the market doesn't care about fairness; it cares about efficiency and profit.

You can see how this plays out in the world of public services. Liberalism believes that healthcare, education, and infrastructure are essential rights—things that governments should protect and provide, so that everyone has equal access. But Neoliberalism? It looks at those same services and says, *"You know, there's a lot of money to be made here."* Why let the state provide healthcare when you can sell it off to private companies, where efficiency means cutting costs and profit means higher prices for the rest of us?

Let's take a look at the UK's NHS, which has traditionally been a pillar of Liberalism—the belief that healthcare is a human right. Under Neoliberalism, however, that pillar has been chipped away at for decades. Services are being outsourced, private healthcare firms are creeping in, and the idea that profit should dictate how the system is run is becoming more and more entrenched. It's a classic Neoliberal move: take something that's supposed to benefit everyone, hand it over to the market, and let the law of supply and demand determine who gets access to care and at what price.

It's a similar story with education. Liberalism sees free education as a cornerstone of democracy—a way to ensure that all citizens have the tools they need to succeed. But Neoliberalism views education as just another commodity. Why have state-funded schools when you can have a system of for-profit academies, where students are treated more like customers than learners? And higher education? It's no longer about expanding access; it's about tuition fees, student loans, and profit margins for universities that run more like corporations than centres of learning.

This is where the distinction really comes into play: Liberalism seeks to protect the individual from oppression—whether that oppression comes from the state or from powerful private interests. Neoliberalism, on the other hand, has no problem with powerful private interests. In fact, it actively empowers them by removing regulations that might limit their ability to exploit public goods for private gain.

Under Neoliberalism, you're not a citizen—you're a consumer. And everything, from your health to your education to the roads you drive on, is up for sale. The ideology has taken the language of freedom from Liberalism and twisted it into something that benefits corporate power at the expense of public welfare. It's as if the ideals of freedom and self-determination have been hijacked by a system that measures success by corporate profits and stock market gains, rather than by how well it actually serves the people.

And like we've already mentioned, Neoliberalism is global. In the US, the gap between Liberalism and Neoliberalism is stark.

Liberalism gave the US things like civil rights and workers' protections. But Neoliberalism took that same country and turned it into a place where healthcare is a for-profit industry, where public infrastructure is crumbling because the government doesn't want to spend the money, and where private prisons are incentivised to lock people up because it makes shareholders happy. It's the embodiment of how far Neoliberalism is willing to go in the name of profit.

So, to put it bluntly: Liberalism is about balancing freedom and fairness, about using the power of government to ensure that individual rights are protected, and that public services remain public. Neoliberalism, on the other hand, is about stepping back, letting the market run riot, and hoping that somehow, everything will turn out alright—despite all the evidence to the contrary.

--Interlude Ends--

And so, we go back to the conference room where we started, which is packed now. The smooth edges of the table feel tighter, as more figures from Neoliberalism's glittering history shuffle in. There's a hum of anxiety, as if the promises of prosperity are wearing thin, but no one dares to say it aloud. Margaret Thatcher and Ronald Reagan sit proudly at the head of the table, their confidence unwavering. But now they're joined by Tony Blair, his eyes flicking nervously to Bill Clinton who's paging through an economic report that neither of them seem too keen to discuss.

Blair clears his throat, speaking as though he's trying to convince himself as much as anyone else in the room. "Neoliberalism has lifted millions out of poverty, right? I mean, we embraced the free market, reduced regulations, and modernised the state... It's brought progress, hasn't it?"

The others nod, but the unease is palpable. The promises feel hollow. Gordon Brown, seated awkwardly in the corner, mutters something about "the crash of 2008" before silencing himself with a sip of water.

In the midst of it all, you find yourself staring at the report in front of you. The charts don't lie. Inequality is growing, public services are crumbling, and corporate profits are soaring. You can see the NHS fraying at the edges, chipped away bit by bit by privatisation. Rail fares have skyrocketed, and the energy companies are making obscene profits while people struggle to keep the lights on.

Blair, catching your gaze, suddenly sounds defensive. "We modernised healthcare, didn't we? Public-private partnerships are efficient. The market can deliver better services—just give it time."

You can feel the temperature in the room shift. Reagan, once so certain, is now quietly fidgeting. Even Thatcher, the Iron Lady herself, is frowning slightly, as if the invisible hand of the market has been a little too heavy-handed. You glance down at your notes, remembering how austerity was sold as the cure, only to find it bled the patient dry. Public services cut to the bone, all in the name of efficiency. The promise was prosperity—the reality was food banks.

Clinton, always the pragmatist, breaks the silence. "Sure, the crash hurt, but the market bounced back, didn't it? The banks were saved."

He says it like it's a triumph, but the nervous glances around the table suggest otherwise. The room knows better. The public paid for those bailouts. And the poorest, as always, were left footing the bill.

A voice from the back—was that David Cameron?—pipes up with a familiar refrain: "Austerity was necessary. We **had** to cut back."

Thatcher perks up at this. "Yes. Exactly. It was a small price to pay to keep the system stable."

You look at the figures in front of you again. Stable for whom? Not the NHS, still buckling under the strain of underfunding. Not the teachers and nurses, or the millions squeezed by soaring rents and stagnating wages. The wealthy, though—they've done just fine.

Blair, ever the politician, tries to rally the room. "The key is to believe in the system. We're just in a rough patch, that's all."

But no one's buying it, not anymore. The air is thick with nervous tension. Everyone knows the promises have worn thin, but no one dares say it aloud. The free market was supposed to fix everything, remember? Competition was supposed to make services better, not worse. Yet here you are, staring at a report that tells the real story: Neoliberalism has left the public behind, and it's the corporations that are reaping the rewards.

As the room grows increasingly quiet, a flicker of panic crosses Blair's face. He knows the game's up, even if he won't admit it. The free market didn't solve climate change. It didn't save the NHS. It didn't bring equality. It just made a few people very rich, while the rest of us were left holding the bag.

The mood in the room shifts, the polished veneer beginning to crack. Someone—the nervous intern in the back, perhaps—mutters something about "rising populism." The others pretend not to hear it. But they all know. Neoliberalism didn't just fail—it's been creating the very discontent that's fuelling the far-right resurgence, the anger and the disillusionment.

You glance around the room. The once-confident faces now seem unsure, hesitant. They've built their careers on this ideology, and yet here it is, teetering on the edge. The facts are undeniable: inequality is worse, public trust in government is shattered, and the system they've championed is cracking under its own weight.

A final voice speaks up. "What now?" it asks, almost in a whisper. The question lingers, heavy in the air.

Before anyone can answer, the door creaks open. A figure steps in—Communism, old and scarred, clutching a tattered manifesto. The next chapter of the story has arrived. Where Neoliberalism promised freedom and delivered inequality, Communism promised equality and delivered oppression. Two ideologies, both claiming to be the way forward. And yet, here we are, with corporate power on the rise, workers disenfranchised, and democracy teetering on the edge.

As Thatcher, Reagan, Blair, and the others stare nervously at the newcomer, you wonder: Is there another way? Or are we stuck in this endless loop of promises, betrayals, and crises, repeating themselves through history like some cruel joke?

And with that, the room empties, leaving you alone with the bill. The cost of Neoliberalism? So much higher than they let on.

Communism

The Utopian Dream (Or Not)

> "For us in Russia, communism is a dead dog, while, for many people in the West, it is still a living lion."
>
> Aleksandr Solzhenitsyn

I imagine a world where everything is perfect. No one has to worry about rent, because no one *owns* anything. Food is always on the table, delicious and plentiful—though, of course, no one has more than they need. Every person is equal. There are no billionaires hoarding obscene amounts of wealth while the rest of us scramble to pay bills or afford basic necessities. The concept of poverty? Gone. Landlords? A relic of the past. It's paradise, a utopia where everyone works for the greater good and reaps equal rewards. All problems have been solved, society functions like a well-oiled machine, and we all live in perfect harmony. No competition, no exploitation, just endless equality and the warm embrace of collective joy. Beautiful, isn't it?

That, my dear reader, was the dream of Communism—the promise of a world so ideal that even the most cynical among us could briefly believe in its magic. The workers control everything, the state withers away, and we live happily ever after, dancing around bonfires[1] and singing songs of unity and brotherhood. The perfect society, free from oppression, inequality, and, well, any semblance of a class system.

It all sounds so lovely, doesn't it? A utopia where everyone has their needs met, and wealth inequality is nothing more than a distant memory. Where the system never breaks down, there's always enough to go around, and no one ever feels the need to question the rules. Communism, in theory, is like the world's greatest group project. Everyone works together, shares equally, and the end result is a perfectly fair and just society where no one goes hungry, and no one gets left behind. It's a foolproof plan, really.

Except, well... *not quite.*

You see, Communism is the kind of plan that looks fantastic on paper, but when you try to put it into practice, it all starts to unravel. It's like one of those Pinterest projects that promises a glamorous result, but by the time you're halfway through, you're drowning in glue, paint, and existential despair. In real-world Communism, that *"perfect group project"* quickly turns into a nightmare, where one person—usually the guy with the most power—takes control, and everyone else is stuck doing the grunt work.

As much as many would love to believe in the dream, the harsh reality is that Communism never quite lived up to its hype. Instead of a happy collective where we all sing kumbaya and share equally, it became something much, much darker. So on that note, welcome to the chapter where we unpack the myth of Communism, explore its spectacular failures, and try to understand why, even after all this time, people still get confused about what it actually is. Because while the dream of equality is beautiful, the reality? Not so much.

---

1. Clothing is *not* optional, Kevin.

The Great American Confusion

Before we dive into the history, let's clear up a little something. If you've tuned into US politics in 2024—or had the misfortune of spending more than five minutes scrolling through Twitter—you'll know that any suggestion of left-leaning policy is enough to get you branded a *"dirty Commie."* It's as if Joe McCarthy himself has risen from the dead, poltergeist-style, to haunt the American political landscape. And here's the most amusing bit of it all: Kamala Harris, currently standing as the Democratic nominee, has been repeatedly accused of harbouring radical communist ideas. Now, let's be clear—Kamala Harris is as much a communist as I am a bright blue reclining armchair. Yet, somehow, in the fevered imagination of certain political circles, anyone who even hints at wanting a healthcare system that won't bankrupt you is halfway to leading a revolution, red flag in hand.

It's a bizarre spectacle, really. On one hand, you've got Trump, whose MAGA movement loves to throw around the word *"communist"* like it's the ultimate insult. And on the other, large sections of Twitter gleefully parrot the same lines. Elon Musk, ever the master of chaos, has been known to dabble in these *"commie-bashing"* waters as well, adding his voice to a chorus that increasingly feels like a never-ending reenactment of 1950s McCarthyism. Honestly, we're going to need a helluva exorcism to purge the ghost of McCarthy from the political discourse at this rate. It's like they've collectively forgotten what communism actually is, preferring to wield it as a catch-all term for any policy that dares to challenge the almighty free market.

And here's where it gets even more ridiculous: in the US, *"communist"* has become shorthand for anything remotely progressive, from universal healthcare to affordable education. Suggest that maybe, just maybe, people shouldn't have to choose between feeding their families and paying their medical bills, and boom—suddenly you're Stalin. It's a neat trick, really. Take a complex and heavily flawed ideology and use it as a fear-mongering tool to shut down even the mildest of reforms. Never mind that actual communism is about state ownership of the means of production and the abolition of private property. No, no—if you so much as whisper the words *"wealth tax"* or *"income equality,"* you might as well start packing for the gulag.

It's astonishing how a term with such a specific historical and political meaning has been stretched beyond recognition. Communism in practice—whether in the Soviet Union, Cuba, or North Korea—was, and is, a system of total state control, where personal freedoms are traded for collective ownership, and the government dictates nearly every aspect of life. But in the American political imagination, communism has morphed into a sort of bogeyman that can be summoned at will to scare the bejesus out of the electorate. Want to raise taxes on the wealthy? Commie. Support stronger labour unions? Red alert. Advocate for climate action? Well, now you're practically Lenin.

So, let's set the record straight. Calling Kamala Harris a communist is like comparing apples to hand grenades, and most of the policies that get labelled as *"communist"* in the US are, frankly, just common sense in other parts of the world (waves from the UK). But the spectre of McCarthyism still looms large, with political labels being thrown around like confetti at a particularly unhinged wedding. The result? A political discourse that's more about scaremongering than actual substance. And as the US gears up for another election, you can bet that we'll see more of these wild accusations. After all, when you don't have real policy ideas, calling someone a communist is always an easy fallback.

The question is, when will the world finally see through the nonsense and realise that not every whisper of economic reform is a slippery slope to communism? Until then, the ghost of McCarthy lingers on, finding new hosts in Musk, Trump, and the Twitterati.

History in Brief: From Marx to the Bread Lines

The story of Communism begins with Karl Marx who we first met in our chapter about socialism—the bearded philosopher who sat down, gazed at the industrial revolution chewing up workers and spitting them out, and thought to himself, *"There's got to be a better way."* And, in fairness, he believed he'd cracked the code for human society. In *The Communist Manifesto*, Marx laid out a vision of a classless, stateless society where the working class (or the proletariat) would rise up, overthrow the bourgeoisie (the capitalist class), and take control of the means of production. In Marx's ideal world, there would be no private property, no exploitation, and no inequality. The workers wouldn't just work *for* a company—they'd *own* it, ensuring that wealth was shared equally among all, rather than being concentrated in the hands of a wealthy few.

Marx's utopia was one where everyone contributed according to their ability and received according to their needs. Gone would be the days of backbreaking labour that benefited only the rich, while the poor barely scraped by. Instead, society would become a harmonious collective where everyone got exactly what they needed based on their contributions. It sounds almost idyllic, right? Well, there was one small problem: Marx didn't exactly leave a step-by-step guide for how to achieve this worker's paradise. His ideas were more like a dream without instructions—a rough sketch of a future society, but without the IKEA assembly manual to put it together.

And as we all know, when you don't have instructions, things can get messy. Enter Vladimir Lenin. Lenin, a revolutionary leader in Russia, took Marx's ideas and thought, *"Sure, but maybe we need the state to take charge first, you know, just to make sure everything runs smoothly until the workers figure out how to manage things themselves."* It was the political equivalent of asking your overbearing friend to hold onto your new house keys while you figure out how to live in it. What was supposed to be a temporary measure of state control to help ease the workers into power quickly spiralled into something much darker. The revolution, which had begun as a movement for worker empowerment and equality, morphed into a system of authoritarianism and state control.

Lenin's revolution in Russia, with its cries of *"power to the people,"* led to some rather unintended consequences[2]. Instead of the workers rising up and taking charge of their destinies, the state—under Lenin and later Stalin—took control of everything. What started as a noble pursuit of collective ownership quickly descended into bureaucratic control, secret police, and those infamous bread lines. It was like signing up for a workers' utopia and getting a dictatorship instead.

But, if Lenin's revolution was the moment Communism lost the plot, Joseph Stalin was the man who turned that loss into a full-on descent into authoritarianism. Stalin didn't just believe in state control—he took it to terrifying extremes. His version of Communism was less about Marx's dreamy equality and more about consolidating his personal power. Under Stalin's rule, millions were purged, dissenters were sent to the gulag, and any whispers of Marx's vision of freedom were buried under a mountain of state oppression and fear. The collectivisation of agriculture? That led to famine and the deaths of millions. The five-year plans? They were less about lifting up the working class and more about meeting insane production quotas at the cost of human life. Stalin wasn't just the man at the helm of the revolution—he *was* the revolution, and everything was to bend to his will.

Funny how every revolution that promises equality and shared power somehow ends with one person calling all the shots, isn't it? It's as if there's some unwritten rule that any movement for collective ownership inevitably turns into one man—or one party—taking control and making sure that no one else gets a say. From Lenin's early attempts to centralise power to Stalin's

---

2. Doesn't overthrowing a government always?

brutal consolidation of it, the path of Communism seems to have veered far from Marx's original dream. What was supposed to be about workers' liberation turned into state control, with a side order of mass purges and some of the longest bread lines history has ever seen.

In the end, the grand dream of Communism as Marx envisioned it—a world where the workers are in charge, free from exploitation, living in collective harmony—was strangled by the very states that were supposed to bring it into being. Instead of a classless society, we got gulags. Instead of collective ownership, we got centralised control. And instead of equality, we got one-party rule, where dissent was met with bullets or a trip to Siberia.

As much as we might want to romanticise the idea of a classless, egalitarian society, the reality is that every time it's been attempted, the results have been far less utopian than advertised. And yet, despite its failings, Communism still exerts a strange allure. After all, who wouldn't want to live in a world where everyone gets an equal share, where the rich don't hoard wealth, and where your contribution to society is valued above your bank account balance? It's a beautiful dream—just one that's proven incredibly difficult to bring to life without devolving into authoritarian rule.

Dialectical Materialism and Historical Materialism

If you want to understand why Marx thought communism was a done deal, you need to start with dialectical materialism—his grand theory of history, where class struggle takes centre stage. According to Marx, history isn't shaped by noble ideals or moral enlightenment, but by cold, hard material conditions. From the moment someone realised they could hoard more resources than their neighbour, humanity has been locked in an endless tug-of-war between the haves and the have-nots[3].

Marx's view was that history moved through predictable stages: feudalism gave way to capitalism, which would eventually collapse under its own weight, leading to the final stage—communism. And why wouldn't it? According to Marx, capitalism was essentially a ticking time bomb, doomed to self-destruct once the working class woke up and realised they were being fleeced[4]. Once that happened, the proletariat would rise up, overthrow their capitalist overlords, et voilà—*utopia*. Sure, it sounds a bit idealistic now, but to Marx, this wasn't some vague hope for a better tomorrow; it was a scientific certainty. He had the theory (he called it scientific socialism), and if you squinted hard enough, the data *almost* made sense too.

Of course, the reality of history wasn't exactly as neat as Marx predicted, but he didn't care. For him, the revolution was inevitable because the contradictions within capitalism were bound to rip it apart. Dialectical materialism wasn't just some philosophical quirk—it was the very logic of human progress. Every epoch contained the seeds of its own destruction, which meant that capitalism would inevitably give way to communism, just as night follows day. Simple, right?

Understanding this dialectical thinking sheds light on why Marx was so very confident. Communism wasn't just a utopian fantasy to him—it was the next unavoidable step in humanity's grand evolution. Capitalism was doomed, and the revolution was just waiting for its cue. Of course, reality had a few curveballs in store that Marx didn't see coming, but no theory's perfect, is it?

---

3. It's basically Game of Thrones with fewer swords and more labour disputes.

4. Yeah, we're still waiting on that...

Leninism, Stalinism, Maoism, and Trotskyism

You'd think communism, with all its promises of equality and a workers' utopia, would be a simple, straightforward ideology. Just follow Marx's blueprint, overthrow the bourgeoisie, and boom—paradise for all, right? Wrong. Turns out, every revolutionary leader had their own special recipe for achieving Marx's dream, because why stick to the original plan when you can throw in a few personal twists? Marx provided the foundation, but Lenin, Stalin, Mao, and Trotsky couldn't resist the urge to remodel the house. And surprise, surprise—the results were often less utopia and more authoritarian hellscape.

Leninism was the first remix of Marxism, and Lenin's big innovation? The vanguard party—because you can't *exactly* trust the working masses to lead themselves, can you? According to Lenin, the revolution needed a bit of top-down guidance, courtesy of a tightly-knit group of professional revolutionaries. You know, just to make sure things didn't go off the rails. And by *"make sure,"* we mean controlling the whole process. Democracy? Sure, but only after the professionals have taken care of the messy bits.

Then there's Stalin, who looked at Lenin's vanguard idea and thought, *"Why stop there? Let's focus on building socialism in just one country—specifically mine."* Thus, Socialism in One Country was born, complete with forced collectivisation, purges, and a delightful array of gulags. Stalin's innovation was essentially communism with a side of brutal repression. The working class was still central, of course—mostly as the group building his five-year plans while trying to avoid starving or getting disappeared by the secret police.

Mao, meanwhile, decided that communism needed a rural makeover. Forget the industrial workers; in China, it was the peasants who were destined to lead the revolution. Why should factory workers have all the fun? Mao's brand of communism shifted the focus from urban to rural, dragging China through the Great Leap Forward[5] , a plan so disastrous it led to one of the deadliest famines in history. But hey, it was revolutionary, right?

And then there's Trotsky, the idealist who couldn't settle for just one revolution. Nope, Permanent Revolution was his answer to Marxist stagnation. Trotsky believed that revolution should be an ongoing process, rolling from one country to the next like some endless, exhausting global tour. His ideas didn't win him many friends in Moscow—least of all Stalin, who eventually had Trotsky exiled and assassinated for being a *bit* too idealistic for his liking.

Modern Communism: The Bizarre Hybrids

So, what's left of Communism today? Well, not much—at least, not in the way Marx originally intended. But there are still a few countries that proudly wear the Communist label, even if their version of it looks less like a workers' utopia and more like a survivalist's guide to running a state. Let's take a quick tour through the most famous (or infamous) Communist holdouts: Cuba, North Korea, and China.

Let's start with Cuba, where the ideals of Fidel Castro's revolution are still clinging to life, though it's hard to say if the island is surviving *because* of Communism or *in spite* of it. Cuba's revolution in 1959 was meant to create a classless society free from American imperialism and capitalist exploitation. And to be fair, they've managed to hang on to their socialist identity in a world that's overwhelmingly capitalist. But the dream of an equal society has faced some serious challenges. The US embargo hasn't helped, of course, but even within Cuba, there's been a noticeable gap between the revolutionary ideals of collective ownership and the harsh reality of economic stagnation and

---

5. A name that is very, very misleading – unless you're describing jumping into a very deep ravine.

shortages. Sure, healthcare and education are universally available and often praised, but the Cuban people face daily struggles that make it hard to romanticise their brand of Communism. It's less about workers owning the means of production and more about workers waiting in line for basic goods.

Then, there's North Korea, a country that technically claims to follow the tenets of Marxist-Leninist thought, but we can all agree—there's nothing remotely socialist about the brutal, dynastic dictatorship of the Kim family. If Marx were alive to see North Korea today, he'd likely need a stiff drink to cope with the fact that his dream of workers' liberation has turned into a regime of oppressive control, nuclear brinkmanship, and poverty. North Korea is one of the most isolated countries on the planet, where the state controls not only the economy but every aspect of life. The people of North Korea aren't controlling the means of production—they're just trying to survive under a regime that insists on absolute loyalty to the Supreme Leader, with a heavy dose of propaganda to keep up the facade of a *"workers' state."* In reality, the country has less to do with Marxist theory and more to do with totalitarianism. But, hey, the word *"Communist"* is still in their official documents, so that counts for something, right?

And now we come to China, where Communism has taken on a curious life of its own. On paper, China is still a Communist state, with the Chinese Communist Party firmly in control of both the government and the economy. But in practice, China has embraced elements of capitalism with a fervour that would make even Adam Smith blush. Since Deng Xiaoping's market reforms in the late 1970s, China has experienced staggering economic growth, much of it driven by private enterprise and competition. In other words, China's brand of *"Communism"* involves a thriving consumer goods market, private billionaires, and state-run enterprises that operate more like corporate conglomerates. Nothing says *"workers of the world, unite"* quite like Alibaba, Temu, and a flourishing middle class that's fully invested in the global economy.

China's Communist Party maintains control, but the country's economy looks more like a hybrid of state capitalism and authoritarianism than the collective ownership Marx envisioned. It's a paradox, really—China still flies the Communist flag, but its policies would make Marx spin in his grave. After all, Marx's vision was for a stateless, classless society, not a one-party state with billion-dollar tech companies and a government that uses capitalism as a tool for national growth[6].

And while these countries struggle with their own unique versions of *"Communism,"* let's not forget the absurdity of how the word is wielded in the US. In the American political discourse, *"Communism"* is less about state ownership or class struggle and more about scaring people into believing that universal healthcare and affordable education are the first steps on the road to gulags. Any hint of left-wing policy is instantly branded as *"Communist"* by certain sections of the media and political establishment, despite the fact that modern leftist movements in the US are more about social democracy than anything Marx would recognise.

The long and short of it is that Communism in practice has drifted so far from Marx's original ideas that calling any of these regimes *"Communist"* feels like a bit of a stretch. What's left of Communism today is a far cry from the classless, stateless society that Marx dreamed of. Instead, we're left with a strange mix of authoritarian rule, state control, and, in some cases, a heavy dose of capitalism. It's almost as if the term *"Communism"* is more of a label than a reality—used by both the regimes that claim it and the critics who fear it.

What It's Not: Modern Socialism

---

6. But hey, if you squint hard enough, maybe you can still see some traces of Communism beneath the glittering skyscrapers and luxury malls. Maybe.

Let's clarify a quick small point here for a second—Communism is not just Socialism taken to the extreme. They may share the same ideological family tree, but these two systems are quite distinct once you get into the details. Where Socialism is like your idealistic friend who wants to make sure everyone has access to healthcare and education, Communism is the more radical cousin that believes the entire system—capitalism, private ownership, the works—needs to be dismantled completely[7]. So, let's stop using them interchangeably. Socialism, especially in places like Scandinavia, has shown it can play nice with capitalism and create functioning, prosperous democracies. Communism, on the other hand, takes a far more revolutionary approach, aiming to flip the entire structure on its head.

The real difference here is in the end goals. Socialism seeks to redistribute wealth and ensure that essential services like healthcare, education, and social security are available to everyone. It works within the system to make it fairer. Communism? Communism wants to tear the whole thing down and start over—no private ownership of land or businesses, no class divisions, no capitalist structures at all. It's a full-blown revolution, not just a shift in tax policies.

And while we're at it, let's clear up the other common misconception: Communism isn't about everyone sharing the same ratty towel or living in some sort of commune where personal possessions are doled out equally. The idea, in theory, is collective ownership of the big stuff—the factories, the land, the means of production—so that wealth isn't concentrated in the hands of a few. In reality, however, this often means the state steps in to decide who gets what, and that's where things get a little... uncomfortable.

In places like the former USSR and North Korea, this *"collective ownership"* has typically translated into the government owning everything and distributing goods and services according to its

---

7. We all have that one cousin – bless their revolutionary cotton socks.

own set of rules—whether the people agree or not. That's a far cry from the dream of voluntary cooperation Marx envisioned. Instead of a happy, cooperative society where everyone contributes according to their abilities and receives according to their needs, it's more like one big bureaucracy deciding who gets bread, who gets cars, and who gets a one-way ticket to Siberia if they don't toe the party line.

So, no, Communism doesn't mean giving up your personal possessions or being forced into communal living. But in practice, it often involves a level of state control that takes away the freedoms and choices many of us take for granted. And for all its talk about eliminating class divisions, it tends to replace one hierarchy with another—a new ruling elite that controls everything from the top down.

Factors Leading to Collapse

The Soviet Union—once the gleaming beacon of communism, promising equality, prosperity, and the workers' paradise—went out with a bang, not a whimper, in 1991. After nearly 70 years of trying to prove Marx right, it all came crashing down like a poorly built house of socialist cards. So, what went wrong[8]?

For starters, the economy was a disaster. Central planning looked good on paper, but in practice, it left the USSR in a perpetual state of stagnation. Imagine trying to run an entire economy by committee—everything slowed to a crawl, inefficiency became the norm, and innovation? Forget it. When your five-year plan involves producing more tractors than you have farmers to use them, you know you're in trouble. Then there was the arms race—the Soviet Union poured so much money into keeping pace with the West militarily that it didn't leave much room for things like, oh, feeding its people.

---

8. In short, *everything*.

And let's not forget the nationalist movements that sprang up like weeds in every Soviet republic. Once the iron grip of Moscow started to loosen, regions like the Baltics, Ukraine, and Central Asia seized the opportunity to break free. These nationalist movements, tired of being under the thumb of the Kremlin, were like cracks in the Soviet dam, ready to burst the moment there was even the slightest slack in control.

But it wasn't just Cold War pressures or nationalist uprisings that did the USSR in. No, this collapse was largely self-inflicted. The Soviet system was packed with internal contradictions—an economy that couldn't feed its people, a political system that couldn't innovate, and a government that treated dissent like a pest problem to be exterminated rather than an issue to be addressed. Repression was always the first option[9], and when you're more interested in silencing complaints than solving them, eventually the complaints get loud enough that even a gulag can't contain them.

By the time the Berlin Wall fell in 1989, the writing was on the wall for the entire Soviet experiment. It became painfully clear that the system had been running on fumes for decades. What was once the proud vanguard of communism was now a hollow shell, collapsing under the weight of its own dysfunction. In the end, it wasn't the CIA or Reagan's "evil empire" speech that brought the USSR down—it was the contradictions at its very core.

Why It Matters: The Dream Lives On

Despite Communism's well-documented failures—famines, authoritarian regimes, gulags, and all—it still casts a long shadow over modern political discourse, particularly on the left. The dream of a classless, equal society where no one is left behind remains alluring to those who look at the widening gap between

---

9. Let's be honest, it was the only option.

the rich and the poor and wonder how we ended up here. In a world where the wealth of a handful of billionaires outstrips the combined GDP of entire nations, it's not hard to see why people are still drawn to the ideals of collective welfare, worker rights, and economic equality. The promise that everyone could have enough if we just distributed things more fairly? It's appealing—especially when capitalism seems to be doing the opposite, hoarding resources at the top.

But here's the catch: Communism and Socialism, two distinct ideologies, are often treated as one and the same, particularly in the United States, where any whiff of a left-wing policy gets you labelled as a *"dirty Commie"* faster than you can say *"universal healthcare." Take* a look at the way progressive movements are demonised in the US. Policies like Medicare for All—hardly a radical proposal by European standards—are smeared with the dreaded *"communism"* label, as though ensuring that people don't die from treatable conditions is one slippery step away from gulags and secret police. This has a lot to do with the lasting effects of McCarthyism, which, even decades later, has left many Americans deeply suspicious of anything that hints at collective action or public ownership.

But while Communism is used as a bogeyman to shut down debates about basic human needs, its ideals continue to shape the conversation, even in the most capitalist of societies. Worker's rights, labour protections, the very concept of a minimum wage—all of these have their roots in the same class struggle Marx was banging on about in the 19th century. Even in America, where capitalism reigns supreme, the presence of labour unions, the fight for better healthcare, and the pushback against corporate greed can trace their origins, at least in part, to the legacy of Communist thought.

It's ironic, really. In its purest form, Communism advocates for a society where the workers control the means of production, but in practice, it led to state control and authoritarianism. Meanwhile, in modern capitalist countries, the most vocal proponents of worker rights and collective welfare often have to tiptoe around the C-word, lest they be accused of wanting to turn the country into a Soviet-style hellscape. It's a delicate balance, this dance between capitalism and the lingering influence of Communism's more appealing ideals. Because while no one wants bread lines, the reality is that people still want fairness. They want a system that doesn't leave them behind while the wealthiest individuals build rockets for fun.

And so, even in the most capitalist corners of the world, echoes of Communism persist. Not the purges and the personality cults, but the desire for a more equal society, where workers aren't exploited and where economic inequality isn't so glaring. It's a legacy that remains relevant, even if Communism itself is widely regarded as a failed experiment.

Fascism

The One We Really Don't Want to epeat

> "Fascism is not in itself a new order of society. It is the future refusing to be born." - Aneurin Bevan

Cut to a family dinner, the table groaning under the weight of too much roast beef and not enough salad. The air is thick with tension—those who've been here before know exactly what's coming. At the head of the table, Uncle Fascism is already in full flow, his voice booming like a drill sergeant, as the rest of the family exchanges nervous glances, too polite—or too terrified—to interrupt. He's the kind of guy who, no matter the topic of conversation, finds a way to steer it back to one of his favourite subjects: discipline, order, and the good old days when "people knew their place."

Uncle Fascism slams his fork down and starts waving his hands, punctuating every word as though his point isn't already clear.

"Look at what's happened to this country," he says, jabbing his finger at an invisible enemy. "Everyone's running wild! No respect for authority, no discipline. Back in my day—now that was a time when people understood real values. People worked hard, and if they didn't, well, they knew the consequences. If you let people do whatever they want, chaos reigns."

Across the table, Cousin Liberalism shifts uncomfortably, clearly trying to muster the courage to respond. But Uncle Fascism has spotted the movement, and like a hawk, he pounces.

"Liberalism! Don't even get me started on all this talk about freedom and equality. You think that's what people need? No, what they need is order. They need strong leadership—someone to take charge and set things straight."

At this, the younger family members—the ones who've seen too many dystopian movies—share uneasy glances. You know the type: sleek haircuts, trendy glasses, the kind of people who shop at farmer's markets but also have a sneaky subscription to Amazon Prime. They know where this conversation is going. They've heard it before. It's never just about "strong leadership," and it certainly isn't about benevolent discipline.

"You're talking about dictatorship, not discipline," says one of the more outspoken nieces, who's fresh out of university and still optimistic about the world. Her tone is cautious but firm. "People want freedom, not... whatever this is."

Uncle Fascism's face flushes. "Freedom? Oh, freedom is overrated. Look where your so-called freedom has gotten us. Chaos in the streets! Immigrants pouring in, people rioting, everyone thinking they can say or do whatever they want. Well, not in my house!" He hits the table with a meaty thump for emphasis. "What we need is **control**. Structure. And yes, discipline. These people you're talking about? The immigrants, the dissidents—they need to be put in their place. They're the ones ruining everything."

Cue a nervous silence. No one's quite sure how to respond to Uncle Fascism's thinly veiled calls for authoritarianism without kicking off a full-blown argument, but the disdain is clear. Especially for anyone who dares to deviate from the script of rigid conformity Uncle Fascism so desperately clings to.

Behind Uncle Fascism's bravado is the heart of the ideology itself—this desire for complete and total control, an obsession with order at all costs. But for all his talk of strength, what really lies at the core of his belief system is fear. Fear of difference, fear of change, fear of anything that challenges the rigid social hierarchy he's built his identity around.

In Uncle Fascism's world, there's always a scapegoat—someone to blame for why things aren't perfect. Whether it's immigrants, minorities, or just people who won't fall in line, they're the source of all society's problems. And the solution, according to him? Crack down. **Hard.**

"Look, Uncle," pipes up the sensible middle child, a blend of cautious conservatism and pragmatic liberalism. "I get it. People are scared of the world changing too fast. But we can't just throw away democracy and freedom because things are tough. Authoritarianism doesn't solve problems—it just creates new ones. You're not fixing anything by getting rid of dissent. You're just silencing voices."

Uncle Fascism huffs, crossing his arms in defiance. "Silencing the **wrong voices**, you mean. There's a reason certain people shouldn't have a platform—because they're the ones tearing this country apart! If people don't like it, they can leave."

There it is—that line, the catchphrase of authoritarianism: "If you don't like it, leave.[1]" No room for compromise, no room for debate. Just unquestioning obedience to the state. Because at the end of the day, Fascism isn't about strength or security. It's about submission—everyone fitting into neat little boxes, doing as they're told.

The dinner ends, as it always does, with Uncle Fascism retreating into angry silence, the room thick with unspoken disapproval. Everyone leaves with a sense of unease, knowing that

---

1. Now where have I heard this before...

even though the conversation has ended for now, the ideology still lurks at the edges of political discourse, waiting for the right moment to rear its head again.

Philosophical Foundations of Fascism

Fascism is the unruly, illegitimate, and, quite bluntly, evil offspring of radical authoritarianism and ultranationalism, raised on a steady diet of flag-waving and intolerance. It rejects everything that makes modern democracy bearable—like individual rights or, heaven forbid, social safety nets. Liberalism's annoying obsession with personal freedoms? Fascism rolls its eyes. Socialism's lofty dreams of workers' paradise? Fascism sneers. None of that matters if *The Nation* isn't perched on its imaginary throne of glory, and anyone who isn't on board can expect the boot of the state on their neck.

Enter Giovanni Gentile, who gave fascism its fancy ideological polish. Gentile wasn't interested in collectivism where you share things with your neighbour—this wasn't a socialist potluck. No, Gentile's collectivism was the kind where the individual exists for one reason only: to serve the almighty state. Want freedom? Fascism has just the thing for you—freedom to obey without question. Anything else would be selfish, unpatriotic, and—let's face it—dangerous to the perfect harmony of a nation-state that demands your complete submission.

Gentile's philosophy was a bizarre cocktail of ultranationalism spiked with spiritual drivel about the state being the *"ethical"* entity above all else. His intellectual gymnastics were just what Mussolini needed to transform Italy into a well-oiled police state. Why bother with pesky individual rights when you can have mass loyalty and unwavering devotion to the state? And questioning authority? Perish the thought. After all, Gentile argued, if the state says it's ethical, who are you—just a lowly individual—to say otherwise?

Understanding the basics of this philosophical mess is key to grasping why fascism still manages to seduce some parts of society. It sells a seductive cocktail of national pride, a sense of belonging, and the illusion of strength—all while erasing individuality. By scaring the living daylights out of people with talk of societal chaos and instability, fascism swoops in with its authoritarian *"solutions[2] "* that just so happen to involve violence, censorship, and your very soul bowing to the almighty state.

Marching Towards Disaster: A Brief History of Fascism

Fascism didn't just emerge out of thin air; it was born from the wreckage of a Europe ravaged by World War I, where national pride was shattered, economies lay in ruins, and millions of people were left disillusioned and desperate. The promises of liberal democracy seemed hollow, and as the old order crumbled, people sought radical alternatives. Enter Benito Mussolini, the Italian strongman who forged the first Fascist state, and in doing so, gave the world a blueprint for authoritarianism dressed up as national revival.

Mussolini's promise? To restore Italy's lost glory, a rallying cry for a nation still reeling from its perceived humiliation in the Great War. Fascism, as he envisioned it, would unite the country not through messy democracy, but through strict discipline, hierarchy, and militaristic zeal. He created a state where the individual was subsumed by the needs of the nation, where dissent was crushed, and where public life became little more than a stage for endless parades, martial vigour, and nationalist propaganda. The trains might not have actually run on time, but Mussolini made sure everyone thought they did.

But Fascism didn't stop at Italy's borders. It caught the attention of another disillusioned European: Adolf Hitler. If Mus-

---

2. And no, these solutions have never and will never work.

solini's Fascism was an iron fist of authoritarianism, Hitler's Nazism was the fist wrapped in a swastika, wielding a terrifying weapon: racial hatred. Where Mussolini sought to revive Italian pride through discipline, Hitler took that basic formula and infused it with a lethal cocktail of antisemitism, racial purity, and genocidal nationalism. For Hitler, Fascism wasn't just about order; it was about eliminating anyone who didn't fit his twisted vision of Aryan supremacy. What followed, as we know too well[3], was one of the darkest chapters in human history: the Holocaust, a war of conquest, and the brutal subjugation of millions.

Yet, Fascism wasn't limited to Italy and Germany. It was a political virus that spread across Europe and beyond. In Spain, General Francisco Franco rose to power after a bloody civil war, establishing a fascist dictatorship that would last until his death in 1975. Across Eastern Europe and even parts of South America, authoritarian regimes took root, often adopting the militaristic, nationalist trappings of Fascism. Though they wore different faces and marched under different flags, they shared a common DNA: the rejection of democracy, the embrace of authoritarian control, and an obsession with creating a homogenous national identity by excluding or violently erasing those who didn't fit.

What all these regimes had in common—whether it was Mussolini's Italy, Hitler's Germany, or Franco's Spain—was that they promised order, unity, and strength in a time of chaos and uncertainty. And what they all shared, too, was the way they ended: in catastrophe. Fascism may have claimed to restore national greatness, but it dragged countries into wars, crushed civil liberties, and left scars that have yet to heal. The promise of order came at the cost of unimaginable human suffering.

---

3. And if you know or deny it for your own purposes, then you are in no uncertain terms an awful human being.

Fascism is NOT a Left-Wing Ideology

And now, before we get too deep into this chapter, let's address one of the most pervasive conspiracy theories circulating today: the idea that Fascism is somehow a left-wing ideology. It's a myth that refuses to die, often promoted by those with little grasp of history or political theory. Yes, the Nazi Party had the word *"socialism"* in its name—*National Socialist German Workers' Party*—but don't be fooled by that superficial detail. Hitler's *"socialism"* was a grotesque distortion, a tool to rally support while crushing the very working-class movements that real socialism aimed to empower. Fascism, at its dark-hearted core, was about preserving and strengthening hierarchies, *not* dismantling them. It was about propping up the elites, not empowering the masses. It was a movement of brutal repression, designed to maintain the power of the few at the expense of the many.

Far from being an ideology of the left, Fascism was the workers' worst nightmare. It shattered trade unions, suppressed strikes, and turned the state into an instrument of violent repression, ensuring that any challenge to the status quo was met with the full force of the law—and often, far worse.

Fascism doesn't just prey on nationalism and fear—it's also remarkably good at manipulating capitalism to serve its authoritarian goals. In Nazi Germany, Hitler promised jobs, infrastructure, and prosperity, but behind the scenes, the regime was working hand-in-hand with industrialists and the economic elite. Major corporations—like Krupp and IG Farben—profited *enormously* from Hitler's war machine and were more than happy to fund a regime that would keep workers in line and boost their profits.

The fascist state claimed to champion the *"common man,"* but in reality, it was a corporate dream: trade unions were crushed, strikes were outlawed, and the state dictated labour policy to ensure a docile, productive workforce. Far from empowering workers, fascism used the illusion of national unity to protect the interests of the wealthy, all while pretending to care about economic equality. It was a brilliant con, one that still echoes today as far-right movements continue to co-opt economic discontent while selling out to the highest bidder.

So, the next time someone named Brian88149492[4] on Twitter tells you that *"Fascism is left-wing you simping cuck"*, maybe ask them why Hitler's regime executed communists, sent trade unionists to concentration camps, and aligned itself with the industrialists and aristocrats. The reality is that Fascism was, and remains, the enemy of progressive movements. Its central tenet has always been the consolidation of power in the hands of a select few, achieved through violence, fear, and division.

Manipulation of Media and Symbols

Fascists may be many things—ruthless, authoritarian, power-hungry—but one thing they excel at is *salesmanship*. Joseph Goebbels practically invented the art of political branding, turning propaganda into a weapon so effective it would make Orwell's worst dystopias look like a children's puppet show. The secret? It's not rocket science—just lie. A lot. Repeat the lie enough times, slap it on every available surface, and voilà, it becomes *"truth."* In a fascist regime, facts are more dangerous than dissenters, so they bury them under a pile of patriotism, fearmongering, and endless praise for the glorious leader. If people start thinking for themselves, the whole dictatorship gig might fall apart.

Symbols become omnipresent in this nightmare marketing campaign. Take your pick: swastikas, black shirts[5], or those disturbingly choreographed parades where everyone salutes in

---

4. With 14 followers all of whom are sex robots making promises they can't keep.

5. Or perhaps red caps with a certain four word slogan...

perfect sync, as if individual thought were a deadly disease. These symbols aren't just badges of loyalty—they're the psychological chains that bind individuals to the fascist state. And if you're not marching in lockstep with the crowd, you're probably next on the state's hit list.

Rallies, meanwhile, are fascism's bread and butter. Nothing says *"cult of personality"* like a stadium full of people screaming their adoration for the dear leader. Goebbels, ever the master propagandist, knew that the trick to maintaining power was simple: control the media, and you control the masses. Every radio broadcast, every newspaper headline, and every film was just another cog in the machine, designed to drown out dissent and ensure that the only voice people heard was the state's.

Propaganda isn't just a tool for fascism—it's the *oxygen* that keeps the regime alive. Understanding how these regimes manipulated media and symbols is essential if you want to grasp why fascism works so effectively. The methods Goebbels perfected didn't vanish when the Third Reich collapsed—they're alive and well. Just look around. Nationalist symbols still dominate public spaces, state-controlled media spreads the official narrative, and leaders frame any criticism as a betrayal of the nation. The fascist playbook? Still depressingly relevant.

Gender Roles and Fascism

Fascism didn't just want to control the state—it also had grand plans for your personal life, right down to the bedroom. Fascist regimes promote a rigid, joyless version of gender roles, hammering patriarchal structures into place with all the finesse of a drunk carpenter. In the fascist playbook, women were seen as baby factories first, human beings second. Mussolini, Hitler, Franco—they were all obsessed with birth rates, convinced that the only way to secure the nation's future was for women to pump out as many patriotic offspring as possible. Preferably boys, of course, to fuel the next generation of soldiers and obedient citizens who would die for the fatherland.

In fact, the more children you had, the better. In Nazi Germany, if you managed to produce four or more kids, you'd be rewarded with the *"Mother's Cross"*—because apparently, the best way to measure a woman's worth was by counting the number of blonde-haired, blue-eyed babies she could churn out. Who needs career aspirations or personal autonomy when you can have a shiny medal for your uterus?

And let's not forget the LGBTQ+ community, who were treated as walking threats to the perfect, heterosexual family unit. Homosexuality wasn't just frowned upon—it was criminalised. Brutally. Anyone who dared defy traditional gender norms was persecuted with brutal efficiency. The message was clear: step outside the rigid, state-approved family structure, and you weren't just different—you were a danger to the nation itself.

Fascism's obsession with gender roles is just another way of asserting control. Individual freedom, whether political or personal, was the enemy. By forcing women into traditional roles and crushing anyone who deviated from the norm, fascist regimes made it clear that they weren't just interested in controlling your vote—they wanted control over your most private choices, too[6].

Modern Fascism: Same Old Tricks, New Branding

Fascism didn't die with Hitler in his bunker or Mussolini hanging from a lamppost in Milan. It didn't fade quietly into the annals of history, a tragic lesson never to be repeated. Instead, it rebranded. Fascism evolved, slipped into new clothes, and learned to speak a different language while clinging fiercely to the same authoritarian playbook. In today's world, you're less likely to see fascists openly waving swastikas or parading

---

6. And if this all sounds spine chillingly familiar, it's because well known and prominent reactionary movements today still push the same tired *"family values"* rhetoric. It's just fascism with better PR.

through the streets in brownshirts, but the underlying messages remain disturbingly familiar: hyper-nationalism, authoritarian leadership, and a deep-seated distrust of immigrants, minorities, and anyone deemed an *"other."*

Let's start with a clear example: Hungary. Under Viktor Orbán, Hungary has increasingly moved toward what Orbán himself proudly calls *"illiberal democracy."* Nationalist rhetoric, a crackdown on independent media, the demonisation of immigrants, and sweeping control over the judiciary have all become part of Orbán's governance style. He positions himself as the defender of European Christian values against the *"threat"* of multiculturalism and Islam. It's a play straight from the fascist handbook, just with fewer armbands.

Then there's Poland, where the ruling Law and Justice Party (PiS) has systematically undermined judicial independence and cracked down on LGBTQ+ rights, all while positioning itself as the protector of the Polish nation against external threats—be they the European Union, migrants, or liberalism itself. Nationalism has been weaponised, and once again, the idea of the nation-state, pure and indivisible, is pitted against an imagined enemy that threatens to destabilise *"traditional values."*

Across the Atlantic, Brazil has flirted with its own brand of fascist tendencies under Jair Bolsonaro. His presidency was marked by extreme right-wing populism, nationalist rhetoric, and a dangerous disregard for democratic norms. Bolsonaro consistently undermined democratic institutions, demonised political opponents, and fuelled division, all while riding a wave of economic discontent and fear. His rule was a mix of militaristic nostalgia and authoritarian governance that should send shivers down anyone's spine. And even with him out of office, the political ecosystem that allowed him to thrive hasn't disappeared.

And then, of course, there's the United States, where fascist ideas have found new life under the guise of populism. Donald Trump's presidency brought authoritarianism back into the mainstream in a way that hadn't been seen in generations. From his open disdain for democratic norms—encouraging violence, threatening opponents, undermining elections, and appealing to white nationalist sentiments—to his use of scapegoating immigrants and Muslims, Trump's America walked perilously close to the fascist edge. Even after losing the 2020 election, Trump's influence on the far-right continues to cast a long shadow. The Capitol insurrection of January 6, 2021, was a terrifying display of how far-right populism, fuelled by lies and conspiracies, can spiral into open violence. The spectre of fascism has re-emerged in America's far-right movements, like the Proud Boys, white supremacist groups, and other militia-style organisations emboldened by Trump's rhetoric.

France has also seen the rise of far-right populism with Marine Le Pen's National Rally. Though she's attempted to soften the image of her party by dropping overtly racist language, her platform remains grounded in anti-immigrant, nationalist, and anti-EU policies. Le Pen has carefully repackaged far-right ideas into a brand more palatable for mainstream voters, but the underlying themes of exclusion, control, and national supremacy are all too familiar.

Even in Germany, a country that has tried to reckon deeply with its Nazi past, the far-right Alternative für Deutschland (AfD) has gained a troubling foothold. Openly xenophobic, anti-immigrant, and nostalgic for a Germany of the past, the AfD has used economic discontent and fears about immigration to rally support. It's a chilling reminder that even in a country where the horrors of Fascism are part of the national memory, authoritarian nationalism can still rear its ugly head.

What's frightening is that these movements aren't confined to a fringe—they've made their way into the political mainstream. Politicians, eager to capitalise on growing fear and economic insecurity, have adopted fascist rhetoric in their appeals to voters. Calls for militarisation, crackdowns on dissent, and the erosion of civil liberties in the name of *"security"* are all straight from the Fascist playbook. Once confined to the extreme right, these ideas are now openly discussed in parliaments and campaign trails across the world.

And then there's the internet. In the digital age, the rise of fascism has found a new, terrifyingly effective battleground online. Far-right extremism has spread faster than ever, with online echo chambers amplifying nationalist, xenophobic, and violent rhetoric. Social media platforms have become recruitment tools for fascist movements, allowing them to exploit economic instability, racial anxieties, and social unrest to stoke division and hatred. Platforms like Twitter, Reddit, and even private messaging apps have enabled fascists to find each other, organise, and radicalise others.

This online breeding ground for extremism has already had real-world consequences. From mass shootings inspired by white supremacist ideologies to the open embrace of *"Great Replacement"* theories by far-right leaders, the internet has proven to be a powerful weapon in the fascist arsenal. It's no longer just the strongman leaders we need to fear—it's the countless anonymous voices online, radicalising a new generation and bringing fascist ideologies into the homes of millions.

What's most terrifying is how normalised these authoritarian tendencies have become. In the rush to capitalise on fear and economic uncertainty, mainstream politicians are increasingly borrowing from the Fascist playbook, all while disguising it with more palatable language. They talk about *"law and order," "national pride," "wanting our country back",* and *"protecting our way of life,"* but the echoes of Fascism are unmistakable.

The risks we face are clear: when authoritarianism becomes mainstream, democracy itself is at stake. Fascism may have rebranded, but its core remains unchanged—a belief in power, control, and division. If we don't confront it head-on, we may find ourselves marching once again towards disaster.

What Fascism Is (and Isn't): The Ever Present Myth of *"Strong Leadership"*

Let's clear something up that drives me a bit mad: *Fascism is not about "strong leadership"*. It's easy to confuse the two because fascists often elevate a single, domineering figure to rally around, but strong leadership in itself isn't inherently fascist. The reality is far more sinister. Fascism isn't just about a leader calling the shots—it's about total, uncompromising control. Fascism doesn't simply want to lead a nation; it wants to dictate every aspect of life, from your political beliefs to your personal relationships. It's not enough to fall in line; you have to *believe* in the system. The leader becomes the embodiment of the state, the law, and the future, with no room for dissent.

Fascism's goal isn't just to create order—it's to create an obedient, unquestioning society. The kind where opposition isn't just silenced but erased. Forget about freedom of speech or assembly, because in a fascist regime, those are luxuries that threaten the very order they've built. Imagine a world where your thoughts, your movements, and your identity are all carefully curated by the state. That's not strong leadership. That's authoritarian control at its most brutal and intimate.

Then there's the idea of the scapegoat. Fascism always needs an enemy—someone to blame for the ills of society. In Nazi Germany, it was Jews, Roma, disabled people, and political dissidents. In Italy, it was Communists and socialists. Fascism thrives on division—it's not about bringing the nation together in a meaningful way but rather excluding and dehumanising anyone who doesn't fit the rigid national mould. There's always an *"other"* that must be purged to preserve the purity and unity of the state. So, no, Fascism isn't simply about patriotism or national pride; it's about forcing everyone to conform to an idealised and often twisted vision of what the nation should be—one that's built on fear, exclusion, and violence.

In Fascism, the individual is always subservient to the state, and any notion of equality is tossed out the window in favour of national or racial supremacy. Far from being a movement that uplifts the working class, Fascism has historically used the working class as a pawn—riling them up with promises of economic security, only to subjugate them once power is consolidated. Fascism champions the elite, the ruling class, and the idea that only a select few are fit to rule over the many. It's about power for the few at the expense of the many, with a boot forever pressing down on those who don't comply.

So, no—Fascism isn't about community or solidarity. It's about exclusion, domination, and a strict hierarchy that punishes anyone who dares to step out of line. It's not the promise of a better future for all; it's the demand for unwavering obedience to a regime that demands total control over life, thought, and identity. The strength of Fascism lies not in its leadership but in its ability to crush dissent and control society from the top down.

Modern Fascism and the Myth of Protest: Riots, Crackdowns, and Convenient Scapegoats

In recent months, we've seen the word *Fascism* thrown around in ways that almost seem designed to drain it of all meaning. Particularly in the UK, there's been a dangerous misuse of the term in relation to the crackdown on violent orchestrated far-right riots, which some are now bizarrely labelling as *Fascism under Keir Starmer*. Let's be clear: this isn't Fascism, and conflating it with actual fascist ideologies does a grave disservice to historical and present-day understanding of what the word truly means.

These right-wing riots weren't your average protests—far from it. What we witnessed was mob violence incited by far-right groups targeting migrants and Muslims. Hotels housing asylum seekers were set on fire, masked men rampaged through towns, and yes, in the middle of this grotesque spectacle, Lush stores were looted—because apparently, nothing says *"defending your country"* quite like grabbing a bath bomb in the middle of a riot. These weren't political demonstrations in any meaningful sense; they were acts of disorder and violence that put lives at risk.

When police cracked down on these violent mobs, the usual suspects—online reactionaries, conspiracy theorists, and those with a dangerous misunderstanding of both politics and history—started yelling that Starmer's government was showing fascist tendencies. This, of course, is utter nonsense. The violent incitement against vulnerable communities wasn't some brave stand against tyranny—it was targeted, racially motivated violence, plain and simple. And yet, somehow, the focus has shifted to whether stopping these riots was an authoritarian overreach.

Compare this to the rhetoric we saw under the previous government. Suella Braverman, who made headlines with her hard-line stance on immigration and crime, referred to peaceful pro-Palestinian marches as *"hate marches"* while overseeing the introduction of a policing bill that has made the very act of protest more illegal. The bill, passed under the Tories, gives police sweeping powers to clamp down on any form of public dissent that's deemed too disruptive or too loud—basically, any protest that's not convenient for those in power. That is where the creeping authoritarianism lies. It's in the erosion of basic democratic rights, like the right to protest, especially when those protests don't align with the government's narrative. Peaceful dissent is being reframed as a public order issue, and that's an incredibly dangerous road to go down.

When you look at these two situations side by side, it's clear where the real fascistic tendencies are emerging. A violent far-right mob being stopped by the police is not *fascism*; it's law enforcement doing its job. But when the government redefines peaceful protest as a threat, that's when alarm bells should be ringing. It's a tactic ripped straight from the fascist playbook: recast the dissenters as dangerous enemies of the state and use the guise of public safety to tighten control over personal freedoms.

The real danger is that these terms—*Fascism, protest, freedom*—are being thrown around carelessly, muddying the waters to the point where people can no longer distinguish between protecting democracy and undermining it. While the far right's violent riots were not *protests* in any meaningful sense, peaceful marches and demonstrations should be defended as part of any healthy democracy. The rise of fascist language comes when a government begins to blur the line between legitimate political dissent and disorder, treating both as equally dangerous.

Why Fascism Still Matters: The Authoritarian Temptation

Here's the uncomfortable truth: Fascism never truly disappeared. Like a particularly nasty infection, it went into hiding for a while, only to resurface when the world is at its most vulnerable. In the political climate of 2024, as economic inequalities grow wider and far-right rhetoric finds a home in places it once seemed unthinkable, we can no longer pretend that Fascism is just a relic of history. It's back—and it's creeping into mainstream politics all across Europe and the world.

Why is Fascism still relevant today? Because its authoritarian impulse never really went away. The movement that once marched in lockstep and waved flags emblazoned with swastikas has since learned how to blend in, hiding behind nationalist slogans, populist movements, and convenient scapegoats. This time, the aesthetic might be different—less jackboots, more polished suits—but the underlying message is the same: *"We need control. We need order. **And we'll do it by any means necessary."***

Fascism thrives because it offers simple answers to complex problems. Feeling anxious about your future? Blame immigrants. Worried about the economy? Blame minorities, the global elite, or anyone who isn't part of your ever narrowing definition of *"us."* The seductive appeal of Fascism is that it gives people a target for their fear and frustration. It tells them who's to blame and offers them a way out: conformity and control.

The fact is, when people feel powerless—whether due to economic insecurity, social upheaval, or a perceived cultural threat—they are more susceptible to the authoritarian temptation. The offer is almost irresistible: Sacrifice a bit of your personal freedom, and we'll give you security in return. All it takes is a charismatic leader to stoke that fear, promising to restore national pride, bring back jobs, or "cleanse" society, and suddenly, the impossible becomes plausible.

And that's where the danger lies. Fascism thrives on fear. It is a movement built on exploiting insecurity and offering simple, brutal solutions to the anxieties people feel in their everyday lives. And what's worse, in times of fear, people are often willing to trade freedom for the illusion of security, placing their trust in the very systems that will strip away their rights under the guise of protection.

Take a look around Europe today, and the warning signs are hard to miss. Hungary has seen the rise of a government that openly challenges democratic norms, clamping down on media freedoms and weakening the judiciary in the name of "national security." In Poland, the ruling party pushes an agenda that demonises immigrants, undermines LGBTQ+ rights, and seeks to curtail judicial independence. Meanwhile, in France, far-right figures like Marine Le Pen, while repackaging their rhetoric to appear more mainstream, still rely on a dangerous brand of hyper-nationalism and thinly veiled xenophobia.

Italy, too, is flirting with a dangerous resurgence of authoritarianism, as the far-right continues to gain ground. The new Prime Minister, Giorgia Meloni, is part of the Brothers of Italy, a party with neo-fascist roots. Her rise to power signals that the spectre of Fascism is not confined to the past—it's still here, haunting the politics of a nation that once gave birth to the ideology.

And then there's Germany, where the resurgence of neo-Nazi groups, though officially marginal, still sends a chilling message: the extreme right hasn't gone away—it's simply waiting for its moment to strike.

Let's not forget the UK. The rise of populist, far-right movements that dress up xenophobia as "national sovereignty" is deeply concerning. After all, when groups incite violence against migrants, demonise minorities, or undermine peaceful protests, these aren't political differences—they're dangerous authoritarian tactics. It's a pattern we've seen before: stoke fear, find a scapegoat, and slowly chip away at the foundations of democracy. And the terrifying thing is, many people either don't see it or are too disillusioned to care.

The Loud, Angry Minority

Fascism thrives on the illusion of dominance. It's a movement that shouts the loudest, demands absolute control, and threatens anyone who dares to question it. But here's the truth fascists don't want you to know: they are not the majority. They never have been. For all their bluster about strength, control, and *"the will of the people,"* they are always the ones trying to manipulate fear, to create a sense of overwhelming inevitability.

The reality is, fascism feeds on the margins of society—on the fringes where insecurity, economic hardship, and cultural anxiety fester. It exploits these fears, magnifying them into a crisis, all while pretending to be the only solution. It relies on people feeling powerless, isolated, and angry, so that they'll turn to the authoritarian promise of order in exchange for freedom.

But despite all the noise, the fascist playbook remains the same: lie, distort, and sow division. Convince people that democracy is weak, that diversity is dangerous, and that only a return to "strength" can save society. The truth is, fascists want us to believe that their movement is larger, stronger, and more influential than it actually is. They thrive on the perception of power—because the minute we see through the façade, their influence crumbles.

They are not the majority. They are not invincible. And their cries for authoritarian control are not the will of the people—they are the desperate, angry demands of a movement that knows, deep down, that it cannot survive in the light of freedom, democracy, and unity. Fascism wants to overwhelm us, to make us feel like resistance is futile. But that's the greatest lie of all.

So, while the threat is real, so is the resistance. And the best way to fight fascism isn't through fear, but by holding firm to the values it despises: freedom, equality, and the messy, wonderful chaos of democracy. As long as we stand together, we can outlast their shouts and their angry fists on the table. Because in the end, fascism is a movement born of fear—and fear never wins.

Nationalism

The Loudmouth Who Ruins the ame

> "Patriotism is when love of your own people comes first; nationalism, when hate for people other than your own comes first."
>
> Charles de Gaulle

It's a crisp autumn evening outside Twickenham Stadium, where the English rugby team has just suffered a nail-biting defeat to South Africa. The floodlights dim, the crowd slowly disperses, and the air is thick with the scent of spilled beer and sweat. Walking alongside you are two historical giants—George Orwell, ever the observer, hands in pockets, and Oswald Mosley, cape-like Union Jack draped over his shoulders, exuding the fervour of a man who believes England should always come first.

Mosley kicks a discarded can down the pavement with a disgusted snort. "Unbelievable. Losing to South Africa—South Africa! What a disgrace. England should be crushing them. It's like this country's forgotten who it is."

Orwell glances at him, eyebrow raised, lighting a cigarette as if preparing for the inevitable. "Oh, for God's sake, Oswald. It's a rugby match, not the Second Boer War. Both teams played well, and South Africa's strong. It's hardly the end of the Empire."

Mosley whirls around, his face flushed with indignation. "That's the problem right there, Orwell. That attitude! This defeatist, apologetic nonsense. England is supposed to be the best. We are the best. We should never lose to them—or anyone, for that matter."

You, caught between these two, try to offer a gentle nudge back toward sanity. "Come on, Mosley, it's just a game. They put in the effort. Besides, South Africa has a good team—rugby's a level playing field."

"Level playing field?" Mosley scoffs, his voice lowering to a venomous growl. "That's the kind of talk that's turned this country soft. We're not like the others. England is superior, always has been. That's why we're losing—because we've forgotten that."

Orwell, ever the sharp-tongued realist, blows a cloud of smoke and leans in. "Forgotten, have we? Or perhaps we're waking up from the fever dream of thinking we can bully the rest of the world into submission. Patriotism, Mosley, isn't about thinking you're better than everyone else. It's about loving your country enough to criticise it, to want it to be better—for everyone. What you're preaching isn't love for England. It's just hatred for everyone else."

Mosley's eyes narrow, his nationalist fervour palpable. "You never did understand, did you? This is about pride. English blood, English strength. It's about showing the world what we are. If you can't see that, Orwell, then you're part of the problem."

Orwell stops walking, his usual calm now tinged with frustration. "I understand perfectly well, Mosley. What you call 'pride' is just fear dressed up in a flag. You're terrified that England might have to share the world with others, that it can't just stomp around as it pleases. You're clinging to an outdated, dangerous fantasy."

The tension is palpable. You can feel the weight of history pressing down on this conversation, knowing full well that this isn't just about rugby anymore. Orwell's words, sharpened by years of witnessing the devastation of nationalism, cut through the chill in the air.

"Loving your country," Orwell continues, his voice steady, "isn't about thinking it can do no wrong. It's about wanting it to do right, to be just. Patriotism doesn't need an enemy. Nationalism, on the other hand—well, it always needs a scapegoat, doesn't it, Mosley? First, it's the other teams, then the immigrants, and soon it's anyone who dares disagree with you."

Mosley sneers, pulling the Union Jack tighter around himself. "Spoken like a man who has no real pride in his country. England's meant for greatness. You just don't have the spine to admit it."

Orwell stares him down, calm but unflinching. "England's meant for greatness, yes—but not the kind you dream of. Our greatness should come from fairness, from justice, not from pretending we're lords of the world. Nationalism has always been a thin veil for tyranny, Oswald. I've seen it with my own eyes, and I'll be damned if I let it take root here."

You glance between them, feeling the weight of history in the conversation. The street around you is bustling—people laughing, cars honking—but it feels distant, a mere backdrop to the ideological duel in front of you. Mosley, ever rigid in his beliefs, shakes his head in disgust and storms off into the crowd, his flag still fluttering behind him.

Orwell watches him go, flicking his cigarette to the ground. He turns to you, offering a rueful smile. "Do you think he'll come around?" you ask.

Orwell shrugs. "Probably not. Men like him don't come around. They double down, they dig in. But as long as we've still got voices, we can call them out. Make sure they don't get too comfortable."

You both descend into the underground station, the hum of London growing louder as you move away from the flickering streetlights. As the train approaches, you can't help but reflect on the conversation. The world might change, but the fight between patriotism and nationalism is as old as history itself—and it seems Orwell, for all his pessimism, still believes in the possibility of a better England.

--Interlude--

A Personal Journey Through Nationalism's Shadows

Growing up in South Africa under the latter years of the National Party's rule was like living in a world meticulously curated by a propagandist who had mastered the art of stark contrast—black and white, literally and figuratively. No room for grey, no space for doubt. Apartheid wasn't just about keeping people apart; it was nationalism at its most grotesque—stitched together with fear and a bloated sense of superiority, paraded as "patriotism." It wasn't enough to simply love your country; you had to believe that one group was inherently superior to all others, that one race had the inalienable right to rule. Nationalism didn't just thrive under apartheid—it was the blood coursing through the regime's veins.

As a child, you don't question the world you're born into. You accept the absurdities, the inequalities, as the natural order. The "Whites Only" signs on park benches, the separate schools, the clearly divided spaces—they're as ordinary as the sun rising. I remember our housemaid having her own cutlery, kept separate from ours, and how she wasn't allowed to use the toilet in the house. She had to use an outside one, as if proximity to her could somehow taint the purity of our space. And then there was the day she brought her children to our house. I played with them—innocently, without thought—until my uncle saw us and pulled me aside, his face stern. "Go wash yourself," he told me. "They're dirty."

I couldn't understand it then. Why was I dirty from playing with them? Why were they different? I stared at my skin and then at theirs, and I began to see how the world was being divided in ways that made no sense. I knew they were treated differently, but why?

I attended a Model-C school, and I still remember the near panic when the first black children started joining. For years, we had lived in a bubble of assumed superiority, and now that bubble was being pricked, bit by bit. Even by the time I matriculated, a good ten years after the ANC came to power, the divide was still there, unspoken but palpable. There was always *us*—the white kids—and *them*. We may have been in the same classrooms, but the invisible wall between us had yet to crumble.

The propaganda of apartheid wasn't confined to the newspapers or the radio. It seeped into the water, the air, the fabric of everyday life. Afrikaner history was glorified, its "heroes" lionised for their conquests, while the suffering of the non-white population was conveniently scrubbed from the narrative, as if entire lives could be swept under the carpet like dust. It was like reading a history book written by the victors, where the pages detailing the human cost had been torn out and used to stoke the flames of a braai.

The National Party didn't just ask for allegiance; it demanded your complicity. Its ideology was drilled into every aspect of life, from the classroom to the pulpit. Even Sunday sermons became exercises in quiet indoctrination, cloaking nationalism in biblical virtue. National holidays turned into spectacles of white-washed pride, celebrations of victories that, upon reflection, were moral catastrophes dressed up as moments of national glory.

Yet, even in that carefully curated reality, the cracks began to show. There were moments—small, private moments—where the weight of the system faltered. I remember the uneasy whispers at family gatherings, where the adults would speak just softly enough to escape official ears, but loud enough to make me wonder. The brash, uncompromising nationalism that ruled public life didn't match the quiet, creeping doubts expressed at home. The contradictions were everywhere, but as a child, it felt like standing on the shore, watching cracks spread across the ice—slow, imperceptible at first, but growing.

Then came the '90s, and with it, the moment the spotlight was thrown on the whole grotesque farce. When Nelson Mandela walked free, the entire country saw the apartheid set for what it was: an elaborate illusion built on violence, exclusion, and fear. Nationalism, once presented as the glue holding the nation together, was revealed as the very thing tearing it apart. The regime that had prided itself on its strength crumbled under the weight of its own contradictions, leaving behind a fractured, wounded society.

Witnessing the dismantling of apartheid was exhilarating and terrifying in equal measure. It was a testament to the resilience of the human spirit, yes, but also a sobering reminder of how deeply nationalism can poison a society. As we moved into the future, we carried the scars of a nation built on exclusion and division. Healing those wounds would take decades—perhaps even longer.

That personal history is why the line between patriotism and nationalism is so stark for me. Patriotism, for all its complexities, is a love for your country—a love that includes doubt, self-reflection, and a desire to see your country improve, not just for some, but for everyone. Nationalism, however, is patriotism's deluded cousin. It doesn't ask for love; it demands loyalty. It doesn't seek to improve; it seeks to dominate. It turns well-meaning people into agents of exclusion and fear, often without them realising.

When I hear politicians like Lee Anderson or Nigel Farage nat-
ter on about *"national pride"* in a way that diminishes others,
those memories of South Africa come rushing back, vivid and
unsettling. I recognise the early warning signs of an ideology
that, if left unchecked, doesn't just distort reality—it destroys
it. The kind of nationalism that whispers, *"We're better than
them,"* always ends in *"They don't deserve what we have."* And
from there, the road to exclusion, to oppression, is all too familiar.

The Anatomy of Nationalism: Us vs. Them

Nationalism is seductive. It wraps itself in the flag, sings in
rousing choruses, and offers up a version of history where the
nation is always the hero, never the villain. It tells you that you
are part of something special, something uniquely superior. But
nationalism doesn't unite—it divides. It builds a false sense of
solidarity by creating an "other" to fear, to hate, or, at best, to
pity. In the nationalist mindset, your identity isn't defined by
shared values, but by who you're standing against. And that, my
friends, is where things start to get ugly.

In the UK, nationalism has been dressed up in different outfits
over the years—sometimes in the polished uniforms of far-right
groups, other times in the casual slogans of the Brexit campaign.
The message is always the same: *"We've lost control," "Others are
diluting our culture," "We need to take back what's ours."* It's a
refrain as old as empire, as hollow as the promises made by those
who sing it. It's nostalgia for a past that never really existed,
dressed up as a manifesto for the future.

But let's be clear: nationalism doesn't thrive on its own. It
feeds on fear, insecurity, and economic inequality. When people
feel left behind—when jobs disappear and communities fall
apart—it's easy for demagogues to point fingers and say, *"They
are the reason."* Immigrants, international organisations, foreign
cultures—they're all convenient scapegoats for a nation unwill-
ing to confront its own failings.

Take the Brexit[1] campaign, for example. Wrapped in the Union Jack and promising a return to sovereignty, it sold itself as a patriotic movement. But scratch even lightly under the surface and you find a darker undercurrent of nationalism, the kind that says Britain can and *should* stand alone, that foreign influence is inherently corrupting, that our problems are *their* fault. It's an illusion, of course. In a world as interconnected as ours, no nation thrives in isolation. But nationalism doesn't deal in reality—it deals in fear.

What makes nationalism so dangerous is its simplicity. It reduces the world to *"us"* and *"them,"* to black and white. It's the political equivalent of a child's colouring book—except the lines it draws aren't just crude; they're cruel. It's why nationalists struggle with nuance, with empathy. To them, acknowledging complexity is weakness, and weakness is betrayal.

Patriotism, by contrast, is rooted in a love for one's country that embraces complexity. It acknowledges that no nation is perfect but holds a deep, abiding desire to improve it. A patriot looks at their country's flaws and says, *"We can do better."* They don't shy away from criticism; they embrace it as a necessary part of progress. A patriot's love for their country is not blind; it is clear-eyed and compassionate. Patriots seek to build a society that is inclusive, just, and fair for *everyone*.

Nationalists, on the other hand, demand loyalty at all costs. To criticise the nation is to betray it. This is why nationalism is so insidious: it silences dissent and stifles growth. In a nationalist's view, the country is already great—any suggestion to the contrary is not just unpatriotic; it's an attack.

That's the difference. Patriotism strives for betterment. Nationalism demands submission.

---

1. It's always Brexit, isn't it?

The History of English Nationalism: A Fine Tradition of Fear and Loathing

English nationalism is a peculiar beast. Unlike its more flamboyant continental cousins, which tend to throw parades and wave flags as if they're auditioning for a Wagner opera, English nationalism operates with the subtlety of a hangover—quietly pervasive, often unpleasant, and always lurking just beneath the surface. It cloaks itself in nostalgia, pines for an empire long dead, and occasionally bursts into that full-blown fever dream of *"taking back control[2]."* It's as if the nation has been perpetually waking up from a dream where the map was still pink and the sun never set. And yet, here we are, in a country whose national identity seems tied more to what it was than what it is or could be.

The architects of English nationalism read like a who's-who of historical wrong-turns, each contributing their own unique brand of xenophobia, superiority complex, and romanticised imperialism. Let's start with one of the real hallmarks of this tradition: Oswald Mosley—the man we met earlier in this chapter who tried to sell fascism to England like it was the latest trendy gin.

Oswald Mosley: Blackshirts and Black Hearts

If there's a pantheon of English nationalism, Mosley's there, right at the top, polishing his jackboots to a brandishing shine. In the 1930s, Mosley saw an opportunity to feed off a nation reeling from economic depression, and he seized it with both grubby hands. He didn't go for subtlety; oh no, Mosley went full throttle, establishing the British Union of Fascists[3] in 1932.

---

2. And yet, when they have that control, it inevitably doesn't work, and we look for the next thing to leave or take back control of – hence the current conversations about leaving the ECHR.

3. When the name truly does say it all.

His solution to the nation's woes? Blame the Jews, immigrants, and those pesky left-wingers. Because nothing says *"let's save the country"* like borrowing Hitler's playbook and dressing up in black shirts.

Mosley's rallies, full of salutes and bile, were an attempt to inject some continental-style fascism into British politics. But here's the thing—England never *quite* took to the goose-stepping. Sure, there were followers, and enough thuggery to make him dangerous, but there was something about Mosley's act that never quite stuck. It could be the whole dictatorship thing didn't play well in a country that just adored its monarchy too much to swap it out for a wannabe Führer.

His most famous moment, the Battle of Cable Street in 1936, saw thousands of East End Londoners—Jews, socialists, trade unionists—stand shoulder to shoulder to block the Blackshirts' march. In true English fashion, they gave Mosley and his lot a proper battering, as the streets became a battleground not just for territory but for the soul of the nation.

Still, Mosley's black heart continued to beat long after the Second World War, and his ideas of English superiority lingered like a bad odour in the corridors of nationalism. His influence was clear in the post-war years, even as his personal career dwindled into irrelevance. Like any good nationalist, he managed to plant the seeds of division that others would nurture in the decades to come.

Enoch Powell: The Rivers of Blood and a Flood of Fear

If Mosley was England's fascist in a tailor-made suit, **Enoch Powell** was the more respectable face of English nationalism, dressed in tweed and brimming with barely-concealed paranoia. Powell's infamous *"Rivers of Blood"* speech in 1968 was less a political address and more a masterclass in how to whip up fear of immigration and social change with the kind of apocalyptic rhetoric usually reserved for Old Testament prophets.

Powell's speech painted a picture of Britain overrun by immigrants—specifically, people of colour from the Commonwealth—warning that the country was on the brink of racial disaster. *"Like the Roman,"* he pontificated, *"I seem to see 'the River Tiber foaming with much blood.'"* This wasn't a man calmly discussing policy; this was a man trying to turn fear into fact. And tragically, for many, it worked.

The speech ignited a firestorm, and Powell was immediately sacked from the Conservative shadow cabinet. But let's not mistake that for a condemnation of his views—oh no. Powell's ideas found fertile ground among those who felt Britain's identity slipping away, buried beneath waves of immigration and social progress. He became a martyr to the nationalist cause, a beacon for those who believed in the myth of an England that was white, Protestant, and sovereign in all things.

Powell's legacy is still felt today, with his apocalyptic vision of multiculturalism used as a rallying cry for modern nationalists. Every time the far right starts harping on about *"culture wars"* and *"taking back control,"* you can hear echoes of Powell's speech reverberating through the years. The rivers may not have foamed with blood, but they certainly filled with fear.

Margaret Thatcher: The Iron Lady with a Nationalist Spine

Now, some might raise an eyebrow at including Margaret Thatcher here, but the fact is that Thatcher's nationalism was wrapped in the Union Jack, proudly proclaiming that Britain would never be dictated to, either by foreigners or by inconveniently needy miners. While she wasn't as openly nationalist in the blood-and-soil way Mosley or Powell were, her version of nationalism came through in other ways.

Thatcher's defiant stance during the Falklands War—fighting to maintain British sovereignty over a cluster of rocks, a couple of seagulls, a few dozen confused sheep farmers and three stray penguins 8,000 miles away—was an old-school display of imperial hubris. To Thatcher, the Falklands wasn't just about the sheep farmers though; it was about Britain's place in the world, refusing to accept that its imperial power had faded. It was an assertion of British superiority, dressed up as sovereignty, and it played beautifully into a national myth of the island nation standing alone against all odds.

Let's also not forget her often-sarcastic distaste for Europe. Thatcher's nationalism veered into Euro-scepticism long before it was fashionable, and she would no doubt be raising a glass from the afterlife at the sight of Brexit. Her *"No, no, no"* speech in 1990, rejecting the idea of a united Europe, was as much about protecting British identity as it was about economics. Europe was the *"other,"* and for Thatcher, England was always a step above.

Brexit: A Nationalist Dream Come True?

Speaking of Brexit, can we really talk about the history of English nationalism without bringing up that colossal act of national self-sabotage? When the Brexit campaign emerged, it was draped in patriotic language, of course— *"Take back control,"* *"Make Britain Great Again*[4]*."* But make no mistake: the entire Brexit project was a nationalist fever dream.

Figures like Farage—a man who often appears like a cross between a used car salesman and a Victorian villain—championed the idea that Britain was better off without all those meddling foreigners. Farage tapped into a deep well of nationalist sentiment, invoking Powell's rhetoric, though with fewer classical references and more pints down the pub. The EU was portrayed

---

4. Yes, they practically borrowed the slogan from across the Atlantic.

as the faceless bureaucrat that had stolen Britain's sovereignty, but Brexit wasn't just about policy—it was about a vision of a Britain that no longer existed: a nostalgic dream of empire, of global dominance, of an England that led the world, rather than worked alongside it.

And that's the trick of English nationalism, isn't it? Whether it's Mosley's fascism, Powell's rivers of fear, or Brexit's *"control,"* nationalism always promises a return to a glorious past that, when you look closely, was never that glorious in the first place[5]
.

So, what do we learn from all this? English nationalism, despite its various guises, always comes back to the same idea: the notion that England is exceptional, not by virtue of its inclusivity or progress, but because of some mythical superiority tied to blood, soil, or nostalgia. Nationalists—from Mosley's thugs to Powell's prophets of doom—have always tried to sell the country a vision that's narrow, exclusionary, and ultimately self-destructive.

Today, nationalism still clings to that vision. The rhetoric may have evolved slightly (though not by much), but the underlying message remains the same: England should be alone, special, *pure*. It's a message that thrives on fear—fear of immigrants, fear of change, fear of losing control. And while the flag might be waved with pride, what lies beneath is often insecurity, isolation, and a stubborn refusal to face the complexities of the modern world.

But here's the irony: English nationalism is obsessed with the idea of greatness. And yet, history shows us that greatness isn't built on exclusion or fear. It's built on understanding, on cooperation, and yes, sometimes on a good dose of humility. Perhaps, if the nationalists of today took a leaf from history, they'd realise

---

5. Just don't mention that too loudly lest you branded not patriotic enough.

that waving the flag isn't enough—you've got to live up to it, too.

Patriotism vs. Nationalism in Modern Britain: Lessons from the Past, Warnings for the Future

If English nationalism were a pub, you'd still find plenty of folks nursing pints and ranting about how things were better before *"all those foreigners showed up."* But here we are in 21st-century Britain, where the ghosts of Powell and Mosley seem to have found a new batch of living hosts, dressed in ill-fitting suits and fat salaries from GB News, union flags fluttering behind them, and the same tired refrain on their lips: *"We just want our country back."*

Yes, that's the soundbite du jour of **Lee Anderson**, the Conservative MP who has become a poster child for the type of nationalism that wraps itself in the flag but ignores the deeper, complex challenges facing the country. Anderson's plea for Britain to return to some imagined golden age is just the latest incarnation of the *"us versus them"* mentality—except now it's disguised as a plea for sovereignty, culture, or security[6].

When Anderson says, *"We just want our country back,"* what he's really doing is, again, peddling nostalgia for a Britain that never existed in the first place. He and his ilk act as though England in the 1950s was some utopia of community spirit and wholesome values—conveniently forgetting the rampant poverty, class divides, and casual racism. But that's the trick with nationalism: it sells a dream, not a reality.

Nationalists like Anderson thrive on the idea that Britain has lost something—that immigrants, globalisation, and progressive values have eroded the country's *"true"* identity. What they

---

6. It's basically Powell's "Rivers of Blood" speech without the Latin and more grunting.

fail to admit, of course, is that the only thing Britain's lost is the right to trample over other nations without consequence. This *"we want our country back"* rhetoric is less about pride and more about fear—the fear that a more diverse, modern, and interconnected Britain might look different from the sepia-tinted postcards in their minds.

The Modern Faces of English Nationalism

Lee Anderson isn't alone, of course. He's part of a growing movement of politicians and public figures who stoke nationalist fires for political gain, tapping into the same insecurities and frustrations that Powell and Mosley once exploited.

Take Nigel Farage[7], for instance—Britain's most professional nationalist. Farage has built an entire career out of selling the idea that Britain can and should stand alone, that it was somehow shackled by the EU, and that immigrants were to blame for everything from housing shortages and waiting times at the GP to your nan's 22 year old cat mysteriously disappearing with a wink and a nod to how he's heard that immigrants eat pets. His particular brand of nationalism is one that thrives on discontent and division, wrapped up in patriotic bunting with a pint in hand.

We can't forget Suella Braverman, another architect of Britain's increasingly draconian immigration stance and dreamer of Rwanda flights. Her obsession with protecting the *"British way of life"* feels plucked straight from Powell's playbook, except with less classical reference and more fearmongering. Whether it's labelling immigrants as invaders or throwing around phrases like *"cultural dilution,"* Braverman seems intent on presenting Britain as some sort of endangered species, constantly under threat from the outside world.

---

7. It's funny how he keeps popping up, isn't it?

The worrying thing about this modern crop of nationalists is that they've learned how to play the game. Unlike Mosley, they don't march in black shirts. They smile for the cameras, say the right things about *"sovereignty"* and *"British values,"* and present themselves as patriots. But the underlying message is the same: Britain is in danger, and the only way to save it is by closing the doors, shutting the borders, and turning inwards.

The great irony of all this is that true patriotism—the love for one's country—is far removed from the nationalism peddled by Anderson, Farage, and Braverman. Patriotism doesn't mean longing for some mythical past or blaming others for the nation's struggles. It means caring about your country enough to want to fix its flaws, not paper over them with nationalist fantasies.

Take figures like Marcus Rashford, for example. Rashford represents a modern, inclusive patriotism—a vision of Britain that strives to care for its people, to create a fairer society for everyone, regardless of their background. When Rashford campaigned for free school meals for underprivileged children, he wasn't selling nostalgia; he was fighting for a better future. His patriotism is about lifting people up, not dragging them down. And it's precisely this kind of inclusive, compassionate patriotism that stands in direct opposition to the nationalism of Anderson and his ilk.

The younger generation, too, seems to be redefining what it means to be British. For many young people, multiculturalism is a given, and the idea of closing the country off to the world feels not just outdated but absurd. They see Britain's identity as something that evolves—something that includes new ideas, cultures, and people. Their vision of patriotism is about inclusion, not exclusion. It's about embracing the complexities of modern Britain, not retreating into the past.

The Warnings from History

But here's the thing: history has already shown us what happens when nationalism goes unchecked. Mosley's rise in the 1930s, Powell's speeches in the 1960s—both were moments when nationalism could have pushed Britain down a much darker path. And though Britain resisted, these ideologies never truly disappeared. They lingered, mutating into the *"respectable"* nationalism we see today.

If we don't learn from history, we risk repeating it. Nationalism thrives on division, on scapegoating, and on fear. And right now, in the wake of Brexit, with economic instability and social unrest brewing, nationalism is finding fertile ground once again. We see it in the rise of far-right groups, in the hate crimes that spike every time a politician rants about "illegal immigrants," and in the rhetoric that makes patriotism sound like a zero-sum game where someone else always has to lose for Britain to win.

If history teaches us anything, it's that nationalism doesn't end well. It leads to isolation, to exclusion, to policies that hurt the very people nationalists claim to protect. And if we're not careful, if we allow the likes of Anderson, Farage, and Braverman to set the agenda, Britain could find itself on a dangerous road—one where the lessons of Powell's rivers are forgotten and the mistakes of Mosley's blackshirts are repeated.

Britain stands at a crossroads, much as it has many times before. One path leads to the kind of nationalism we've seen throughout history—narrow, defensive, and rooted in fear. The other path leads towards a more inclusive patriotism—one that recognises the value of diversity, of cooperation, and of facing the challenges of the modern world with openness rather than retreat.

The choice, as it always has been, is ours. We can choose to follow the Andersons and Farages of this world, down a road where *"getting our country back"* means shutting it off from progress. Or we can follow the Rashfords, the young, and the compassionate, who see Britain's greatness not in its past, but in its potential to be a fairer, more just society.

If we don't make the right choice, the warnings of history will come back to haunt us. And this time, the rivers may not foam with blood, but the nation could very well drown in its own fear.

The Media's Role in Nationalism's Growth

If there's one thing the British media does well, it's taking complex issues, stripping them of nuance, and turning them into weapons of mass hysteria. When it comes to nationalism, the tabloids and their cronies don't just fan the flames—they dump an entire petrol tanker on the fire and stand back to admire the blaze. From the *Daily Mail* to *The Sun* and the new kid on the nationalist block, GB News, British media has become a well-oiled machine of fearmongering and xenophobia, turning immigration into a national sport and *"us vs. them"* into the main event. And let's not forget our transatlantic friends at Fox News, who've generously exported their brand of polarisation to these shores, because apparently we didn't have enough problems of our own.

Tabloids: The Nationalists' Best Friends

No conversation about British nationalism would be complete without a nod to the tabloids—the original architects of the *"Immigrant Panic"* genre. Take the *Daily Mail*, for example, a paper that's built an entire empire on the premise that Britain is being overrun by anyone who didn't pop out of the womb singing *"God Save the King."* Headlines like *"Migrants Swarm the Channel"* make it sound as though the country's under siege by an army of desperate refugees, armed with nothing but sheer determination and the audacity to seek safety.

Not to be outdone, *The Sun* takes a slightly different tack—less apocalyptic, more *"pub patriot."* Here, nationalism is dished out with a side of football banter and celebrity gossip, wrapped in headlines like *"Britain Facing Migrant Invasion"* and *"Stop the Madness!"* As if complex immigration policy can be reduced to a single page, sandwiched between gossip about the latest Love Island contestant and whatever scandal the royal family is embroiled in this week. It's lazy, it's simplistic, and it works. The more these tabloids hammer away at the narrative that foreigners are ruining everything, the more they stoke the fires of nationalist sentiment, all while raking in profits from the outrage machine.

GB News: The "Alternative" to Facts

Then, there's *GB News*—the channel for people who find *The Sun* a bit too restrained. Marketed as an *"alternative"* to the supposedly liberal mainstream media[8], GB News offers the perfect safe space for nationalist rhetoric to thrive. It's the TV equivalent of that one uncle who thinks the country's gone to the dogs because you can't say anything anymore *"without offending someone."* Cue endless discussions about the erosion of British values, the threat of immigration, and the mythical golden age when the sun never set on the British Empire.

Led by none other than, surprise, surprise Nigel Farage, *GB News* delivers its content with all the subtlety of a man carving a Sunday roast with a chainsaw. Farage's contribution is about as predictable as it is inflammatory—Brexit was Britain's saviour, immigrants are the reason for everything from housing shortages to climate change, and anyone who disagrees is part of the *"liberal elite[9]."* It's a carnival of fear, with Britain cast

---

8. You know, the one that's apparently out to destroy Britain.

9. Which of course causes every single irono-meter within a five male radius to violently explode when we consider that he spent four months on an epic fannywobble about losing his Coutts account.

as the victim, eternally besieged by foreigners, bureaucrats, and the spectre of multiculturalism. The truth doesn't really matter here—what matters is making the viewers feel like they're the only ones who see what's really happening. Spoiler alert: they aren't.

The Echo Chamber of Social Media

If the tabloids are the kindling and *GB News* is the match, social media is the windstorm that turns a minor blaze into a full-blown inferno. On platforms like Facebook and Twitter, nationalist rhetoric doesn't just thrive—it multiplies. The algorithms, ever eager to serve users exactly what they want (or at least what makes them angry enough to stay engaged), push nationalist content right to the top. Click on one inflammatory article about immigrants *"taking over,"* and suddenly your feed is flooded with more of the same. It's like a digital echo chamber where the only voice you hear is the one that tells you what you already believe—immigrants are bad, globalisation is worse, and Britain is the victim in all of this.

What's particularly charming about social media is its ability to strip away every single shred of nuance. Complex discussions about immigration, the economy, and identity are reduced to memes, sound bites, and angry rants. And why bother engaging with facts when you can simply retweet the latest outrage from someone who also thinks Britain is being sold off to the highest bidder? Twitter, in particular, is a breeding ground for over-simplifications, where nationalist slogans can spread faster than you can say *"sovirinity,"* and debates quickly descend into nationalist chest-thumping. Meanwhile, more reasonable voices are drowned out, because nothing kills an echo chamber faster than nuance.

The long and short of this is that the British media isn't just complicit in the rise of nationalism—it's actively fuelling it. Tabloids like *The Sun* and *Daily Mail* crank out nationalist propaganda disguised as news, while *GB News* gives it a shiny veneer of credibility. Meanwhile, social media ensures that the message spreads far and wide, reaching every corner of the country in the form of rage-inducing sound bites and recycled fear. Add in a little Fox News-style hysteria, and you've got the perfect recipe for a nationalist surge.

As long as the media keeps serving up this toxic brew of fear and division, nationalism will continue to flourish. And the best part? The same media that fans the flames will, with a straight face, claim to be baffled by why the country is so divided. Because, after all, why take responsibility when you can keep selling the myth that Britain's problems are all caused by someone else?

National Identity in Flux

British identity is a curious thing—constantly changing, yet somehow the source of endless panic for people who believe it was chiselled into stone tablets by God Himself, presumably alongside the Magna Carta. For all the talk of tradition and continuity, Britain has spent most of its history in a state of glorious flux. But you wouldn't know it from the way modern nationalists bang on about some mythical, unchanging *"Britishness"* that they're desperate to preserve—despite the fact that Britain's identity has been shaped, reshaped, and re-reshaped by everything from foreign invasions to immigrant chefs.

To hear nationalists tell it, you'd think Britain was a pristine little island floating in a sea of barbarians until the unfortunate moment it discovered immigration—sometime around the mid-20th century, apparently. But history tells a different story, one where British identity has been a bit like an overcrowded coat rack, with each wave of immigrants tossing on a new layer. The result? A cultural mishmash that nationalists loathe to acknowledge even exists.

Take the Norman invasion in 1066. Nothing screams *"pure British identity"* quite like being conquered by French-speaking aristocrats. It's almost endearing that modern-day nationalists, the self-appointed guardians of Englishness, would conveniently forget that some of their cherished traditions and words come courtesy of a bunch of Normans who probably couldn't even point out a Yorkshire pudding. But then again, it's easier to pretend *"Britishness"* hasn't been shaped by outsiders when your entire argument depends on it.

Then there were the Huguenot refugees in the 16th and 17th centuries. Fleeing persecution in France, these Protestant refugees brought their odd languages, foreign habits, and new trades to Britain. Today's nationalists would likely have stood at the ports with picket signs reading *"Britain for Britons,"* blissfully unaware that the Huguenots were contributing to the very British identity they claim to defend. The idea that Britain could absorb outsiders and somehow not collapse into an existential crisis was as true then as it is now. But why let facts get in the way of a good, frothy panic?

Fast-forward to post-WWII immigration, when Commonwealth citizens were invited to rebuild the country that had merrily exploited them for centuries. Immigrants from the Caribbean, South Asia, and Africa flocked to Britain, bringing with them not just their labour but their culture. They helped build the NHS, ran the buses, and kept the country functioning—all while being told they didn't quite belong. It's a level of hypocrisy nationalists should admire: invite people to save your nation, then pretend they're the problem. And yet, these same communities, now generations deep, are accused by nationalists of *"changing"* Britain's identity—as if that identity wasn't always changing anyway.

The truth is, Britain has always been a patchwork of cultures, languages, and identities. From Roman legions to Irish labourers, the country's DNA is a historical buffet. Nationalists clinging to the fantasy of a monocultural Britain would do well to remember that their *"pure"* Britain was stitched together by centuries of immigration and exchange. What they see as contamination, the rest of us call reality.

The Role of Empire: Nostalgia with a Convenient Blind Spot

And now, we come to the real heart of the nationalist nostalgia: the British Empire. Ah, the empire—those glorious days when Britain ruled the world, civilising it with trains, tea, and a healthy dose of violence and scorching the earth. For many nationalists, the empire is their happy place, a time when Britain wasn't just a country but a global overlord. The fact that this so-called *"golden age"* was built on exploitation, conquest, and the suffering of millions? Details, my dear. Minor details.

Modern nationalists, bless their selective memories, like to think of the empire as a time when Britain was at its peak—noble, strong, and respected. They conveniently forget that much of the world viewed the Union Jack as a symbol of oppression rather than liberation. Take India, for example, where British policies didn't just exploit the land, they starved its people. But sure, let's focus on the railways. Nationalists seem to think the empire was some benevolent force, handing out cricket and democracy to the savages—ignoring the fact that those savages would have preferred Britain keep its cricket and sod off.

The Mau Mau rebellion in Kenya, another chapter nationalists avoid in their rose-tinted view of empire, saw Britain responding to anti-colonial resistance with torture, concentration camps, and brutal repression. If the empire's defenders are right, and Britain was *"taking civilisation"* to the world, it did a spectacularly violent job of it. But the nationalist nostalgia doesn't like to deal in brutality. It prefers to romanticise empire as the time when Britain was *"in control,"* even though that control was usually imposed by force and backed by cruelty.

And what about, the crown jewel of the British Empire's brutal policies of conquest? While modern nationalists may cheerfully recall the Union Jack fluttering over Cape Town as some beacon of progress, they conveniently ignore that Britain's *"civilising mission"* in South Africa involved scorched-earth policies, concentration camps during the Boer War, and a legacy of racial division that planted the seeds for apartheid. The British didn't bring enlightenment to South Africa—they brought exploitation, imposing control over both the indigenous population and Dutch settlers with a methodical, violent efficiency. The aftermath of their rule didn't exactly leave a nation flourishing in freedom; instead, it left a deeply fractured society, where racial divisions were institutionalised, and the exploitation of resources continued long after the empire had faded. But sure, let's not talk about that. Let's focus on the British contribution to infrastructure, and perhaps the generous introduction of afternoon tea. The reality, of course, is that South Africa is just one more chapter of Britain's imperial hypocrisy—a place where the British system of "civilisation" looked a lot like subjugation, and the Union Jack was less a flag of liberation and more a banner of economic and racial dominance.

Then there's the **hilarious contradiction** at the heart of the nationalist longing for empire: they want Britain to *"take back control,"* while wistfully remembering a time when Britain's entire business model was about denying control to everyone else. It's the height of irony—longing for the days when Britain got to boss everyone around, while being horrified at the idea of Brussels telling Britain what shape its bananas should be. The very people shouting loudest for sovereignty are the ones who'd have been perfectly happy imposing their will on half the globe. The mental gymnastics required to make that make sense could win an Olympic medal.

The Contradictions of Nationalism

And this, dear reader, is the crux of the nationalist mindset: it's an ideological house of cards built on contradiction, selective memory, and outright denial. Nationalists pine for an empire that was morally bankrupt while simultaneously demanding Britain reclaim its lost *"purity"*—as if Britain has ever been culturally or racially pure. They lament the changing face of the nation, ignoring that British identity has always been a revolving door of influences, ideas, and people.

What they truly fear isn't the loss of British identity—it's that they never really understood it in the first place. Britain's strength has always been its ability to adapt, absorb, and evolve. The same people nationalists fear today—immigrants, refugees, outsiders—are the very people who've contributed to Britain's success for centuries. The idea that Britain was once this insular, unchanging bastion of white, Christian values is a fairy tale they tell themselves to feel better about the fact that history is leaving them behind.

Nationalists may long for a Britain frozen in time, but the reality is that the country is—and always has been—a work in progress. And rather than wringing our hands about that fact, we should embrace it. Change isn't the enemy. Stagnation is. A nation that refuses to evolve, that clings to some imaginary past, is a nation that's destined to be left behind. And that, I suspect, is what terrifies the nationalists most of all—not that Britain is changing, but that it's always been changing. And perhaps their fear lies in that they might be the ones who don't belong in this future after all.

--Interlude Ends--

The rain starts to patter down as you and Orwell walk along Westminster Bridge, just close enough to the Houses of Parliament to hear the dull rumble of politics in the background. The streets are quieter now, but you're not alone. There, on the other side of the bridge, is Oswald Mosley, standing with his back to the river, staring at the Parliament building as though he's planning a takeover. His coat is draped around him like an old battle flag, and even in the drizzle, his posture exudes a misplaced sense of grandeur.

Orwell lights a cigarette, more out of habit than need, and gives you a sidelong glance. "There's always one, isn't there?" he mutters, as the two of you approach. Mosley doesn't turn around immediately, but he senses your presence. You brace yourself for another ideological joust, but something feels different this time.

"So, the country's fallen further into ruin since last we spoke," Mosley says, his voice like gravel against a polished floor. "Look at this place—still trying to pretend it's a power when it can't even keep its streets clean."

Orwell takes a drag of his cigarette and blows the smoke slowly, purposefully. "Ah, yes. The streets are dirty, so we must be in decline. It's always something, isn't it, Mosley? First it was the foreigners, then the socialists, and now, what? Litter?" He turns to you. "It's funny how people who claim to love their country are always the ones who seem to hate it most."

Mosley finally looks at the two of you, his eyes flickering with the same cold fire as before. "You mock, Orwell, but you know as well as I do what this country used to be. Before we let everyone else dilute our strength, before we became a shadow of ourselves."

You look at Orwell, but his face remains calm, steady. "What we used to be?" he says softly. "And when, exactly, was this golden age of yours? When we ruled over people who had no say in their own lives? When we exploited half the globe for our own gain? You see, Oswald, I remember that 'great' Britain too, and I remember the cost. Patriotism isn't about pretending your country was always right. It's about making it right, for everyone."

Mosley's lip curls in contempt. "And that's why you'll always fail, Orwell. This softness—this obsession with fairness. Britain doesn't need coddling; it needs strength. Superiority. You've forgotten that."

"Superiority," Orwell echoes, shaking his head. "No, Mosley, that's where you're wrong. Patriotism isn't about feeling superior to others; it's about wanting your country to be the best version of itself. Not just for some, but for all. I don't want to 'take Britain back'—I want to take it forward."

You glance at Mosley, waiting for the inevitable sneer, the usual diatribe about lost greatness. But for the first time, he's silent. Perhaps it's the rain, or perhaps it's the way Orwell is speaking now, not with the sharp edge of intellectual debate, but with the quiet, unshakeable certainty of someone who's seen the worst of nationalism and come through the other side.

"Take it forward?" Mosley scoffs, though the venom is gone from his voice. "Forward to what? More of this?" He waves a hand at the skyline, dismissing the city before him, as if London itself had let him down.

Orwell smiles faintly. "Yes, forward to this. To a Britain where people like Marcus Rashford fight for kids to have food on their tables. To a Britain where the NHS still stands, a testament to what we can build when we care about each other. Not a Britain that looks backwards, clinging to its fading memories of empire, but one that embraces the future."

Mosley looks away, staring back at the Parliament building as though it might offer him some kind of answer. "Your future sounds like weakness," he mutters.

"And yours sounds like fear," Orwell replies gently, stubbing out his cigarette on the bridge's stone. "You talk about strength, Mosley, but I've only ever seen you afraid. Afraid of change, afraid of difference, afraid of a world where Britain doesn't stand over everyone else. True patriotism isn't about fear. It's about hope. It's about pushing your country to be better than it was, not just for a few, but for everyone who calls it home."

The rain falls a little harder now, and Mosley turns to leave, his coat flapping behind him like a ragged flag that's long lost its meaning. For a moment, you almost pity him—trapped in a vision of a Britain that never really existed, and powerless to stop the march of time that leaves him behind.

As he disappears into the mist, Orwell exhales softly and nods toward the river. "You know," he says, "people like him will always exist, but they don't win. Not in the long run. The future isn't his. It's the people who fight for what Britain can be—not what it used to be."

You both stand there in the rain for a moment, watching the city move around you—alive, complicated, and constantly changing. It's a mess, yes, but it's a beautiful one. A Britain that's growing, evolving, built by people who don't look or sound the same, but who all belong to it nonetheless.

Orwell lights another cigarette and looks over at you. "We don't need to 'take our country back,'" he says with a quiet smile. "We just need to move it forward."

Anarchism

The Rebel Without a Cause (Or Is here One?)

> "Remove all the traffic lights, yellow lines, one-way systems and road markings, and let blissful anarchy prevail. I imagine it would produce a kind of harmony."
>
> Sadie Jones

Anarchism isn't just a political ideology—it's a full-blown declaration of defiance, the ultimate *"I'm not playing by your rules"* stance against the world. Imagine it: a political theory that doesn't even *bother* pretending it's reasonable by conventional standards. Anarchism isn't trying to win a popularity contest, nor does it care about following the well-trodden paths of democracy, monarchy, or socialism. No, Anarchism is the philosophical equivalent of deciding to run a marathon barefoot, across rocky terrain, because shoes are an oppressive tool of conformity[1]. It's a rebellious, self-destructive, and oddly inspiring middle finger to the system—and that's exactly why it's so damn interesting.

---

1. Which as a South African, I have to agree, they are.

Think about it: Anarchism is like the punk rock of political thought. It's all about chaos and rebellion, but, and this is sometimes left out, with a heart full of idealism. The sheer audacity of imagining a world where no one's in charge, where people just... figure it out on their own, is both laughable and fascinating[2]. No rulers, no police, no government—just people, free from coercion, doing their own thing. It's the dream of ultimate freedom, and yes, the batshit craziness of it is precisely why it's my favourite. There's something so beautifully absurd about the idea that humans could live together in peaceful harmony without anyone keeping them in line. It's utopia, if utopia were written by a group of teenagers at a protest, drunk on the fumes of righteous anger and Red Bull.

But that's the magic of Anarchism. It's not about whether it could work[3]. It's about the glorious, reckless energy that comes with rejecting every single system of control. Anarchism doesn't even pretend to offer a sensible alternative to governance—it's too busy tearing away the idea of governance itself. And there's something refreshing, almost therapeutic, in imagining a world where the shackles of authority have been thrown off entirely.

Picture this: no more politicians to lie to us, no more CEOs hoarding wealth, no more police telling us what to do. It's a fantasy of radical equality and autonomy, where every human being is free to live their life as they see fit. It's like one of those heist movies where everything is so absurdly risky and dangerous that you can't help but be swept up in the thrill of it. You know it's going to crash and burn, but damn, it's going to look incredible while it does.

And that's where the real charm lies—Anarchism knows it would implode within two weeks. We all know. The allure, though, isn't in whether it could actually function in the real

---

2. And intriguing and terrifying!

3. It really wouldn't.

world. The appeal is in its defiance, in its bold refusal to conform to the boundaries set by every other political system. Anarchism is the political movement for people who are tired of the same old structures, the same old hierarchies. It's for those who believe that maybe if you tear down enough walls, you'll find something worth rebuilding underneath all the rubble.

Let's not forget that this ideology has a heartbeat that's difficult to ignore, even if the world is unlikely to ever fully embrace it. The fact that it's wildly impractical doesn't diminish its importance. In a world suffocating under the weight of bureaucracies, surveillance, and state control, Anarchism dares to say that we can do better—if only we had the guts to tear it all down. It's chaotic, it's idealistic, it's completely impractical... and it's utterly intoxicating to think about.

Clarifying Anarchism's Ideals

Before we dive into the delicious chaos that anarchism tends to revel in, it's worth remembering that at its core, anarchism isn't just about smashing things up for fun. Sure, tearing down authority sounds great, but the ideal anarchist society is built on something far more constructive: mutual aid and voluntary cooperation. Anarchists genuinely believe that people, when left to their own devices, can organise themselves without the need for bosses, governments, or coercive institutions. In theory, people don't need someone cracking a whip—they can collaborate, share resources, and ensure equality without the state breathing down their necks.

In this utopia, power isn't centralised in the hands of a few; instead, it's dispersed among individuals and communities, who voluntarily cooperate to meet each other's needs. The idea is that human beings, at their best, are capable of mutual aid—helping one another without being told to do so by some higher authority. This isn't some pie-in-the-sky dream (okay, it mostly is), but it's rooted in a deep mistrust of the idea that hierarchy and authority are necessary for society to function.

History in Brief: A Fight Against Authority Since Day One

Anarchism didn't emerge from some sterile university debate or lofty academic conference. No one was sitting in a wood-panelled study with a glass of brandy, politely musing over the virtues of anarchic thought. No, it was a messy, raw reaction to authority—a big, rebellious *"no thanks"* to anyone who thought they had the right to tell someone else what to do.

The fire was first stoked by Pierre-Joseph Proudhon, a man whose declaration that *"property is theft*[4] *"* still sends certain capitalists into apoplectic fits of rage. And he wasn't talking about your neighbours walking off with your toaster. Proudhon was tackling the idea that when property allows someone to exploit others—whether it's landlords jacking up rent or bosses squeezing profit out of workers—it's inherently unjust[5]. It was a provocative statement, and it threw the doors wide open for anarchism's journey, a journey marked by chaos, idealism, and, well, more chaos.

Enter Mikhail Bakunin, the man who didn't just throw fuel on the fire—he wildly drove a tanker straight into the heart of the inferno. If Proudhon planted the seeds of anarchism, Bakunin was the one who wanted to tear down the entire orchard. Bakunin's message was disarmingly simple: *smash the state, all of it, no exceptions.* He took one look at Marx's grand plans for a worker's state and thought, *"Nope, that's going to end badly too."* For Bakunin, *any* form of authority—even one supposedly run by and for the workers—would eventually become corrupt. His solution? Never let that authority form in the first place. Bakunin's suspicion of power wasn't confined to capitalism or

---

4. Yet another term that gets thrown around when someone gets confused with communism.

5. And let's be very honest with ourselves, he really wasn't wrong.

monarchy—it extended to everything. The man was allergic to authority in all its forms.

It's no wonder that Bakunin and Marx didn't exactly get along. Marx envisioned a centrally planned socialist state, while Bakunin was already plotting how to dismantle it before it even existed. Their clash was the stuff of ideological drama, but it highlights a core tension within leftist movements: the anarchists never played well with others. They were too busy tearing down systems to sit still and build them back up. Bakunin believed that even well-meaning revolutionaries would eventually slide into tyranny if given too much power. Better to burn the whole thing to the ground and let people figure it out themselves.

And figure it out they did—at least for a brief moment in history. The Spanish Civil War saw anarchism have its brightest and most fleeting moment in the sun. For a short, utopian spell, anarchist collectives managed to run entire regions of Spain. Workers took over factories and farms, making decisions collectively without bosses or bureaucrats breathing down their necks. It was the anarchist dream in motion: a society without rulers, where people were free to live and work as equals. It was beautiful in its way, proving that perhaps anarchism wasn't so far-fetched after all.

Of course, this idealistic experiment couldn't survive the brutal reality of civil war, Franco's rise to power, and the looming shadow of authoritarianism. Anarchism's brief success was stamped out, but it left a mark, a reminder that a world without bosses, without rulers, without the heavy hand of the state, could exist. Even if just for a little while.

It's the kind of fleeting victory that fuels anarchism's continued, albeit fringe, presence in political discourse. While anarchism has never gone mainstream, it's always there—lurking on the edges, ready to stir things up, challenge authority, and remind the rest of us that power, unchecked, is inherently dangerous. Anarchism isn't just a protest; it's a vision of something radically different. Whether or not it's achievable is almost beside the point. The sheer act of questioning the status quo and refusing to accept hierarchy is enough to keep the anarchist spirit alive.

And frankly, who wouldn't want to manage their own factory or farm, if only the weekly collective meetings didn't end up taking half the day? At the very least, anarchism reminds us that we don't have to accept the world as it is—we can dream of something wilder, more free, even if it only exists in the briefest flashes of history.

Modern Anarchism: Collectives, Direct Action, and the DIY Revolution

Anarchism hasn't faded into the background of political history. In fact, in our turbulent modern era, it's making a bit of a comeback. But you won't find it in political parties or neatly packaged manifestos. Instead, anarchist ideas live on in collectives, direct action movements, and anti-authoritarian protests that challenge the very idea of centralised power and governance.

Take groups like Just Stop Oil, Extinction Rebellion, and even certain factions within the Occupy movement. These aren't your typical political organisations with leaders, hierarchies, and five-year plans. They embody anarchist principles of decentralisation, direct action, and collective decision-making. These are movements where no one is in charge, and yet somehow, things manage to get done—whether it's blocking highways, occupying buildings, or staging climate protests that bring cities to a standstill.

Anarchism thrives in resistance. It's there in the moments when people decide that waiting for politicians or corporations to act is no longer an option. When the system is too slow, too corrupt, or too apathetic, anarchists take matters into their own hands. Whether it's environmental activists chaining themselves to oil rigs or anti-capitalists disrupting the latest G7 summit, anarchists are the ones willing to break the rules in the name of direct, immediate action.

Just Stop Oil is a prime example of modern anarchist principles in action. They don't wait for government policies to change or rely on corporate pledges to go green. Instead, they block roads, disrupt high-profile events, and make it impossible to ignore the climate emergency. Their tactics are disruptive, yes, but that's the *point*. Anarchism doesn't play by the rules, because it doesn't believe the rules are fair in the first place.

Anarchist collectives take this one step further. Rather than rely on leaders or institutions to guide them, they embrace the messy, often exhausting process of consensus decision-making. In these spaces, there's no hierarchy—everyone has an equal say. And while that sounds lovely in theory, it often leads to what we might charitably call *"spirited discussions"* over who's responsible for taking out the bins in the communal kitchen. But that's anarchism in action: decentralised, equal, and painfully slow, but fiercely democratic in its own way.

And let's not forget about the punk scene, one of anarchism's cultural playgrounds. The punk ethos of *"Do It Yourself"* (DIY) aligns perfectly with anarchist values. Why rely on big corporations or institutions when you can make your own music, print your own zines, and organise your own gigs? The punk subculture has long embraced anarchist principles, rejecting authority and corporate control in favour of grassroots creativity and collective action.

Of course, anarchism's favourite tool remains direct action. It's about getting out there and doing something, rather than waiting for a distant politician to solve the problem. Whether that's taking to the streets, occupying a corporate office, or sabotaging infrastructure projects, anarchists believe in making change happen now, not later. And while these tactics often get labelled as extreme or disruptive, they're a powerful reminder that not everyone is content to let the system grind on unchanged.

But here's the thing about anarchism: it's not a coherent, long-term plan for governance. It's not offering a step-by-step guide to running a country, or even a city. It's messy, it's chaotic, and it's often impractical. But that's not really the point. Anarchism exists as a form of resistance, a challenge to power structures that seem unchangeable. It's a refusal to accept that we have to play by the rules set by those in charge.

And in today's world, where political apathy runs high and people feel increasingly powerless in the face of global crises, anarchism offers a different kind of hope—a chaotic, messy hope, but hope nonetheless[6]. It reminds us that systems of power are not immutable, that resistance is always possible, and that sometimes, tearing things down is the first step toward building something better.

Digital Anarchism and Cyber Activism

If you thought anarchists were all about Molotov cocktails and black hoodies, think again. In the digital age, the spirit of anarchy has found a new playground: the internet. After all, why bother smashing up a Starbucks when you can hack its customer database from the comfort of your mum's basement? The internet provides anarchists with the perfect decentralised platform for communication, collaboration, and resistance—no centralised authority, no middlemen, and absolutely no need to listen to anyone who thinks they know better. It's anarchism's dream home.

Enter *hacktivism*. Instead of waving protest banners, groups like Anonymous and LulzSec are exposing government secrets, crashing corporate servers, and leaking data faster than politicians can claim their emails were *"hacked by the Russians."* In this version of anarchism, it's not about toppling physical in-

---

6. Yup. We are indeed at that point where anarchy is looking mighty attractive these days.

stitutions; it's about peeling back the layers of modern power structures, one data leak at a time. Need to challenge state surveillance? There's a script for that. Want to embarrass corporate overlords who've built an empire on exploitation[7]? That's just a matter of finding the right password.

Of course, digital anarchism isn't just about gleefully taking down Big Brother. At the heart of it is a deeper commitment to open-source software—the DIY of the tech world. Forget your corporate monopolies like Microsoft or Apple—anarchists are all about technology that's built by the people, for the people, with no Silicon Valley overlords hoarding the source code. Programs like Linux or peer-to-peer platforms are free, open, and anyone can improve them. It's the software equivalent of an anarchist commune where everyone pitches in and no one tries to sell you a premium version with 20% more features for an extra £9.99 a month.

Anarchism in Non-Western Contexts

Contrary to popular belief, anarchism isn't just the intellectual playground of disgruntled Western academics with more theory than practical experience. While it's true that the likes of Proudhon and Bakunin laid much of the ideological groundwork, anarchism's spirit of rebellion has found fertile soil in far-flung corners of the globe. Anarchism has, rather ironically, spread far beyond the armchairs of European radicals, popping up in places where people have much more pressing concerns than whether or not they can brew kombucha in their living rooms.

---

7. Yes, please and thank you.

Latin America: Anarchy with a Dash of Decolonisation

Take Latin America, where indigenous communities have been practising a version of anarchism since before anyone in Europe even *dreamed* of overthrowing a king. They didn't need a manifesto to tell them that centralised power was bad; they'd already figured that out after several centuries of imperialism, colonisation, and being told they needed saving by conquistadors with an unhealthy obsession with gold crosses.

Consider the Zapatistas in Mexico. They've created autonomous zones where indigenous people govern themselves through direct democracy, without the interference of the state. It's like anarchism, but with added resistance to imperialism and a strong side of *"don't tread on us with your colonial boots."* In Zapatista communities, they've rejected the entire concept of state control. Who needs a government when you can run things yourselves, based on collective decision-making and mutual aid? It's anarchism, but with fewer lengthy debates about what Bakunin would have thought about TikTok.

Africa: Anarchism Meets Anti-Colonialism

In Africa, anarchism intersects with anti-colonial struggles. Here, it's not just about rejecting the state; it's about rejecting the entire colonial framework that propped up those states. Kenyan activist Ngugi wa Thiong'o, for instance, has discussed how decentralised governance offers a way out of the colonial mess left behind by European powers. Imagine being told your country is free now, only to find out that *"freedom"* means being ruled by a handful of corrupt elites who learned everything they know about governance from the people who oppressed them. It's like swapping one dictator for another, only this time they've got a nicer accent.

In this context, anarchism isn't just a fancy European theory. It's a survival mechanism. Rejecting the state means rejecting the legacies of colonialism and capitalism, which have done little more than ensure that a select few get rich while the rest stay hungry. Decentralised governance, mutual aid, and communal decision-making aren't just ideological preferences here—they're tools for survival in a world still grappling with the aftershocks of imperialism.

Asia: Labour Struggles and Anarchist Experiments

In Asia, anarchist movements have historically aligned with labour struggles. In early 20th-century Japan and Korea, anarchism wasn't overshadowed by Marxism so much as elbowed aside, like the quiet, idealistic cousin at a family reunion where Marxists took all the attention with their big plans and centralised committees. But anarchism was there, introducing radical ideas of decentralised, worker-led governance at a time when these countries were clawing their way out of feudalism and into the welcoming arms of capitalism's exploitative embrace.

The anarchist movement in Korea, for example, got involved in the fight for liberation from Japanese imperialism, and while it was largely overshadowed by nationalist forces, it left behind a legacy of labour-led revolts and decentralised organising. It turns out, telling people who've been colonised for decades that they could run their own affairs without bosses or bureaucrats is a pretty enticing proposition.

Anarchism is an idea that transcends geography and culture, adapting itself to the specific struggles of the people who adopt it. Whether it's indigenous communities fighting off colonisers in Latin America, anti-colonial activists in Africa, or labour movements in Asia, anarchism's rejection of centralised power and authority resonates with anyone who's ever had to live under the boot of a state, an empire, or a multinational corporation. It's the ultimate political escape plan[8].

Anarchism's appeal isn't limited to Europeans frustrated with the monarchy or disillusioned socialists. Its adaptability across different contexts highlights its universal critique of power, hierarchy, and the idea that a small group of people should tell everyone else what to do. It's a global reminder that people everywhere have always had a deep, instinctual suspicion of anyone claiming the right to govern them—especially when those people are standing on the backs of the exploited, waving a flag, and quoting scripture or ideology.

Art, Literature, and Music: Anarchy's Wild Canvas

The really fun thing about Anarchism is that it's just about toppling governments and throwing Molotov cocktails—it's also about wreaking havoc on the cultural front. Why settle for revolution in the streets when you can disrupt the very foundations of taste, beauty, and acceptable behaviour? Anarchism's influence has seeped into art, literature, and music, pushing the boundaries of creative expression with all the subtlety of a wrecking ball smashing through a royal portrait gallery. It's where rebellion meets creativity, with a healthy dose of middle-finger-to-the-establishment thrown in for good measure.Take the punk movement which we previously mentioned, the snarling love child of anarchy and three guitar chords. Punk wasn't just about making music—it was about making noise. *Loud, chaotic, unapologetic noise* that gave two fingers to corporate-controlled industries, authoritarian governments, and anyone else who had the audacity to hold power. Bands like Crass and the Sex Pistols didn't just scream rebellion—*they lived it*. With lyrics that spit on conformity, DIY production methods

---

8. And who didn't think it was a better solution than what we had during September and October 2022?

that bypassed record labels, and performances that were more riot than concert, punk was anarchism's answer to the bloated, self-indulgent music industry. It wasn't pretty, and it certainly wasn't polished, but that was the point: who needs gloss when you've got rage?

The entire punk ethos is essentially anarchism with a safety pin through its nose, shouting *"fuck you"* to the idea that creativity should come packaged, polished, and sold to the masses. These bands weren't waiting for a revolution—they were making one, three chords at a time, on a budget of about £5.Of course, not all anarchist art is about screaming into a microphone. In the more contemplative corner of anarchism, you've got authors like Ursula K. Le Guin, who managed to explore anarchist ideas without throwing chairs through windows. *The Dispossessed* is her magnum opus in this regard—a utopian novel about a society that has, theoretically, rid itself of hierarchy. It's a world where mutual aid reigns supreme and authority is kept in check. Of course, it's not quite a perfect paradise. The society is idealistic, yes, but also plagued by the messiness that comes from trying to live without power structures[9].

Le Guin's work goes beyond the simplistic, idealised world of *"no government = peace"* that some anarchists cling to. She explores the difficulties of living in a decentralised society, where freedom and equality are hard-won and even harder to maintain. It's a sobering reminder that while anarchism offers an alternative to hierarchy, it doesn't come with an easy-to-follow instruction manual[10]. Meanwhile, in the visual arts, anarchism got *weird*—delightfully, wonderfully *weird*. Enter the Dadaists and the Surrealists, movements born from the ashes of World War I, when it became abundantly clear that the so-called ratio-

---

9. Le Guin's characters wrestle with the complexities of anarchism in a way that punk rock never quite did—less *"smash the system"* and more *"what do we do after the system's smashed?"*

10. You can almost hear Bakunin sighing from the afterlife: *"Yeah, it's harder than it looks."*

nal structures of society had led to one of the most horrific conflicts in human history. Their solution? Smash the idea of *"rationality"* entirely. Traditional art? Boring. Beauty? Subjective.
Politics? Who cares. The Dadaists especially embraced nonsense
and chaos, throwing out anything that smacked of hierarchy or
established value. Art was no longer about what was beautiful
or prestigious—it was about what could disrupt the status quo.

If you were a well-to-do art collector expecting a tasteful portrait of a horse, the Dadaists were happy to present you with a
urinal signed *"R. Mutt"*. This wasn't just art—it was a rebellion
against the very idea that art should make sense. The Surrealists
followed suit, bending reality itself in their dreamlike, absurdist
creations. Both movements served as an anarchic middle finger
to the structures that dictated what art could and couldn't be.

For these artists, creativity was a weapon—a way to destabilise
the very structures that kept society in line. Why paint a beautiful landscape when you can create something that forces people
to question the nature of reality itself? It's anarchism in paint
and clay, designed to be as unsettling as it is transformative. A
narchism's cultural reach shows that its rejection of authority
isn't confined to political theory—it invades every sphere of life.
Art, music, and literature become playgrounds for anarchist
ideas, offering new ways to challenge societal norms and push
boundaries. From the raw energy of punk rock to the intellectual exploration of Le Guin's anarchist societies, creativity
becomes a form of resistance.

Art is more than just rebellion; it's the reimagining of what
society could look like without the suffocating grip of control, hierarchy, and convention. Anarchism's influence on culture demonstrates that imagination can be just as radical as
protest—sometimes even more so. In the hands of anarchists,
art isn't just about self-expression; it's about self-liberation. It's
about pushing past the limits of what is considered acceptable,
rational, or possible and dreaming of something freer, weirder,
and far less polite.

And that's why I've loved writing this chapter so much—because, it's the perfect playground for chaos. When I started my Twitter account back in 2023, it wasn't to follow the rules. It was to break them. I embraced long-form tweets (despite everyone hating them), hid my identity so I could shout *"CROTCH-GOBLIN!"* at politicians who pissed me off, and threw my calm demeanour to the wind so I could smash through the nonsense and start breaking things down.

What It's Not: Chaos Isn't the Goal (Except When It Is)

If you think anarchism is all about setting things on fire and looting your local supermarket, you've been watching too much Fox and GB News[11]. Anarchism isn't about chaos—at least not in the way most people imagine. It's not an invitation to lawlessness or disorder. Anarchists don't want society to collapse into a free-for-all where the strongest survive and everyone else suffers. What they want is self-governance without coercion—a world where communities take charge of their own lives, free from the oppressive grip of the state, capitalism, or any authority that thrives on hierarchy and control.

Think of it this way: Anarchism is a rejection of the idea that we need someone to be in charge to keep things running smoothly. Instead, it's about the belief that people, when given the chance, can organise themselves cooperatively. It's about creating systems where power is decentralised, where there's no need for bosses, police, or politicians telling everyone what to do. It's a radical trust in humanity's capacity for mutual aid and collaboration, without the constant oversight of a state that can just as easily oppress as it can protect.

---

11. Anarchism: Not chaos, just a really intense meeting about what to do next.

Now, anarchism has always had a bit of a PR problem. Most people hear the word *"anarchy"* and immediately think of rioting, destruction, and societal breakdown. But that's not what anarchism is about at its core. The confusion often comes from the conflation of *"anarchy"* (as in disorder) with *"anarchism"* (as in a coherent political philosophy). Sure, when your symbol is a big "A" in a circle, spray-painted on walls during protests, it's easy for people to get the wrong idea[12]. But at its heart, anarchism is actually one of the most idealistic political ideologies out there. It's the belief that humans, in the absence of authority, can live together in peace and equality.

But here's the tricky part—anarchism isn't afraid of a little chaos if that's what it takes to break down systems of oppression. It's about disrupting the structures of control that keep people in line—capitalism, the state, the police, the military. To anarchists, these are not institutions that protect society; they're systems of coercion that need to be dismantled. And when you're trying to tear down entrenched power, things can look a little messy, especially if you're on the side of those systems.

Why It Matters: Questioning Power, Challenging Authority

Even if you think anarchism is a just completely batshit crazy, it's still incredibly important. Anarchism is the ideological thorn in the side of complacency, forcing us to ask uncomfortable but necessary questions: Why does the government hold so much control over our everyday lives? Why do we accept hierarchies as natural or inevitable? And why should a small group of elite individuals—whether politicians, CEOs, or bureaucrats—get to make decisions that impact everyone else[13]? Even if anarchism

---

12. Like I said, PR Problem.

13. Exactly!

doesn't provide all the neat, tidy answers we're looking for, it at least keeps us focused on the right questions.

In a world where governments often seem more interested in lining their own pockets than serving the public, where corporations wield more influence than some countries, and where the wealth gap grows wider by the day, anarchism's core message feels more relevant than ever. Its fierce critique of power structures—that no one should have control over others—is a reminder that the systems we've grown accustomed to aren't natural or unchangeable. They're constructs. They were built by people, and they can be dismantled by people too.

And let's be perfectly frank: when the state starts cracking down on civil liberties, when corporations treat workers like expendable cogs in a profit machine, and when society feels like it's slowly unravelling under the weight of its own inequality, anarchism's call for autonomy and individual freedom starts to sound like a pretty good idea. Sure, it might not offer the most practical blueprint for running a functioning society in the long run, but anarchism stands as a bold rejection of the systems that have failed us. It's the ideological *"no"* to authoritarianism, to exploitation, and to complacency.

Even for someone like me—who values organisation far too much to hand the country over to an anarchist collective—the sheer audacity of anarchism is something to admire. It's like the political world's ultimate rebellious teenager: irrational, passionate, but often making points that can't be ignored. And in a world that feels increasingly controlled, surveillance-heavy, and dictated by corporate interests, that rebellious spirit is something we desperately need.

Tying It All (Haphazardly) Together

Anarchism is a beautiful contradiction. It critiques power structures with the same breathless energy it uses to imagine a world without them. At its best, anarchism reminds us to question the authority we take for granted, to challenge hierarchies that seem inevitable, and to push for a world where freedom and equality aren't just slogans but lived realities. At its worst, it's hopelessly impractical, a utopian dream that collapses under the weight of its own lofty ideals.

But perhaps the point isn't whether anarchism can work as a long-term governance model. The point is that anarchism forces us to confront the flaws in the systems we live under. It's the ideological sand in the gears of complacency, always reminding us that there's another way to live, even if that way is chaotic, messy, and doomed to implode within two weeks.

Anarchism doesn't *need* to win to be relevant. Its strength lies in its ability to disrupt, to inspire, and to make us rethink what's possible. And who knows? Maybe in the wreckage of old power structures, something better could grow. Or maybe we'll just end up back where we started, but at least we'll have had a hell of a time tearing things down.

Theocracy

God's Kingdom on Earth, Apparently

"The Handmaid's Tale' is not a book or show
advocating enslaving women or creating a theocracy. It's not glorifying that. It's talking about
what happens if that happens."

Laeta Kalogridis

I f you've ever wondered what it would be like to have politicians armed not with policy briefs but with holy books, look
no further than a theocracy. These regimes are less concerned
with the messy realities of governing an imperfect society and
more focused on implementing what they claim to be *"divine
will."* Of course, the divine doesn't actually show up to chair
these meetings—it's always someone's interpretation of scripture that gets the final say. And therein lies the big issue: who
gets to decide what God wants? Turns out, the answer is usually
whoever has the most power, and, wouldn't you know it, "divine will" tends to align rather conveniently with their political
interests[1].

In theory, theocracy sounds like a utopia—God's laws guiding humanity toward peace, harmony, and moral clarity. No

---

1. Because apparently, God has *very* specific thoughts about tax policy and
driving licenses.

corruption, no crime, no suffering. Everything in its perfect place under the watchful eye of the Almighty. But in practice? Let's just say it's a bit less *heavenly* and a lot more *iron-fisted*. Because in a theocracy, questioning the government isn't just treason—it's blasphemy. After all, if God's in charge, who are you to dissent? The answer is no one. No one questions divine authority, and if they do, there's usually a very swift and un-pleasant consequence.

The problem with theocracy is that it assumes two things: one, that divine law is perfect and unchanging, and two, that those interpreting said divine law are somehow infallible[2]. But history has shown us repeatedly that humans are *very* good at bend-ing divine will to suit their own purposes. Funny how God always seems to agree with the king, the priest, or the Supreme Leader, right? And what happens when different people start disagreeing on what God really meant by that one particular verse or law? Spoiler: it doesn't end with a pleasant debate over coffee. More likely, someone's being burned at the stake, exiled, or imprisoned.

In many theocratic states, religious leaders wield more power than elected officials—assuming elections even happen at all. Their authority isn't just legal; it's *moral*. And that's a danger-ous mix. If you think a secular politician is hard to argue with, try telling a cleric in power that their interpretation of divine law might be just a little bit off. That's the thing about theocracy: it elevates government decisions from the realm of policy debates into the sacred, untouchable world of divine judgement.

Let's take Iran as an example. Its government operates under a unique hybrid system, combining democratic elements with theocratic oversight. On paper, you've got a parliament, a pres-ident, and elections. But looming above it all is the Supreme Leader, whose word is final, as he is considered to represent God's will on Earth. The Ayatollah isn't just a political fig-

---

2. They are most patently not.

ure—he's a religious one, and his authority extends far beyond what we typically think of as a head of state. In practice, this means any policy decision can be vetoed if it doesn't align with the prevailing religious interpretation of Islamic law. And what's the recourse for citizens? There isn't much. It's hard to argue with someone when they claim their authority comes directly from the Creator of the universe.

The issue is even starker in places like Saudi Arabia, where Sharia law[3] (as interpreted by the ruling religious authorities) dictates the country's legal framework. The result is a society where certain actions are not just illegal but are considered outright sins against God. Apostasy, homosexuality, and blasphemy can all carry the death penalty, and any form of public dissent is ruthlessly quashed in the name of maintaining religious and political order. It's an efficient way to ensure obedience, but it's also a brutal reminder that theocracy is not about freedom—it's about *control*, under the guise of piety.

And here's the thing about it: even within the same religion, there are often wildly different interpretations of what God's law actually says. In Christianity, for instance, there's the Vatican, where the pope leads with claims of divine authority—yet even within Catholicism, there are disagreements about doctrine and how strictly it should be enforced. Then you've got Protestant theocracies in history, like Calvin's Geneva, where a rigid interpretation of Christianity led to a city ruled by religious austerity, with a fondness for burning heretics. And that's not even touching on the complexities of Judaism, Hinduism, or Buddhism when used as a basis for governance.

Theocratic regimes present themselves as utopias of moral clarity and divine justice. But when you scrutinise even just a little bit, they're often defined by repression and the monopolisation

---

3. As a quick sidenote for anyone about to have a panic attack about Sharia law in the United Kingdom – it's just not a thing, and the chances are exceedingly slim that it would ever be introduced.

cf power by a small group of religious elites. Instead of allowing society to flourish with diverse ideas, they smother it under the weight of rigid dogma. You see, when a state is governed by *"God's law,"* dissent becomes not just a political act but a *spiritual crime*—and when that happens, things get very dark very quickly.

History in Brief: A Divine Right to Rule

Theocracies have been around for as long as human beings have realised they could use religion as a tool to solidify their hold on power. In fact, you could argue that it's one of the oldest forms of governance[4], and while it may not be as prevalent in the Western world today, it's still alive and kicking in various parts cf the globe. The idea behind a theocracy is simple: if the ruler is backed by divine authority, who could possibly challenge them? It's not just the threat of earthly punishment that keeps people in line, but the fear of divine retribution as well. After all, disagreeing with your government is one thing—disagreeing with God? That's a whole new level of terrifying[5].

One of the most iconic examples of theocratic rule is, of course, the Vatican. For centuries, popes didn't just wield religious influence but political power as well, often in equal measure. The pope wasn't just a figurehead or spiritual leader; he was the absolute authority, considered by many to be God's representative on Earth. Divine rule wasn't just a theological concept—it was a very practical way to maintain control over kingdoms, empires, and even entire continents. The pope's word wasn't just law—it was believed to be God's law. And in a world where most people believed that eternal damnation was a very real

---

4. Which is, after all, exactly what we did in *Medieval Political Thought* right at the beginning of our adventure together.

5. Imagine making Margaret Thatcher omniscient and omnipresent – no wonder Starmer was compelled to take her portrait down in Downing Street – yikes!

possibility, crossing the pope was a direct line to hellfire and brimstone.

During the height of the Vatican's power, there was no real separation between the religious and the political. The pope had the authority to depose kings, excommunicate rulers, and excommunicate entire nations if he so wished. The pope's ability to wield this power was unparalleled; he wasn't just an advisor to kings and emperors—he could make or break them. And let's not forget the Crusades, where papal decrees weren't just spiritual commands but calls to arms, leading to centuries of bloody conflict in the name of God.

Of course, the even darker side of the Vatican's theocratic rule came in the form of church-run courts, inquisitions, and religious wars that ravaged Europe. The Inquisition is a particularly bleak chapter, with its witch hunts, forced conversions, and torturous methods of rooting out heresy. People lived in fear—not just of earthly punishment, but of the eternal consequences of being on the wrong side of the church. The church's power to enforce what it claimed to be God's will meant that dissent wasn't just political—it was spiritual. Questioning the church was to question God himself.

The Reformation and the Enlightenment eventually started to pry apart the marriage between church and state in Europe. Martin Luther's 95 Theses in 1517 didn't just ignite a religious reformation—it sparked a political revolution. When the authority of the pope was challenged, it opened the floodgates for the questioning of religious authority more generally. Enlightenment thinkers like John Locke (who we know) and Voltaire (who we know of) pushed the idea that governance should be based on reason and human rights, not divine decree. Secularism began to take hold as Europe grew tired of centuries of religious wars, inquisitions, and a church that seemed more interested in maintaining its own power than in providing spiritual guidance. Gradually, religion and state were separated—at least, that was the idea. But even today, the scars of religious governance still run deep in many European societies.

While Europe moved on from overt theocratic rule (for the most part), theocracy found new homes in other parts of the world. Perhaps the most notable modern theocracy is Iran, where the 1979 Islamic Revolution transformed the country into a hybrid system of governance—part theocracy, part republic. The revolution was a reaction to the secular, Western-backed Shah, whose reign was seen as a betrayal of Islamic values. Ayatollah Khomeini stepped in with his vision of an Islamic state where Shia clerics would have ultimate authority. The result was a unique system where religious leaders, headed by the Supreme Leader, have final say over all matters of state. Iran's system allows for elected officials, but the clerical establishment can overrule any decision that doesn't align with Islamic law. In this way, the will of the people is always subject to the will of the religious elite.

And let's not forget Saudi Arabia, where the monarchy and Wahhabism—a strict interpretation of Sunni Islam—are so intertwined that the legal system is essentially an application of Sharia law. There's no constitution in Saudi Arabia—the Quran serves as the guiding legal document. The monarchy rules with the understanding that their authority is divinely sanctioned, and the religious police enforce strict moral codes based on Wahhabi interpretations of Islamic scripture. Here, every aspect of life—from women's rights to what you can wear in public—is dictated by religious doctrine. It's not just about governing a state; it's about ensuring that society conforms to a specific set of religious ideals, with little room for dissent or deviation.

In both Iran and Saudi Arabia, religious law isn't just a moral guide—it's the law of the land. And if you think secular governments can be oppressive, you haven't seen anything until you've lived under a regime that claims to speak for God. In a theocracy, blasphemy isn't just a crime—it's a capital offence. Apostasy (leaving the faith) can get you executed, and questioning the legitimacy of the regime isn't just sedition—it's heresy. There's a reason why theocracies don't tend to be bastions of free speech or human rights: when the government claims divine authority, any disagreement becomes sacrilege.

But theocracies aren't just confined to the Middle East. Even in the United States, religious rhetoric plays an outsized role in politics. While the U.S. is technically a secular country, the influence of the Christian right has shaped everything from abortion laws to the debate over same-sex marriage[6]. Politicians openly invoke God's will in their speeches, and many laws are framed in moral, often religious, terms. It's not a theocracy in the strict sense, but the blending of religious authority with political power is alive and well in many parts of the world, even in democracies.

And then finally, as someone who grew up in South Africa during the final years of apartheid, I witnessed firsthand how powerful the grip of religious authority can be on a political regime. The National Party, which enforced apartheid, was heavily influenced by the Dutch Reformed Church (NG Church), a religious institution that justified racial segregation as part of God's will. It wasn't just a political system of oppression—it was underpinned by a belief that divine authority was on the side of the regime. The NG Church acted as a moral enforcer for the National Party, making it nearly impossible to challenge apartheid without also challenging deeply entrenched religious beliefs. For me, this was a direct example of how theocratic influence can be used to entrench power, silence dissent, and create a society where questioning the government meant, in many people's minds, questioning God himself.

This raises the question: why is theocracy still so appealing in certain places? The answer likely lies in the human desire for order, certainty, and moral clarity in a world that often feels chaotic and unjust. Religion provides a framework for understanding the world and our place in it, and for many, it's comforting to

---

6. If you weren't aware, the idea of two men or two women getting married can get this particular group of people into a weapons-grade froth.

believe that there's a higher power guiding human affairs. But when religion becomes the *foundation* for political governance, things get complicated. Theocracies claim to offer divine justice, but in reality, they often serve to entrench the power of a small religious elite while oppressing anyone who doesn't conform.

In a theocracy, personal freedoms take a back seat to religious conformity. Dissent isn't just discouraged—it's often violently suppressed. And while theocracy promises a society based on divine laws, what it usually delivers is a rigid, oppressive system where the lines between faith and power blur to the point of erasing individual rights altogether.

What It's Not: God's Law ≠ Peace

There's a persistent and rather naïve misconception that theocracies are inherently peaceful as if following *"God's law"* would lead to an idyllic society where everyone is united in faith and harmony[7]. This couldn't be further from the truth. Theocracies are often anything but peaceful. In reality, they operate under strict, rigid interpretations of religious texts that leave very little room for disagreement or dissent. If you challenge the system, you're not just being politically rebellious—you're being heretical, and in a theocracy, heresy is a crime against both the state and the divine. The punishment? Let's just say it's rarely lenient.

The rigidity of theocratic law means that everything is black and white. There's no room for nuance, no grey area where interpretation or debate can exist. In a secular legal system, laws evolve based on changing social norms, values, and human experience. Not so in a theocracy. Here, laws are seen as unchangeable because they are, supposedly, ordained by a higher power. This makes dissent not just an act of civil disobedience,

---

7. For anyone who has ever read the Old Testament, it would be very clear that God is not what you would necessarily describe as "peaceful"...

but an existential threat to the very foundation of society. Disagreeing with the law means disagreeing with God, and that's not something a theocracy can tolerate. It's not a political debate; it's spiritual warfare.

In theocracies, the enforcers of these laws—the clerics, priests, or religious police—act as intermediaries between God and the people. They're the ones who *"know"* what God wants, and they wield that knowledge like a weapon. This creates a chilling atmosphere where citizens are forced to toe the line or face brutal consequences. Freedom is stifled, creativity is crushed, and any form of rebellion is met with swift and often violent repression. The threat of divine punishment looms over everything, and with that comes an intense pressure to conform.

Take our earlier example of Iran, for instance, where the morality police enforce dress codes and public behaviour with an iron fist. If you're caught flouting the rules—wearing too much makeup, failing to wear a headscarf properly, or holding hands with someone in public—you're not just breaking the law; you're defying God's will[8] .. And when dissenters protest against such repression, as we've seen in the recent waves of demonstrations against the compulsory hijab laws, the state cracks down hard, arresting, imprisoning, and in some cases, executing those who dare to oppose the system. There's no room for dialogue in a theocracy; there's only submission or punishment.

The myth of peaceful theocracies also ignores the fact that religious law often justifies violence. Holy wars, inquisitions, and persecutions are all hallmarks of theocratic governance. Look no further than Saudi Arabia, where punishments like public floggings, amputations, and executions are part of a justice system that claims to be carrying out God's will. In a theocracy,

---

8. Conveniently as interpreted by a group of men who happen to have control.

violence is not just permitted; it's sanctified, a necessary part of maintaining order and purity in society.

Let's not forget that theocracies aren't peaceful because they operate on a shared moral code—far from it. They are often peaceful on the surface because they enforce strict social control through fear. The people live under the constant threat of punishment, and this fear keeps them in line. It's not peace through harmony; it's peace through oppression. The silence you hear isn't the result of everyone living in perfect religious alignment—it's the result of everyone being too scared to speak up.

And here's the thing: theocracies are very rarely religious utopias. It's not as though these societies are living in harmony with divine principles, whatever those might be. Theocracies are political systems that use religion as a tool to consolidate power. Religion is the means to an end—control. The ruling class, whether they're clerics or kings, use the language of faith to justify their rule and maintain their grip on power. This isn't about fostering spiritual enlightenment; it's about ensuring that no one questions the authority of the state.

This is why theocracies are dangerous. They masquerade as societies built on moral or divine principles, but in reality, they're just authoritarian regimes dressed in religious garb. They use faith to control the masses, and they shield themselves from criticism by claiming to act on behalf of a higher power. You can argue with a politician; you can't argue with God—or at least, that's the narrative they push.

This is particularly concerning when we consider how theocratic tendencies are creeping into modern politics, even in places that pride themselves on secularism. In some parts of the United States, for instance, religious fundamentalism has made its way into lawmaking, with politicians using their personal faith as a justification to restrict reproductive rights, roll back LGBTQ+ protections, and curtail the separation of church and state. Margaret Atwood's *The Handmaid's Tale* was meant to be a warning, but it's starting to look more like a playbook for certain corners of the political world. When lawmakers say they are acting on "God's will," democracy takes a backseat to dogma.

The rise of Christian nationalism in the U.S. is an alarming trend that mirrors theocratic regimes in other parts of the world. While America is not (yet) a theocracy, the increasing influence of religious fundamentalism on policy decisions is concerning. The argument that laws should be based on religious beliefs rather than democratic consensus threatens to erode the very foundation of secular governance. And the danger of this, as history has shown, is that once religious law takes root in governance, it's almost impossible to pull out. It spreads, infecting everything from the justice system to education, all under the guise of moral authority.

Theocracies are not peaceful havens of religious purity. They are authoritarian regimes that use the weight of divine law to justify their oppression. They crush freedom, they suppress creativity, and they stifle any form of dissent. The real question isn't whether theocracies are peaceful; it's whether they can ever truly deliver on their promise of divine justice without descending into tyranny[9].

Broader Cultural Perspectives:

Now, when we think of theocracies, it's easy to get stuck on Christianity and Islam. After all, nothing says *"theocratic dystopia"* quite like centuries of inquisitions or the idea of religious police chasing you down for holding hands. But don't worry—theocracy is far more versatile than that. It's not just limited to the Bible and the Quran; turns out, plenty of other belief systems thought it would be a great idea to mix God with governance.

---

9. And judging by the history books, the answer is a resounding "Nope".

Take Tibet, for example, before China decided to step in and replace spiritual rule with its own brand of authoritarianism. For centuries, Tibet was essentially a theocracy, led by the Dalai Lama. Here, the idea wasn't that the ruler was a dictator with a direct line to God's wrath, but more like a spiritual guide who also happened to run the government. A peaceful, enlightened theocracy, you might think. And while it's certainly a gentler form of religious rule than what you'd find under, say, Saudi Arabia's hard-line clerics, it was still very much a system where religious authority dictated governance. You could almost imagine the cabinet meetings: half spiritual meditation, half policy briefing, with plenty of sage nodding and chants. Enlightenment might sound lovely, but power is power, and combining spiritual authority with political rule inevitably comes with its own set of hierarchies and complications.

And speaking of hierarchies, let's not forget the divine right of kings, especially in Hindu monarchies. These rulers didn't just claim to represent God—they claimed to *be* God[10] . Imagine having a ruler who was believed to be a living deity on earth, their every decision imbued with divine authority. You couldn't exactly stage a protest when the king literally claimed he was doing the gods' will. These monarchies were steeped in spiritual lineage, so no matter how benevolent or incompetent the ruler was, they had a celestial stamp of approval that put them beyond reproach.

Sure, these systems weren't always run by tyrannical zealots smiting unbelievers left and right, but they were still deeply rooted in unshakable spiritual hierarchy. Reverence may sound better than fear, but it's hard to feel *that* warm and fuzzy about a political system that insists the king is an avatar of Vishnu. Whether it's wielding spiritual enlightenment or the promise of divine retribution, the bottom line is that religious rulers, no matter the faith, often end up using their *"godliness"* to cement power. And no matter how you package it—whether through

---

10. Or at least a convenient incarnation.

heavenly enlightenment or fire and brimstone—theocracy is still about control. Just because your king wears robes instead of a crown doesn't mean you're not under his thumb.

Intersection with Indigenous Beliefs: Theocratic Exceptions that Prove the Rule

Now, as has become abundantly clear, when we think of theocracy, we usually picture stern-faced clerics or fire-and-brimstone sermons followed by some poor soul getting dragged off for blasphemy. But, there are minor exceptions. In many indigenous cultures, the relationship between governance and spirituality takes on a much less dystopian vibe. Instead of a rigid hierarchy where a single spiritual leader calls the shots, indigenous theocracies are more about balance, respect, and keeping the peace with the natural world.

Take the Hopi in North America, for example. Their governance wasn't exactly a *"do this or face divine wrath"* kind of setup. Instead, it was built on the belief that humans, nature, and the spiritual realm were all deeply interconnected. Their leaders, known as *kikmongwi*, were spiritual figures who guided communities based on shared values and traditions, not by imposing rigid laws. These spiritual leaders didn't wield power like a sceptre but rather acted as keepers of balance, ensuring that the community didn't fall out of harmony with the natural world. You could almost say it was a theocracy where the main concern wasn't breaking the rules, but offending Mother Earth. Imagine trying to explain *that* to the pope.

Over in South Africa, the Zulu kingdom had its own unique brand of theocratic governance. The *inkosi* (king) wasn't just a political leader but was seen as divinely sanctioned. However, unlike in more rigid theocracies, Zulu leadership was also accountable to the people. There was a reciprocal relationship between the leader and the led, with spiritual rituals and consultations to ensure that harmony within the kingdom was maintained. It's not exactly a democracy, but it wasn't pure authoritarianism either. You had a king who was supposedly in with the gods, but who also had to make sure the gods weren't displeased by, say, overtaxing his people or disrespecting a sacred cow.

These indigenous systems were theocracies of a different flavour—more free-range than force-fed, so to speak. Spiritual leaders had authority, but their power came from their ability to maintain harmony with the world around them, not from threatening divine punishment for stepping out of line. It was a lot more about respect for natural law and tradition than about absolute control. If theocrats in Europe had adopted this model, maybe we'd have fewer inquisitions and more campfire ceremonies.

Of course, the appeal of these systems is that they show a more cooperative relationship between spirituality and leadership. But let's not romanticise it too much. Indigenous theocracies still rested on spiritual authority, which, at the end of the day, meant that those in charge had a say in how you lived your life. Whether it's being told you can't fish in sacred waters or that you need to perform a ritual to ensure a good harvest, theocratic governance in any form always comes with a set of rules. They just might be delivered with fewer smitings and more drumming circles.

Impact on Minority Groups

Something I think we can all agree on is that theocracies aren't exactly known for their tolerance, are they? When one religion holds all the political cards, anyone outside the faith is dealt a pretty rubbish hand. Religious minorities—be they Baha'is in Iran or Christians in Saudi Arabia—end up facing everything from social exclusion to imprisonment, all in the name of *'divine justice'*. It's not just about living in a society with different beliefs; it's about being constantly reminded that, in the eyes of the state, you're one heresy away from a death sentence.

Take Iran's treatment of Baha'is: denied education, jobs, and dignity, simply because their faith isn't *"approved"*. Meanwhile, in Saudi Arabia, non-Muslims don't just face exclusion—they face public floggings if they dare practise their beliefs openly. It's not just persecution; it's persecution wrapped in sanctimony. The state isn't just right—they're divinely right.

And it's not just about religion. Ethnic minorities, like the Kurds in Iran, find themselves on the receiving end of both sectarian and racial discrimination, a double-whammy of marginalisation. Add women and LGBTQ+ individuals to the mix, and you've got a theocratic greatest-hits album of oppression. Saudi's guardianship laws and Iran's morality police exist to ensure everyone knows their place, especially if you're a woman or, heaven forbid, gay.

Theocracies cling to the notion that their leaders are infallible, divinely chosen vessels of God's will. Dissent isn't just political—it's blasphemous. Which is a neat trick, really, because who needs a reasoned debate when you can just call your opponents heretics and be done with it?

It's not a new trick either. From medieval Europe's Inquisitions to modern-day India's rise of Hindu nationalism, the marriage of politics and religion always ends in a tyrannical love-child. And theocrats everywhere seem to agree on one thing: the more divine the regime, the more brutal the punishment for anyone who dares to be different.

Why It Matters: Because It's Still Creeping into Modern Politics

Even in the 21st century, theocratic tendencies have proven remarkably resilient, creeping into political systems that outwardly claim to be secular. You don't have to live in Iran or Saudi Arabia to see religious influence seep into government decisions. In fact, it's happening all over the world in subtler, yet equally concerning ways. We already know about the situation in the United States, where debates over abortion, LGBTQ+ rights, and *"religious freedom"* are constantly skirting the edges of theocratic influence. Politicians routinely cite their personal religious beliefs to justify policy decisions, and in doing so, they blur the line between church and state in ways that would make the Founding Fathers break out in a cold sweat.

Something to always remember is that the United States was founded on principles of secularism, with the Constitution establishing a clear separation of church and state. The very idea was to prevent the kind of religious authoritarianism that had dominated Europe for centuries. Yet, today, we see lawmakers invoking their faith to shape public policy, from limiting reproductive rights to challenging the rights of same-sex couples. When policies are built on religious doctrine rather than on the principles of democracy and individual rights, you're walking a very fine line into theocratic territory.

And it's not just the United States. Across Europe, the rise of far-right movements has brought with it some worrying parallel theocratic tendencies. In countries like Poland and Hungary, religious conservatism has become deeply intertwined with political nationalism. Leaders like Viktor Orbán in Hungary have framed their hardline, authoritarian policies as a defence of *"Christian values,"* positioning the state as a guardian of both national identity and religious morality. This blend of nationalism and religion, though not a full-blown theocracy, draws dangerous parallels with theocratic governance, where dissent is framed as not just unpatriotic, but immoral.

Poland, too, has seen its government leverage Catholicism to justify restrictive laws on abortion and LGBTQ+ rights. The influence of the Church on politics is so strong that Poland's secular legal framework is increasingly subverted by religious principles. In these countries, the rise of far-right ideologies has walked hand-in-hand with religious conservatism, using *"moral"* justifications for policies that infringe on individual rights and freedoms. The message is clear: not only is dissent unpatriotic, but it's also an affront to religious values.

Here's the real danger of theocracy, whether overt or creeping in under the guise of *"traditional values"*: it's absolute. When religious law becomes state law, dissent isn't just political—it's spiritual. Disagreeing with a theocratic government doesn't make you a rebel; it makes you a heretic. And the punishments for heresy, historically speaking, have been far more severe than those for political rebellion. This is why theocracy is such a perilous road. Once you grant a government the power to act in the name of divine authority, you remove any possibility of debate or dissent. After all, how do you argue with God?

The far-right's rise has brought with it a brand of religious conservatism that is, at its core, deeply authoritarian. These movements claim to defend national identity and cultural values, but what they're really doing is building the foundations for a society where freedom is restricted, and dissent is criminalised in the name of religious orthodoxy. The blending of religious rhetoric with far-right populism is not just a troubling trend—it's a direct challenge to the very principles of secular democracy.

And don't be fooled into thinking that this is just about religion. Theocratic regimes, or those inching in that direction, aren't really about spiritual salvation—they're about control. Religion is the tool, the cloak of legitimacy used to justify authoritarianism. When governments start playing the God card to justify their policies, it's not just democracy that's at risk—it's freedom of thought, speech, and action. The more a government leans on religion to validate its authority, the more dangerous it becomes.

Not for Me, Thanks

As someone who's had their fair share of religious baggage, theocracy doesn't exactly strike me as the most welcoming of political systems[11] . I used to believe in a higher power—until, of course, that higher power supposedly decided that loving my husband was enough to condemn me to eternal damnation. Funny how divine will always seems to line up with the biases of those interpreting it, right? So no, I'm not particularly enthused about the idea of running a country based on someone else's view of God's will. There's just too much room for abuse, for those in power to conveniently forget about compassion while clinging to their "divinely inspired" laws.

And here's the thing—even for the devout, theocracy is a dangerous game. It's not just about faith, it's about control. A theocracy doesn't leave room for spiritual growth, for questioning, or for debate. It's the merging of the absolute authority of religion with the unchecked power of the state—a cocktail that's rarely about bringing people closer to God and almost always about making sure they fall in line. Sure, it's dressed up in righteousness, but underneath it all, it's just another way to keep the powerful on top.

In a world already rife with inequality, repression, and authoritarianism, adding divine authority to the mix only worsens the cocktail of control. The last thing we need is more theocratic meddling, more religious figures dictating policies that affect everyone, regardless of their faith.

---

11. Putting it *exceptionally* mildly.

Libertarianism

Freedom! (But Who's Going to Pay for t he Roads?)

"I mean, I've always been a libertarian. Leave everybody alone. Let everybody else do what they want. Just stay out of everybody else's hair".

Clint Eastwood

The scene unfolds in a dimly lit pub, where smoke from cigarettes curls lazily through the air. Somewhere, between London and New York, a peculiar crossroad of time and ideology, where Ayn Rand and John Maynard Keynes sit opposite each other at a well-worn table. At first glance, they could be mistaken for any two pub patrons—Keynes, gently stirring his pint, with that unmistakable air of calculated ease; Rand, cigarette held aloft, smoke dancing above her like a crown. The tension between them, however, is palpable.

Rand takes a long drag, her eyes narrowing as she glances disdainfully towards the pub's window. Outside, the faint flicker of government-funded streetlights illuminate the night, and Rand, ever the purist, can't help but sneer. "This is the problem with society today," she begins, her voice sharp and deliberate, "this blind obsession with sacrifice. Everyone's scrambling to serve some imaginary 'greater good.' It's disgusting, really. The individual should be free, unburdened by the chains of the state."

Keynes raises an eyebrow, clearly amused, though not entirely surprised. He sips his pint with the sort of nonchalance that comes from years of knowing better. "Ah, the greater good," he muses. "I suppose you're talking about the very roads you used to get here tonight? The pint you're enjoying now, brewed in a facility adhering to safety standards set by—what was it again? Oh yes, the government."

Rand exhales, flicking ash from her cigarette onto the table with a touch of disdain. "Safety standards? Pah. If a business can't be trusted to ensure the quality of its own product, it deserves to fail. The market will correct itself. The strong survive, and the weak crumble. It's the natural order."

Keynes leans back, a grin tugging at the corners of his mouth. "The invisible hand! How quaint. But you see, Ayn, that invisible hand doesn't seem to know how to build bridges or hospitals. When the free market is left entirely to its own devices, you don't end up with utopia—you end up with potholes and pandemics." He sets his glass down firmly. "Do you remember 1929? The free market brought the world to its knees."

Rand, ever unshaken, flicks her cigarette toward an unseen ashtray, her voice cold. "The crash of '29 was the fault of government intervention. Had the market been left alone, we wouldn't have been saddled with the disgraceful New Deal."

At this, Keynes laughs—a soft, knowing chuckle that seems to echo off the pub's walls. "The New Deal saved millions from ruin, Ayn. The infrastructure your beloved businesses now rely on? That's thanks to those very policies. You can't claim that individualism is the answer when we live in a world that relies on collective action—roads, clean water, education. Shall I go on?"

Rand's lips tighten into a thin line. "Education should be earned," she snaps. "Not handed out like government cheese. And don't get me started on roads. If people want them, they should pay for them directly, not through the tyranny of taxes."

Keynes lets out a sigh, his patience wearing thin but still intact. "You see, that's where your vision fails. In your world, it's every person for themselves. But when the bridges collapse, when the streetlights go dark, what happens then? Will you build your own road to freedom, Ayn?"

Rand's eyes narrow as she leans forward, her voice low and unyielding. "Yes. Private companies would compete to provide better roads. Only those willing to pay would get access."

Keynes shakes his head, the smile fading as his tone becomes more serious. "So, in your utopia, every road would be privatised? Every pothole a business opportunity? And what of those who can't afford to pay for access? Will they simply stay put, stranded in your glorious free market?"

Rand leans back, folding her arms as though the conversation bores her. "If you can't afford a road," she says coldly, "then perhaps you shouldn't be driving. It's not society's job to hold your hand."

Keynes takes one final sip of his pint, a deep sigh escaping his lips. "Ah, Ayn, you're so obsessed with the notion of freedom that you've twisted it into something almost unrecognisable. Freedom isn't just the right to succeed; it's the right to live in a society where collective needs are met, where we aren't all one bad day away from anarchy. You can't have one without the other."

Rand, unwavering, flashes a sharp smile. "Freedom is sacred. Taxes, regulations—they're just chains disguised as progress. Bitcoin," she adds with a glint in her eye, "now that's true freedom. Decentralised. Beyond the reach of your meddlesome state."

Keynes can't help but laugh, a full-throated sound that rever-berates through the pub. "Bitcoin? Oh, Ayn, that's the Liber-tarian's wet dream. Free from taxes, free from oversight—but entirely dependent on the infrastructure of the state you claim to despise. It's quite the paradox, really. You want to be free from the state, but you still want its roads, its internet, its safety nets."

Rand's smile grows even sharper, her eyes gleaming with con-viction. "The state will crumble, John. Its inefficiencies will be its undoing. The market will prevail."

Keynes raises his glass one last time, as if to toast the absurdity of it all. "And when it does, Ayn, I'll be here, offering govern-ment-funded repairs for your crumbling roads. Because even Libertarianism can't fix a flat tire."

The Roads We Travel

Libertarianism, in its purest form, is like a fantasy where free-dom is an endless buffet but no one bothers to clean up after. Ayn Rand's extreme individualism and disdain for collective action might appeal to those who've never had to rely on public services, but when you scratch the surface, even the staunchest Libertarians start to reveal their hypocrisy.

When the tyres start falling off—whether it's roads, public health, or social safety nets—the true cost of *"freedom"* with-out responsibility becomes glaringly obvious. The reality is, we don't just live in a society because it's convenient. We live in one because it's necessary.

So, the next time someone waxes poetic about the wonders of Libertarianism, ask them: *"Great, but who's going to pay for the roads?"*

--Interlude--

The Gospel of Ayn Rand: Extreme Individualism for the Win (Unless You Need Help Moving)

Ayn Rand—the high priestess of radical individualism, the queen of *"me, myself, and I."* If Libertarianism were a cult (and quite honestly, it often feels that way), Rand would be the charismatic figurehead, standing on a windswept cliff, *The Fountainhead* in one hand and *Atlas Shrugged* in the other, doling out sermons to her devoted acolytes. Picture her, wrapped in the finest metaphorical silk spun from her own self-importance, telling us all that the only moral obligation is to oneself. Don't worry about others; they'll figure it out—or perish—and either way, it's none of your concern. You have more important things to do, like building skyscrapers or perfecting your disdain for those lesser, needy folk who insist on things like community or compassion.

Her basic philosophy, if you can call it that without bursting into ironic laughter, is that life's simply too short to be weighed down by the needs or feelings of anyone else. Why bother with trivialities like empathy or, heaven forbid, social responsibility? In Rand's utopia, the mere concept of *"altruism"* is treated with the same suspicion most of us reserve for wet socks, delayed trains, or people who play ukuleles at parties. It's not just frowned upon—it's an existential threat to the divine power of the self. To her, the very notion of considering another person's well-being is akin to shackling yourself to mediocrity. It's a kind of sacrilege. You might as well commit to self-immolation if you dare suggest that society is a thing worth saving.

Rand's philosophical concoction—objectivism, as she grandly labelled it—was, at its core, a celebration of the rugged individualist, that mythic hero who conquers the world on the strength of their sheer willpower and complete indifference to the suffering of others. Personal achievement isn't just a good thing; it's the *only* thing. Your moral compass should point solely toward your own advancement, and anyone who dares suggest that we owe anything to society is, in her mind, basically a moustache-twirling villain in a second-rate melodrama.

Sure, it's an appealing idea if you're someone who fancies themselves a lone wolf—the kind of person who might have a framed picture of John Galt on their desk and a secret and visceral disdain for public libraries. Why should you care if society crumbles? You're too busy constructing your own tower of success, brick by brick, fuelled by coffee and self-satisfaction.

But—and here's the issue—in practice? Running a society like a collection of lone wolves doesn't exactly foster, you know, functioning infrastructure[1] . You can't pave roads with pure individualism, as much as Libertarians might wish otherwise. You can't run hospitals on bootstraps[2] and self-reliance, unless you think surgery can be outsourced to an online marketplace with a five-star rating system. Rand's heroes are always going off to their fantasy Galt's Gulch utopias, isolated havens where they can live out their lives in blissful freedom from the burdens of the unwashed masses. Who needs roads, schools, or functional hospitals when you've got the intoxicating fumes of individual freedom, right? Never mind that, in the real world, these *"heroes*[3] *"* would likely find themselves living in a dilapidated cave, wondering why the local utility company hasn't built them a power grid.

Rand's ideal society, if it were actually built, would be a glorious monument to freedom—until the first bridge collapses because no one wanted to pitch in to maintain it. Or the streets flood, because who needs drainage systems when you have personal

---

1. You generally can't have one small section of bridge all on your own.

2. Though let's be honest, it's not as though the Tories haven't tried to force the NHS to do so.

3. Usually going by the name of *"FREEDOM-OR-DEATH-PATRIOT-4556090"* on Twitter that has a remarkably similar output to *"FREEDOM-OR-DEATH-PATRIOT-4556091"*...

autonomy? It's certainly an alluring fantasy, this Libertarian dreamworld, where everything is driven by personal achievement and the free market solves all problems. Except, of course, the ones it doesn't, like building the basic necessities that keep us all from slipping into medieval chaos. And when that happens, you can bet the rugged individualists will be the first ones wondering why no one else is stepping up to fix it.

Ron Paul's Legacy: A Libertarian Folk Hero (But Don't Ask About Social Safety Nets)

If Ayn Rand is Libertarianism's philosopher queen, then Ron Paul is its charming, if slightly dotty, grandfather—the sort of figure who'd smile warmly at you while handing out leaflets titled *"Freedom Isn't Free (But Roads Should Be)."* Paul took Libertarianism from its fringes and gave it a folksy, approachable face during his U.S. presidential campaigns in 2008 and 2012. His message was clear and simple: less government, more freedom. Fewer regulations, more decisions driven by the magic of the free market. Less foreign intervention, more isolationism. It was Libertarianism distilled into its purest form—the *"let people do whatever they want"* approach to governance, even if that means leaving society to fend for itself like a neglected houseplant.

Paul's faith in free markets bordered on the religious, a kind of rose-tinted view of capitalism where every problem, from healthcare to housing, could be solved by the invisible hand—though in practice, that hand usually turns a blind eye to the poor. Critics of this worldview often pointed out the glaring issue: if you leave everything to the market, it's usually the rich who end up thriving while the rest, well... don't. But Paul's answer to that? *"Let the market decide!"* [4] "A phrase which, translated from Libertarian, means *"good luck, you're on your own."*

---

4. Sounds familiar that...

He wasn't just promoting small government; he was envisioning a government so shrunken it could be mistaken for your local parish council, if that. Taxes? Practically theft in his book. Regulation? That's just government telling you what you can't do. The welfare state? Don't even mention it. Paul's ideal government was so minimalist that it could barely manage to fill a pothole, let alone provide healthcare or social services. And yet, his message found traction, especially with voters who saw the federal government in the United States as an overbearing nanny, sticking its nose where it didn't belong—in their paycheques, in their medical bills, and most controversially, in foreign conflicts. Paul's call for non-interventionism resonated with those who had grown tired of endless wars, particularly in the Middle East.

What made Paul different from the Randian libertarians, though, was his ability to wrap these otherwise harsh ideas in a populist, almost avuncular charm[5] . He wasn't barking commands from a high tower of philosophical purity; he was the Libertarian you could imagine inviting you over for a barbecue, telling you to *"take back control"* over a cold beer. His version of Libertarianism wasn't just for the elites; it was for everyone[6] .

Paul's enduring appeal came from making Libertarianism seem like a genuine alternative to the suffocating bureaucracies of modern government. For those tired of taxes, wars, and endless regulation, Paul offered a vision of freedom that was light on government interference and heavy on personal responsibility. It all sounded great—until, of course, you hit a pothole and realise that freedom from taxes also means freedom from well-maintained infrastructure.

---

5. Giving credence to the belief that you can sell anything with a jolly accent.

6. At least, everyone who could afford to live without the safety net he was so eager to dismantle.

Libertarianism, Liberalism and Neoliberalism

Libertarianism is *not* Liberalism, and it certainly isn't Neoliberalism. Let's be clear about that from the start. These three may seem like cousins at first glance—after all, they all like to throw around words like *"freedom"* and *"choice"* with the casual enthusiasm of a drunk philosopher at a dinner party—but in reality, they wouldn't be caught dead at the same family reunion. Libertarians might show up in a *"Taxation is Theft"* T-shirt, Liberals with a tote bag of social justice pamphlets, and Neoliberals? Well, they'd be busy making sure no one's taxing their stock portfolio *too* aggressively.

Libertarianism: The "Leave Me Alone" Ideology

Libertarianism is, at its heart, the political philosophy of people who just want to be left the hell alone. Government? Too big, too nosy, too interested in how you live your life. Libertarians view the state with the kind of suspicion most people reserve for door-to-door salesmen. Their dream world is one where you can keep all your earnings, not worry about pesky things like national health services, and drive on toll roads you personally choose to pay for—except, of course, when no one can be bothered to pay, and all the roads collapse into anarcho-potholes.

For Libertarians, personal freedom is everything. You are a sovereign entity, and no one—least of all the government—should tell you what to do with your life, your money, or your crypto. Unlike Liberals, who are quite keen on using government to create a bit of fairness and equality, Libertarians think that fairness is what you get when you're left to the whims of the free market. If you're rich, that's because you deserve it. If you're poor, well, better luck next time—unless the next time involves healthcare, in which case, best start a GoFundMe.

Liberalism: Freedom, But with a Bit of Help

Liberalism, in contrast, believes that freedom is nice, but it's even nicer when you've got a few guardrails to make sure everyone gets a fair shake. Liberalism thinks of the government as the helpful friend who shows up with a casserole when you're down on your luck—not too intrusive, but enough to keep you from starving to death in the alley behind your house. Liberals are keen on personal freedom too, but they also recognise that society is a bit more complicated than everyone just doing their own thing. Sure, you can be as free as you like, but you're going to need a bit of collective effort to build those roads, run those schools, and keep the lights on.

For Liberals, the government isn't the problem; it's the tool for solving problems. They're the ones who see the potholes and think, *"We should probably fix that. Also, shouldn't everyone have access to healthcare? And maybe education too?"* Libertarians, of course, see all this and roll their eyes. *"Freedom is the solution,"* they'd say, while Liberals respond with a slightly patronising pat on the head: *"Yes, yes, but freedom doesn't pave roads.[7] "*

Neoliberalism: Freedom for the Market, Not So Much for You

Now, Neoliberalism—don't let the *"liberal"* part fool you—has very little to do with actually caring about people's freedom in the way Libertarians or Liberals do. Neoliberalism is what happens when you take the free market and let it run wild, drunk on deregulation and privatisation. Neoliberals don't mind a bit of government intervention, so long as it's helping businesses

---

7. Don't lie, you've said pretty much exactly the same thing to the weird Libertarians that call Twitter home.

and markets *"thrive"*[8]. They're the architects of the modern economic system, the ones who told us that deregulating banks was a great idea and that we should really give more power to private companies because they know best. It's the ideology that looks at a multinational corporation and thinks, *"What if we gave it more tax breaks?"*

For Neoliberals, freedom means freedom *for the market*, not necessarily for *you*. It's the freedom for massive corporations to rake in profits and maybe, just maybe, trickle some of those profits down to the rest of us[9]. It's the freedom to privatise public goods—healthcare, education, transport—and sell them back to us at a premium, all in the name of *"choice."* Want to take the train? You have choices! Three different companies, all equally extortionate. Congratulations, consumer, your freedom has been served—just don't mind the fact that the train's late, the ticket price is obscene, and the carriage smells like someone's last attempt at freedom involved a bottle of gin and a kebab.

Where Libertarians scream *"hands off!"* and Liberals say *"hands on, gently,"* Neoliberals just nod approvingly as long as someone is making a profit. In fact, Neoliberals are what happens when Libertarianism gets drunk on corporate power and wakes up the next morning in bed with Goldman Sachs[10]. The individual freedoms espoused by Libertarianism are here, sure, but *only* if you can afford them. The rest of us? Well, we get to enjoy the exciting world of *"market solutions*[11]*"* for our public needs, like privatised water companies that can't stop pumping raw sewage into the rivers.

---

8. Read: letting corporations do whatever they want while the rest of us fight over the crumbs.

9. Which we're all still waiting to happen... Gagging for it, in fact.

10. I mean, to be fair, who *hasn't* found themselves in that exact same position?

11. Read: being gouged relentlessly.

The Fine Distinctions: Freedom, for Whom?

So, what's the fine line that divides these ideologies?

Libertarians want to be left alone—completely. They see the government as the enemy of freedom, full stop. Personal liberty is the only thing that matters, and the rest of the world can fend for itself. It's a lonely sort of freedom, where community and cooperation are sold off in favour of *"rugged individualism"*—which is great until you need someone to patch the roof after a storm.

Liberals, on the other hand, see freedom as something that needs a little structure. It's all well and good to be free, but what's the point if you're free to live in poverty, to be priced out of healthcare, or to drive on roads that could swallow your car whole? Liberals believe in creating a system where everyone gets a fair start, using government intervention to smooth out the worst inequalities and give people a fighting chance at success.

And Neoliberals? Well, they'll talk about freedom, sure, but what they really mean is *"freedom for capital."* It's the ideology of late-stage capitalism, dressed up in the language of choice and opportunity but designed to funnel wealth upward, leaving the rest of us to fend for ourselves in the trickle-down drizzle. You're free, alright—free to work harder for less, free to compete in a global marketplace where the odds are stacked against you, and free to wonder why every "choice" involves paying more for basic services.

So, while Libertarians, Liberals, and Neoliberals may all talk about freedom, it's clear they're speaking very different languages. Libertarians are living in a fantasy where every individual is an island. Liberals are trying to build bridges between those islands. And Neoliberals? They're selling the bridges back to us at a price we can't afford.

Modern Libertarianism: Bitcoin, Taxes, and the Tech Bro Paradise

For the modern Libertarian, the *real* revolution isn't happening at the ballot box—it's happening in the murky waters of cyberspace, where tech utopians have found a way to dodge that most egregious of governmental overreaches: taxation. Enter Bitcoin[12], the digital currency that promises to free us from the tyranny of fiat[13] money controlled by the dreaded state. It's like Libertarian catnip. No central banks, no regulators, no pesky oversight from elected officials who insist on things like monetary policy. Bitcoin embodies everything a Libertarian cherishes: decentralisation, anonymity, and, most importantly, a way to keep the government's sticky fingers out of their hard-earned digital cash.

To a Libertarian, Bitcoin isn't just a currency—it's a middle finger to the state, a declaration of financial independence. In the cryptosphere, every transaction is a small act of rebellion against the forces of government control. Taxes? They're for the uninitiated masses still using *real* money. In the world of Bitcoin, the state doesn't get a cut, and that's exactly how Libertarians like it. Why contribute to public funds when you can revel in the joy of decentralised wealth? Roads, hospitals, public schools—these are mere trivialities for the unenlightened. Bitcoiners are out there stacking satoshis, free from the tyranny of the taxman.

But here's the thing: for all its hype, Bitcoin hasn't exactly created a functioning society. Sure, it's great for buying obscure

---

12. I'll be very honest, I'm still not 100% sure what Bitcoin is beyond what trolls troll about, and it's been so long I'm too afraid to ask.

13. No, not a tiny Italian car. *Fiat currency* is money because governments *say* it's money. Unlike the good old days when cash was backed by gold, now it's just paper (or digital numbers) that we all agree has value—because, well, the government told us so. It's like Monopoly money, but with central banks in charge and no one ever really winning, except maybe the hedge fund managers.

digital art or speculating wildly in the financial markets, but it hasn't replaced the need for roads, healthcare, or anything that requires, you know, actual public funding. While Libertarians like to imagine a world where Bitcoin replaces all forms of state currency, what they don't talk about is how all of the essentials—hospitals, schools, clean water—are still largely dependent on that boring old thing they claim to despise: government infrastructure.

In their crypto utopia, Libertarians picture themselves floating free from the oppressive grip of the state. But even the most ardent Bitcoin advocate still lives in a world where the ambulances that arrive after a crypto trader faints from their latest market crash are paid for with—brace yourself—taxes. They drive on roads built by the government, attend universities funded by public money, and even access the internet—a network originally developed with taxpayer dollars. The dirty little secret of Bitcoin Libertarians is that their entire rebellion only works because the system they're rebelling against hasn't collapsed under the weight of their idealistic fantasies.

It's a clever dance of rebellion that only works as long as the state they despise doesn't vanish entirely. After all, someone still needs to maintain the infrastructure for their libertarian paradise. Let's say the state really did pack up and disappear overnight. What then? Will they crowdsource road repairs via Bitcoin donations? *"Donate 0.05 BTC to fix the pothole outside your house, or face the consequences![14] "* will become the new mantra of community action.

Tech Bro Paradise: Libertarianism and Silicon Valley's Love Affair

Now, let's talk about **Silicon Valley**, the Libertarian Mecca where everyone's convinced that the market can solve all of

---

14. Spoiler: that road's never getting fixed.

humanity's problems—except, of course, when it doesn't. The tech bro class has adopted Libertarian ideals with the enthusiasm of a start-up founder discovering microdosing. In their world, the government is too slow, too clumsy, too...well, human. But technology? *Technology* can save us all! Self-driving cars, algorithms, and cryptocurrencies are the answers to everything, and regulation is just the annoying hurdle that prevents *disruption*.

For the Silicon Valley elite, Libertarianism is perfect because it validates their belief that innovation is the new religion, and they're the high priests[15] . They envision a world where entrepreneurs—read: themselves—are freed from the meddling hands of bureaucrats, where markets are left to do their thing without the dull thud of government regulation interfering with progress. In this tech bro utopia, everyone is a winner if they just innovate hard enough. Your startup failed? No worries—bootstraps are provided at the door.

But there's a catch. These tech bros, just like their Bitcoin-loving Libertarian cousins, still rely on that dreadful thing called public infrastructure. They may dream of floating cities and Mars colonies, but until Elon[16] finally gets his act together, they're still stuck here, using the roads, hospitals, and public services provided by the very governments they claim to despise. Their companies thrive because of state-funded research, education, and, yes, regulations that keep society functional.

And here's where the Libertarian fantasy collides with reality: for all their talk of innovation and freedom, the Silicon Valley Libertarians conveniently forget that their tech empires were built on the back of public investment.

---

15. And we've already learnt what happens when you base your system of governance on religion – even if it is a belief in AI being a benevolent overlord (it is not).

16. AKA: Cissy Spacek, Space Karen, Elmo Husk.

In the end, the tech bro Libertarians and the Bitcoin Libertarians are fighting the same fight: a battle for *"freedom"* that overlooks the fact that society runs on cooperation, not competition. While they're busy disrupting industries and all tweeting exactly the same thing about decentralisation, the rest of us are left wondering how they plan to fix the potholes when their brave new world finally arrives. Perhaps they'll invent an app for that, but I wouldn't bet my Bitcoin on it.

A Moment of (Reluctant[17]) Praise: What Libertarianism Gets Right (Sort Of)

Now, before I consign Libertarianism *entirely* to the dustbin of political absurdities, it's only fair to admit that not every idea it puts forward is entirely without merit[18]. Despite its self-defeating obsession with dismantling the state, there are a few aspects of Libertarian thought that, in moderation, are worth paying attention to—if only to remind us that not all government intervention is automatically a good thing.

At its core, Libertarianism champions personal freedom and autonomy. The belief that individuals should have control over their own lives, without excessive interference from the state, resonates with many who have experienced the heavy hand of government overreach. The desire for privacy, for example, is a valid concern in an age where surveillance seems to be everywhere—from your phone to your fridge. Libertarians are often at the forefront of debates about privacy rights, arguing that the state (and the corporations that feed off it) should not have unchecked access to our personal information. It's a good reminder that freedom from control, in certain contexts, is something worth fighting for.

---

17. *Very* reluctant.

18. I was genuinely going to end the chapter there, but a certain husband noted that a bit of balance would be good.

Then there's the matter of economic freedom. Sure, Libertarians may take it too far, imagining a world where the market solves all problems, but their scepticism of bloated government bureaucracies isn't completely off the mark. When government grows too big, it *can* become sluggish, unresponsive, and prone to inefficiency. In certain sectors, particularly in innovation and technology, too much red tape can stifle progress. Libertarian critiques here can serve as a check against overregulation that kills creativity and entrepreneurship.

And let's not forget non-interventionism. Ron Paul's brand of Libertarianism was built on the idea that government should stay out of not only our wallets but also the business of other nations. The push for isolationism may seem extreme, but the core idea of restraint in foreign policy—of not meddling in the affairs of other countries at every turn—is one that many of us could support, especially after decades of costly and often disastrous military interventions abroad.

So, while Libertarianism often takes its principles to laughable extremes, there is a nugget of wisdom buried beneath the potholes. The desire for individual autonomy, for a government that isn't constantly overreaching, and for a foreign policy that's less trigger-happy are all worthy goals—if applied in moderation. The trick, of course, is balancing these ideas with the recognition that we still need a functional society. Libertarianism may offer some valuable lessons in how to keep the state in check, but it's no substitute for the complex web of cooperation and collective responsibility that actually makes modern life possible.

--Interlude Ends--

When Reality Collides with Libertarian Fantasy

The pub has quieted. It's well past closing time, and the dim glow of the remaining streetlights barely manages to keep the creeping shadows of decay at bay. Outside, the roads have deteriorated into a patchwork of craters, flickering lights casting uneven shadows over the asphalt. The hum of the city has dulled, replaced by the unsettling sound of silence and distant rumblings of a society coming undone.

Inside, Ayn Rand sits rigidly, cigarette long burnt out but still clutched between her fingers like a badge of stubborn pride. Across from her, Keynes swirls the dregs of his pint, his earlier amusement now giving way to a more profound exasperation laced with pity.

"Well, Ayn," Keynes says, leaning back into his chair, his voice carrying a heavy dose of irony, "here we are. The roads are falling apart, the hospitals are barely functional, and even the streetlights seem like they're on their last leg. Your Libertarian utopia's not looking too sharp."

Rand doesn't look at him, her gaze fixed somewhere far beyond the pub's window. "Nonsense," she replies, her voice steely. "This is all part of the natural order. The weak systems are being purged. What remains will be stronger. Innovators will rise. The market always corrects itself."

Keynes chuckles, a sound filled with disbelief. "Innovators? Really? I'm watching people trip over potholes big enough to swallow cars, Ayn. And what of your digital libertarians, your Bitcoin champions? Still trading their 'freedom' over government-funded internet, I see."

Rand turns toward him, an almost mischievous glint in her eyes. "Potholes are just part of the journey, John. They build resilience. And soon, people will monetise them. Private companies will jump in, and we'll have sponsored potholes, crowdsourced road repairs—total freedom. No need for your meddling government."

"Sponsored potholes?" Keynes shakes his head, genuinely incredulous. "Maybe we'll auction off sections of the sewer next.

Let's not pretend the market is going to fix anything, Ayn. The world you envision, where people 'innovate' through suffering, doesn't inspire genius—it inspires desperation. They're **surviving**, not thriving."

Rand leans in, her eyes gleaming with defiance. "Oh, they'll innovate. Private ambulance services are already stepping in where your so-called 'universal' healthcare has failed. Sure, it costs more, but why should everyone have access to the same services? If you can't afford it, you haven't worked hard enough. That's how the world should be."

Keynes arches an eyebrow, the faintest smirk on his face. "Ah yes, a world where only the wealthy survive past middle age. A true paradise. And the rest of us? We're just supposed to bootstrap our way through life, while your tech billionaires retreat to their bunkers, safe from the chaos they've helped create?"

Rand's smile grows wider, embracing the absurdity with unshaken conviction. "Exactly. It's a game, John. And those who aren't smart enough to play... well, that's their problem. Hospitals? Who needs them when we've got entrepreneurial spirit? Someone's probably working on a medical app for DIY surgeries as we speak. Pure freedom—no regulations, no red tape."

Keynes laughs, more out of disbelief than humour. "DIY surgery kits? That's your big solution? A future where the strong 'earn' the right to survive, and the rest are left to fend for themselves with a YouTube tutorial and a set of kitchen scissors?"

Rand shrugs, nonchalant. "Why not? If you can't figure out how to stitch yourself up, maybe you don't deserve to be driving—or surviving. It's called personal responsibility, John."

Keynes sighs, shaking his head. "You really do sound like one of those internet trolls, Ayn. The kind that insists everyone can make it if they just 'try harder,' while conveniently ignoring the fact that not everyone has a private island to trade Bitcoin from.

But tell me, when all the roads have crumbled and the hospitals are gone, who's going to be left to pick up the pieces?"

Rand, ever defiant, stands up, brushing imaginary dust from her sleeve. "The strong will be left. And they'll build something far better than this society you cling to. Who needs roads when you can fly over them in privately-owned drones, built by the free market?"

Keynes raises his pint in a mock toast, a tired grin spreading across his face. "Ah yes, Ayn. When the drones come, I'm sure everything will be just fine. Until then, though, I'll be here, filling in the potholes and funding hospitals with boring old taxes. Because, in the end, even the strongest individualist can't build a bridge alone."

Rand gives him one final, resolute glance before turning on her heel. "I don't need anyone, John. The future belongs to those who take it, not those who wait for handouts.[19]" And with that, she strides out of the pub, her back straight, as though the cracks forming beneath her feet are nothing but illusions.

The Libertarian Endgame

And so, the Libertarian dream marches on—fuelled by defiance and denial, much like Ayn Rand herself. Even as the world around her crumbles, Rand insists that the market will fix everything, clinging to the fantasy that freedom without responsibility is the ultimate solution. It's a philosophy that works best when nothing's actually broken, when society is running smoothly, and the roads are freshly paved.

---

19. Despite her lifelong disdain for government programs, in 1976 she enrolled in Social Security and Medicare—with the help of a social worker. Turns out, those "chains of government" feel pretty comfortable when you need them.

But when the cracks start to show—when the potholes grow, the hospitals close, and the infrastructure falls apart—it turns out we all need a little cooperation. Even the most rugged individualist eventually runs out of Bitcoin to spend when there's no one left to fix the bridges. And while Ayn Rand may walk away from the wreckage, convinced she's proven her point, the rest of us are left to patch up the holes—with our taxes, our neighbours, and the very collective efforts Libertarians seem so eager to dismiss.

Because at the end of the day, even the strongest individual can't build a society on stubbornness alone.

Technocracy

The Engineers Have Taken Over

"Technocrats live their lives abstractly, even while
they are managing their own sphere. For them, all
problems are intellectual."

George Friedman

L et's make up an image of our minds of the Technocrat.
They're the straight-A student who not only reminded the
teacher about the homework, but also provided an annotated
bibliography—just for fun[1]. They've never missed a deadline,
never failed a test, and probably organised their class notes using colour-coded tabs. Fast forward a few decades, and now
they're running your country. Not because the public found
them charming or inspiring (please, that's so inefficient[2]), but
because they were *"the most qualified."* In a world of bumbling
politicians getting stuck on ziplines and getting lost in a room
with one entrance, the Technocrat is out there with their trusty
Excel spreadsheet, running the numbers, optimising society like
a particularly complex financial model.

---

1. Considering the number of footnotes and the fact that there is a bibliography and a glossary attached to this book, I'm not in any position
whatsoever to judge.

2. Also, very unlikely.

They don't do emotional speeches. They don't do handshakes or public rallies. They do PowerPoint presentations with bullet points and bar graphs. The Technocrat is the ultimate pragmatist, the one who treats society like a machine to be tinkered with, improved, and, if necessary, rebooted. They're the political equivalent of your company's IT guy—constantly muttering that *"if people would just stop touching things, this system would run perfectly."*

I have to admit, if I were ever to go into politics (don't worry, I won't), this is *exactly* the ideology I'd follow. I am, after all, Spreadsheet-Guy. I live my life on Excel. My idea of a productive afternoon is running statistical analyses and making sure every data point is colour-coded for maximum efficiency. There's something comforting about it—about the neat, orderly world of data, where every problem has a solution, as long as you just *run the numbers* one more time.

But, as my husband is always so fond of pointing out, there's a little thing called *thinking like a human being* that doesn't always align with the joys of spreadsheet life. He likes to remind me, often with a raised eyebrow, that there's more to the world than graphs, data sets, and mathematical precision. There are feelings, emotions, and irrationalities. People—annoyingly—don't fit neatly into rows and columns.

Now, this is where Technocracy hits its first real snag. The appeal is obvious, right? Who *wouldn't* want the experts in charge? Surely things would go more smoothly if we put the nerds—the logical, data-driven problem solvers—in control of everything. No more political grandstanding. No more emotional speeches about *"the will of the people."* Just good, clean, efficient governance, led by people who actually know what they're doing.

But here's the thing. As much as I love a good graph, humans aren't graphs. They're not even *pie charts*, and trust me, I've tried to make that analogy work. The more you try to cram people into data sets, the more they resist. People have this annoying habit of not behaving like variables in an equation. They have emotions, they make irrational decisions, and they don't always choose the most efficient option. In fact, they rarely do. Just try creating a spreadsheet that predicts human behaviour and see how long it takes for the whole thing to devolve into chaos.

Now, imagine the Technocrat stepping into power. They've got all the data. They've run the numbers, consulted the experts, and have a plan. They're going to streamline the economy, reduce inefficiencies, and optimise public services. Everything's going to run like a finely tuned machine. And for a while, maybe it does. Decisions are made based on cold, hard facts. Budgets are balanced. Infrastructure projects are rolled out with military precision. Society hums along like a well-oiled machine.

But then, something happens that wasn't on the spreadsheet. People—those damned, unpredictable creatures—start to complain. Maybe it's because the new data-driven healthcare system has reduced their wait times, but also cut out those *"inefficient"* human doctors who actually listen to their patients. Maybe it's because the algorithm deciding who gets public housing doesn't quite account for the messy reality of human lives, like trauma, family connections, or—dare I say it—empathy.

You see, while Technocracy is brilliant in theory (and honestly, who wouldn't prefer a well-organised, data-driven government to the usual mess of populist politics?), it's not foolproof. At some point, you have to take off the Excel goggles and realise that humans don't fit neatly into models. They defy categorisation. They reject optimisation. And they sure as hell don't like being reduced to numbers.

Now, I'm not saying we should ditch technocratic thinking entirely. Far from it. I'm still firmly in the camp that believes the experts should be making the big decisions—climate policy, public health, economic planning. Let's leave that to the professionals, not the politicians whose idea of expertise is shouting the loudest on Twitter. But technocracy, like my love for a well-formatted spreadsheet, has its limits. You can't always govern from the data *alone*.

It's a tough pill for a data nerd like me to swallow. I want to believe that everything can be solved with the right model, the right algorithm, the right formula. I *want* to believe that if you just analyse enough numbers, you'll find the answer. But then my husband, ever the realist, reminds me that not everything is a numbers game. Sometimes, you have to think like a human. You have to consider the emotional, the irrational, and the downright illogical.

This is where Technocracy needs a reality check. As much as I want to hand the world over to the experts and let them fix everything with data and reason, I also know that people don't live their lives in a bubble of rationality. They're messy, emotional, contradictory beings who don't always do what's best for them. And that's okay. Sometimes, the most efficient solution isn't the best one. Sometimes, what we need is a bit of chaos, a bit of unpredictability. We need to *feel* like we're part of something bigger than just a well-run machine.

So yes, while I love a good graph and can happily spend hours tweaking a spreadsheet until it's perfect, I also know that governance requires more than just data. It requires humanity. It requires leaders who can step away from the numbers and see the people behind them. Because, in the end, no matter how much we want to optimise society, people aren't just variables. They're the reason we need to get it right.

The Technocrats of the 1930s: The Best and Brightest, Solving the Depression... or Trying To

Let's throw ourselves back to the 1930s[3] —a time of mass unemployment, breadlines, and governments flailing about like toddlers trying to manage an economic crisis they barely understood. Capitalism was in freefall, socialism was gaining traction in the streets, and democracy? Well, it looked like it might keel over at any moment, coughing up its last, pitiful breath. Enter the technocrats—the straight-A students of society who stared at this mess with a mixture of pity and superiority. The world, they thought, didn't need these emotional, ideological politicians flailing about. No, what the world needed was scientists with calculators, engineers with slide rules, and experts who could solve all the problems if everyone would just *shut up* and let them do their thing.

Their grand plan? To run society like the before-mentioned well-oiled machine—literally. The technocrats envisioned a world where every decision, every process, every moment of daily life could be optimised and quantified. Everything would be measured, from the energy output of factories to the calories people consumed. They believed they could plan society down to the last kilowatt of energy, carefully balancing supply and demand as if the world were one big engineering problem to be solved. And why wouldn't it work? After all, chemical reactions are predictable, mathematical equations always balance out, and engines always run perfectly—assuming no one touches anything, of course.

If humans had the predictability of a steam engine, this plan might have been brilliant. Unfortunately, people are not steam engines. They are notoriously difficult to optimise, and they

---

3. Don't worry, this is the last time I'm going to be shoving you into a Time Machine.

do irritating things like *having emotions*[4] and making irrational
decisions. But the technocrats of the 1930s had faith in their
methods. They truly believed that by removing messy things
like politics and ideology from governance, they could create
a society where everything ran smoothly, efficiently, and, most
importantly, under the benevolent guidance of experts who
knew better.

The irony, of course, is that while technocrats believed they
could plan society to the last detail, society wasn't particularly
interested in being planned. People didn't want to be reduced
to numbers on a spreadsheet, and they certainly didn't want to
live in a world where every aspect of their lives was subject to
cold, calculated efficiency. The technocrats' dream of a perfectly
planned society never took off—not because their math was
wrong, but because their understanding of human nature was.
It turns out that people enjoy a bit of chaos, unpredictability,
and the occasional emotional decision.

But the technocrats weren't completely defeated. They may
have failed to solve the Great Depression, but they left behind a
legacy—a belief that experts, not politicians, should be running
the show. And as the world plunged into World War II and
emerged battered and broken, the technocrats would find a new
stage for their expertise.

Post-WWII Technocrats: Rockets, Economic
Planning, and Government by Slide Rule

If the technocrats of the 1930s were a bit ahead of their time,
the post-World War II era was their moment to shine. The world
was rebuilding from the ashes of war, and who better to lead the
way than the experts? This was the golden age of technocratic
thinking. Governments around the world realised that perhaps
letting scientists and engineers take the lead *wasn't* such a bad

---

4. Which is the worst!

idea—at least when it came to things like space exploration, economic planning, and grand public works projects.

The United States had NASA and the Apollo Program—a shining example of technocracy at its best. This wasn't about ideology; it was about getting to the moon before the Soviets. And who could argue with that? Technocrats designed the rockets, ran the numbers, and, in 1969, put a man on the moon. It was a triumph of science, engineering, and the belief that experts could achieve the impossible if only you gave them enough resources and didn't ask too many questions.

Meanwhile, in the Soviet Union, technocrats were running the show in their own way. Five-year plans, centrally managed economies, and the cold, logical precision of scientific socialism. The Soviet technocrats believed they could control not just space exploration, but entire economies. They planned production quotas, allocated resources, and optimised agriculture. And, in theory, it was brilliant. On paper, everything worked perfectly. In reality? Well, let's just say the Soviet citizens didn't always appreciate being part of a grand technocratic experiment. Human desire doesn't fit neatly into production quotas, and breadlines have a way of souring people's enthusiasm for scientific planning.

But the technocrats didn't just stop at space exploration and economic planning. They were quietly running the show from the back rooms, planning cities, managing economies, and generally being the people who made sure everything functioned. This was the era of government by slide rule. And in many ways, they were at their best when they stayed in their lane—designing rockets, building infrastructure, mapping out economic growth. They were good at solving problems that could be solved with data, logic, and a bit of technical know-how.

The problem, as always, came when they tried to apply their methods to *people*. You can plan for production quotas, but you can't plan for human desire. People are unpredictable. They don't always choose the most efficient option, and they don't always behave in ways that make sense on a spreadsheet. The technocrats learned the hard way that society doesn't always follow the most efficient path. People like things messy, and no amount of scientific planning can change that.

Still, the post-war technocrats left their mark. They proved that experts could do incredible things—build rockets, rebuild economies, and, in some cases, run entire countries. But they also learned that human society is not a machine to be fixed. It's a living, breathing organism, and sometimes, even the best-laid plans can fall apart when confronted with the irrationality of the human heart.

The Rise of the Expert Class: From Climate Change to Economic Policy

Fast forward to the 21st century[5], and technocratic thinking is alive, well, and powering your local government algorithm. Whether it's climate change, economic policy, or public health, we've seen the rise of the expert class—the firm belief that those with technical knowledge should be the ones steering the ship. And honestly, on paper, it's hard to argue against. Who wouldn't want scientists running the show when it comes to climate change? Economists handling the economy? Doctors overseeing public health?

There's an undeniable appeal to handing the reins over to the people who, well, actually know what they're talking about. Surely, it's better to let people with degrees in the relevant subjects make the big decisions, rather than leaving it in the hands of career politicians who seem to get by on charisma alone. This is the dream of technocracy in action: informed, data-driven decision-making that cuts through political nonsense and gets to the facts.

---

5. Okay, *that* was the last time you get shoved into the Time Machine.

But, as we're learning, the shiniest graph can't solve everything.

The Sunak Problem: When Technocrats Forget to Be Human

Take Rishi Sunak, the UK's former Prime Minister, for example. Sunak was the poster boy for technocratic governance. As Chancellor of the Exchequer, he was lauded as the numbers guy—a data-driven technocrat who could crunch figures with the best of them. He had a reputation for being smart, efficient, and meticulous—exactly what you'd expect from a leader who spent his career navigating spreadsheets and financial forecasts.

Sunak seemed to have all the hallmarks of a successful technocrat: clear-headed in a crisis, able to handle economic turmoil with the precision of a surgeon wielding a scalpel. His policies were technically brilliant, at least on paper. If anyone was going to lead the UK through a financial storm, surely it would be Sunak, right?

Wrong.

Because, despite his technical brilliance, Sunak's leadership faltered when it came to one glaring problem: people. While he was busy solving the UK's financial woes like an equation in a ledger, the human element—those damned, irrational beings—were left in the cold. Sunak's reliance on data and technocratic solutions left him appearing cold, robotic, and, at times, shockingly out of touch with the real-world frustrations of ordinary citizens.

Take his handling of the **cost-of-living crisis**. From a purely technocratic perspective, Sunak's policies did make sense—he adjusted taxes, balanced the books, and made sure the numbers all added up. But in the process, he forgot that people aren't data points. His policies might have looked great on a spreadsheet, but they lacked empathy, leaving millions of Britons struggling to heat their homes and put food on the table.

It was a classic technocratic failure: Sunak made decisions based on logic and numbers, without considering the emotional toll those decisions would have on the public. He failed to connect with people, to show that he understood their struggles[6]. For Sunak, it was all about *"efficiency"*—a buzzword that might make sense in an office, but is of little comfort to a family facing skyrocketing energy bills.

And that's where technocracy often falls short. It's efficient, yes. It's rational. Very. But it forgets that humans aren't just variables in a financial model. They have fears, frustrations, and emotions that don't always conform to what the data says they should feel. Sunak's economic models couldn't account for the very real fact that, in times of crisis, people need more than balanced budgets—they need hope, and they need to feel heard.

The Brilliant Technocrats: When Expertise Meets Humanity

Now, it would be unfair to suggest that all technocrats fall into the same trap as Sunak. In fact, some of the most successful leaders in history have been technocrats who understood that data is only half the equation.

Take Mario Draghi, for instance. As the former head of the European Central Bank and later Italy's Prime Minister, Draghi proved that technocratic leadership can excel when balanced with political acumen. Known for his decisive role in saving the euro during the European debt crisis, Draghi was more than just a numbers guy. While his policies were driven by data and financial expertise, he understood the importance of reassuring the public, building trust, and making difficult decisions with empathy for how they would affect ordinary citizens. His leadership showed that technocracy can be effective when it's not

---

6. Aside from those who had the horror of growing up without Sky of course – bless his out of touch cotton socks.

just cold, calculated logic, but also deeply attuned to the human consequences of policy decisions.

Or look at Lee Kuan Yew, the founding Prime Minister of Singapore. A master technocrat, Lee managed to transform Singapore from a struggling former colony into one of the most prosperous and well-governed nations in the world. Lee was all about efficiency, governance by experts, and long-term planning—but he never lost sight of the fact that his citizens weren't just passive recipients of his policies. He understood the importance of social harmony, of making people feel like they were part of something greater, even if that "something greater" was being planned down to the last detail by a team of technocrats.

The difference between a Draghi or a Lee and a Sunak is clear: successful technocrats know that spreadsheets, while important, don't tell the whole story. You can have the most logical policies in the world, but if you fail to connect with people—if you can't show them that you understand their lives beyond the numbers—you'll lose them[7]. It's the human element that makes technocracy work, and without it, all the algorithms in the world won't save you.

AI and Data in Governance: Are We Getting Closer to Technocratic Rule?

If you think technocracy has reached its peak, oh boy. We are now in the era of big data and artificial intelligence, and the technocrats are more powerful—and more data-driven—than ever. From healthcare to law enforcement, algorithms are increasingly making decisions that were once the domain of human judgment. AI can predict crime patterns, determine creditworthiness, and even decide who gets access to healthcare. To

---

7. And you're going to especially lose them if you come across as a malfunctioning tetchy robot that keeps repeating *"The plan is working, we've turned a corner, the plan is working, we've turned a corner the-plan-is-working-we've-turned..."*

a technocrat, this is the ultimate dream: removing human bias, emotion, and that inconvenient thing called *"the human factor"* from the equation. Why trust fallible human beings when cold, hard data can drive decisions? It's efficiency on steroids.

Now, I have to confess—there's a part of me that *loves* this. I'm not immune to the seductive allure of data and AI. When it comes to healthcare diagnostics, for example, I am fully on board with the idea of artificial intelligence helping to detect diseases more accurately and quickly than a human ever could. We can all admit—machines are brilliant at spotting patterns in data. Imagine a world where AI systems, fed by millions of medical cases, can diagnose cancer or heart disease with near-perfect accuracy. It's a technocrat's paradise, and honestly, it's a dream I would happily live in.

But—and this is where my love of spreadsheets needs to take a backseat—I also know that no machine, no matter how sophisticated, should be trusted to make life-and-death decisions on its own. AI in healthcare diagnostics? Great, as long as there's a *qualified doctor* or healthcare professional in the driver's seat. The AI should be the passenger, not the pilot. It can assist, but ultimately, a human needs to be the one making the final call. Someone with compassion, experience, and the ability to understand the messy, unpredictable nuances of human life that no algorithm can ever fully capture.

It's the same principle when AI is applied to governance, particularly in areas like social support and welfare. The idea of using AI to assess who gets welfare assistance may sound efficient, but this in particular terrifies me. Why? Because AI, for all its brilliance, doesn't have *empathy*. It doesn't understand what it's like to live in poverty, to struggle with mental health, or to face systemic inequalities. It sees numbers, not people[8] . And when AI is fed biased data—which, let's face it, most of our societal

---

8. Because AI *is* numbers, not people.

data is—it simply reinforces the very inequalities we're trying to address.

Take predictive policing, for example—an AI-driven system used in law enforcement to predict where crimes are likely to occur. On paper, it sounds like a great idea. The AI looks at historical crime data, analyses patterns, and predicts future hotspots. It's efficient, logical, and seemingly objective—exactly what a technocrat would love. But here's the problem: the data is already biased. Historical crime data reflects systemic inequalities, including over-policing in certain communities, particularly those of colour. So, when the AI crunches the numbers, it doesn't remove the bias—it *amplifies* it. The system ends up disproportionately targeting already marginalised communities because the algorithm is doing exactly what it was programmed to do: following the data.

This is where the technocratic dream starts to look rapidly more like a dystopia. In the quest for efficiency, technocrats risk creating a world where humans are reduced to data points, where morality and empathy are outsourced to machines, and where we lose sight of the very people we're supposed to be helping. The AI-driven systems may be efficient, but they often miss the bigger picture. Efficiency and fairness aren't the same thing.

Take AI in credit assessments, another classic technocratic move. The idea is simple: let AI analyse your financial data, your spending habits, and your payment history to determine if you're creditworthy. Efficient, right? Sure, but again, the data is often biased. What about people who don't have a long credit history because they've been systematically excluded from the financial system? Or those who've fallen on hard times due to circumstances the algorithm can't understand—like a medical crisis or sudden unemployment? Or a migrant who has just moved into the country? To the AI, these people are just numbers that don't add up. The technocrat might argue that the data doesn't lie, but it's only as good as the systems—and the society—that produced it.

And that's the crux of the problem. Data may be objective, but the systems that generate it, and the people who interpret it, are not. We can't pretend that AI is a perfect solution just because it spits out results that look rational and unbiased. AI reflects the world it's built from, and that world, unfortunately, is far from perfect. Without human oversight—without someone who understands the deeper context—AI can reinforce existing inequalities, not fix them.

This is where I find myself torn. I love the idea of AI-driven healthcare. I'd love to see artificial intelligence help us solve complex, technical problems with precision. But when it comes to the human side of governance—when it comes to deciding who deserves welfare, who gets credit, or who should be policed—AI falls painfully short. These are decisions that require empathy, understanding, and nuance. No algorithm can calculate that.

So while the rise of AI in governance may seem like the technocratic dream come true, we need to tread carefully. Because behind every data point is a person. And if we forget that, we risk creating a world where efficiency reigns supreme but humanity is left behind.

A Tempered Technocracy: Balancing Expertise with Humanity

Now, as you may have noticed throughout this chapter—I'm a fan of technocracy, at least in principle. Give me a room full of scientists, engineers, and economists making decisions about climate policy, public health, and economic planning over populist politicians any day. I trust the data-driven, peer-reviewed rigor of the experts far more than I trust the politician who thinks a gut feeling or a catchy soundbite is a valid policy-making tool.

Technocracy, at its core, is about letting people who know what they're doing take charge. It's about using logic, data, and expertise to solve society's most complex problems. And honestly, who wouldn't want that? In a world increasingly dominated by crises that can't be solved by charisma or ideology alone, we need the experts more than ever. Climate change doesn't care about your feelings, and an economic recession won't be solved by a rousing speech. Data, reason, and technical skill are vital to navigating these challenges.

But here's the catch: expertise, while absolutely necessary, isn't *everything*. Technocracy needs to be tempered with something more human. We need leaders who can read a spreadsheet, yes, but we also need leaders who can read a room. People aren't just numbers in an algorithm. They aren't neat little variables in a model, waiting to be solved by the right equation. They have emotions, desires, and frustrations that don't fit neatly into a data set, and they certainly don't behave in ways that always make logical sense.

Take the allure of AI governance, for example. Like I said, I'm the first to admit that I *love* the idea of artificial intelligence in healthcare diagnostics. Let the algorithms sift through the data, detect patterns, and diagnose diseases faster and more accurately than any human could. It's brilliant—*as long as* there's a doctor, a human being with the capacity for empathy, guiding the process. AI can't understand the emotional weight of a cancer diagnosis, or the need to explain things in a way that a frightened patient can grasp. It's a tool, not the solution.

But when we start applying the same AI-driven efficiency to areas like social support or welfare, things get trickier. There's something unsettling about the idea of an algorithm deciding who deserves help and who doesn't. The efficiency might be appealing, but it risks stripping away the very thing that makes society work: humanity. An algorithm can't understand the nuance of someone's personal struggles. It can't grasp systemic inequality or account for the emotional toll of poverty. It sees numbers, not lives.

The best technocrats, the ones who really make a difference, understand this. They know that data alone can't run a society. They know that people aren't perfect little pieces of a grand social puzzle to be moved around for optimal results. Yes, the data is vital—it's our compass in a world of chaos—but you still need a human to steer the ship. Because people aren't a problem to be fixed; they're a reality to be lived with, in all their messy, irrational glory.

This is where technocracy needs to evolve. We need experts to guide us through the challenges of the modern world, but we also need those experts to recognise the limits of their own methods. Data can inform decisions, but it can't *make* decisions. Algorithms can assist, but they can't *understand*. In the end, society is not a machine to be repaired with logic and precision. It's a living, breathing organism, full of contradictions, emotions, and experiences that no spreadsheet can ever fully capture.

It's a lesson that technocrats like Rishi Sunak never quite grasped. His cold, data-driven approach to the cost-of-living crisis may have made sense on paper, but it didn't connect with the people who were actually living through it. His policies lacked the one thing that can't be quantified: heart. And without that, no amount of efficiency is going to make a government work.

On the other hand, leaders like Angela Merkel and Lee Kuan Yew knew the value of combining technical expertise with a deep understanding of the human condition. Merkel, with her scientific background, understood the data but never lost sight of the people behind it. Lee transformed Singapore into a technocratic wonder, but he also knew that governing was about more than just efficiency—it was about building a society that people felt part of, even if the plan was being crafted behind the scenes by experts.

So, while technocracy offers clear, rational solutions to complex problems, it can also leave humanity behind if it's not careful.

Expertise is essential, yes, but so is empathy. We need technocrats who can step outside the data and see the world as it is—messy, emotional, and filled with people who don't always make sense.

In the end, the dream of technocracy—of a world governed by those who understand it best—is only half the story. We do need experts to guide us through an increasingly complex world. The problems we face today—climate change, global pandemics, economic instability—can't be solved by intuition alone. We need the scientists, the engineers, the economists to lead the way. But we also need leaders who can navigate the messy terrain of human experience.

Because society isn't a machine to be fixed. It's a living, breathing organism. It doesn't run smoothly, and it never will. The machines may be efficient, the data may be perfect, but at the end of the day, it's the people who matter. And if we forget that—if we lose sight of the humanity behind the numbers—we'll find ourselves living in a world that runs like clockwork, but where no one wants to live.

In a world where the technocrats have taken over, the smartest thing we can do is remember that the goal isn't just to build a perfectly efficient system. The goal is to build a society that actually works—for everyone.

Environmentalism/Green olitics

The Planet Is Melting, Karen!

> "Why should we tolerate a diet of weak poisons, a home in insipid surroundings, a circle of acquaintances who are not quite our enemies, the noise of motors with just enough relief to prevent insanity? Who would want to live in a world which is just not quite fatal?"
>
> Rachel Carson

We've all met a Green Politics Karen. She shows up clutching her reusable tote bag, wearing bamboo socks, and sipping kombucha from a stainless steel thermos. Your cheeky Friday night takeaway isn't just a poor choice—it's an environmental crime. Plastic containers, carbon footprints, and the audacity to enjoy yourself without guilt? Outrageous. Karen, of course, is vegan (except for that organic bacon last weekend, but it's artisanal, so it doesn't count).

Karen's life is a mix of earnest intent and eco-hypocrisy. Monday to Friday, she bikes to work, sips oat milk lattes, and lectures on recycling. By the weekend, she's in her diesel Range Rover, heading to an eco-friendly Airbnb in the Cotswolds, calculating how many trees she'll need to plant to offset her emissions. The perfect symbol of performative Green Politics.

Karen means well—she really does. She wants to save the planet. But in her quest for carbon-neutral perfection, she forgets that living sustainably takes more than obsessing over trends or fitting all your waste into a mason jar. Like much of today's environmental movement, she's lost in personal guilt and token gestures, missing the bigger picture: without systemic change, we're all just farting against thunder.

My Thoughts on Environmentalism: Doing What I Can, When I Can... Except for Meat

Let me start by saying I'm an environmentalist—at least, I try to be. I recycle, I use energy-efficient light bulbs, and I do what I can to reduce my carbon footprint. But, and I must stress this, while personal changes are great, if we don't see sweeping global reforms, our efforts are the worst kinds of farting against thunder. I'll sort my rubbish, carry my reusable bag[1] , and proudly show off my bamboo toothbrush, but I'm also excruciatingly aware that it's not going to make much of a dent if entire industries and governments don't change their ways. It's like trying to bail out the Titanic with a teaspoon. It might make *you* feel good, but you're still going down with the ship.

Then, there's the meat issue. Yes, the carbon footprint is massive, and cutting meat is often touted as a top individual action. But let me confess: I'm South African. Meat isn't just food; it's a cultural staple. We braai[2] like it's a national sport, and to me, chicken is practically a vegetable. So, while I'll make changes where I can—sorry, Karen, the braai stays.

---

1. It's a Waitrose one with long handles so I can wear it like a handbag.

2. It's like a Barbecue, just less burning of meat and actual cooking of food.

In my view, environmentalism needs to make room for realism. Not everyone is going to give up meat, not everyone can afford to go zero-waste, and not everyone is in a position to overhaul their entire lifestyle in the name of sustainability. It's the system that needs changing. We can all make small contributions, and yes, they add up—but without international cooperation, corporate responsibility, and large-scale policy shifts, we're essentially rearranging deck chairs on the climate Costa Concordia.

History in Brief: From Early Conservation to the Green Party

Now, let's take a step back—way back to the days before hashtags and virtue-signalling via Instagram stories, when saving the planet was less about getting *"likes"* and more about making sure rivers didn't catch fire. Yes, I'm looking at you, Cuyahoga River[3] . This was an era when the word *"environmentalist"* wasn't automatically accompanied by side-eye and sarcasm. Back then, the big environmental battles weren't about plastic straws, but rather about very tangible threats, like the fact that we were poisoning ourselves into extinction.

Environmentalism, as we know it, was really kickstarted in the 1960s with *Rachel Carson's* iconic book *Silent Spring*. Carson called out the widespread use of pesticides—especially DDT—and how they were quite literally turning the planet into one massive death trap. Carson wasn't worried about her Instagram footprint or going viral for her eco-conscious outfit; she was more concerned about birds falling out of the sky and fish floating belly-up in streams. She wrote her book like it was

---

3. *The Cuyahoga River, infamous for catching fire. Literally. Multiple times. Yes, an actual river, so polluted with industrial waste that it decided to join in on the combustion fun. It's the perfect symbol of unchecked pollution at its finest: when even water starts burning, maybe it's time to rethink a few things.*

a wake-up call, and boy, oh boy, did we hit the snooze button. Repeatedly.

But slowly, and I mean *slowly*, we started to pay attention. Environmentalism began branching out from the initial outrage over pesticides into broader conservation efforts. It was no longer just about saving the critters; it was about *us*. We couldn't keep treating the Earth like our personal rubbish bin without facing the consequences. So, the movement evolved—gradually shifting from protecting forests, wildlife, and rivers to protecting our own future. It wasn't exactly a seamless transition. People were still more interested in bulldozing nature to build shopping centres, but hey, at least they planted a tree afterwards, right?

Now, here's where it all gets a bit paradoxical. The original conservationists, the ones we like to picture as tree-hugging purists, were often the same people who spent weekends hunting or fishing in those very forests and rivers. It's hard to reconcile the image of a rugged outdoorsman in khakis standing over his fresh kill with the fact that he might've donated to the Sierra Club the day before. These early environmentalists weren't eco-warriors chaining themselves to trees—they were more likely to shoot a deer and then have a spirited debate about the merits of protecting natural habitats. For them, loving nature didn't necessarily mean not exploiting it. They loved it pragmatically; it was about preserving the beauty and functionality of nature so that it could be used, not just observed. They were the original *"have your cake and eat it too"* environmentalists, and if we're being honest, a lot of us still live in this contradiction today.

But even with this paradox at its heart, early environmentalism sparked something—an awareness that maybe we were screwing things up on a scale that we couldn't fix with a few tree plantings and a recycling bin.

Fast forward to the 1970s. The world had finally woken up from its post-WWII industrial boom hangover. The oil crises of the 1970s made people realise that maybe endless consumption of fossil fuels wasn't the most sustainable lifestyle. The air was thick with pollution, and rivers were still catching fire (really, it took a while to sort that out). By now, environmentalism had grown from a handful of concerned biologists and outdoor enthusiasts into something of a political force. It wasn't enough just to get a book on the bestseller list or to throw the occasional protest—if the planet was going to be saved, it was going to require some political muscle.

Enter the Green Party. No longer content to sit on the sidelines, the environmentalists decided it was time to crash the political scene. And where better to do it than in Europe, where a love of intellectual debate and bureaucracy are national pastimes? The Green Party emerged in the late 1970s and early 1980s, bringing environmental issues front and centre in the political discourse. In Germany, for instance, the Green Party became a legitimate political player by the 1980s, forcing mainstream parties to at least pretend they cared about the fact that glaciers were melting faster than Karen's resolve when she spots a designer handbag on sale.

The Greens were ambitious. They weren't just about saving trees or getting plastic bags banned; they were out to fundamentally transform society's relationship with the planet. To their credit, they achieved a lot. They dragged climate change from the dusty corner of scientific journals and thrust it onto the political stage. Environmental protection was no longer a fringe concern—it was a key part of national debates. And if you think Greta Thunberg is shaking things up today, imagine what it was like for the staid, suit-wearing politicians of the 1980s to suddenly face a political movement that talked about composting like it was a national emergency.

But as always, politics is a game of compromise, and the Greens were no exception. The idealistic dreams of saving the world through radical environmental policies quickly ran into the reality of parliamentary committees, bureaucratic red tape, and the occasional stubborn farmer who didn't see the point of composting. It's not easy being green when you're stuck in debates about which plastic can go in the recycling bin or whether you can use nuclear energy without feeling like a complete hypocrite.

As the Green Party grew, they had to navigate the treacherous waters of political compromise. Sure, they got people talking about environmental issues, but they also had to make deals with mainstream parties to get anything done. And that meant watering down their ideals—just a bit. Suddenly, saving the planet was a matter of strategy. You can't exactly dismantle capitalism in a day, especially when you're trying to pass a bill that mandates solar panels on government buildings. So, they played the game, trading radicalism for practicality, ideals for incremental progress. It wasn't sexy, but it worked. Sort of.

The truth is, the Greens accomplished more than their critics like to admit. They made environmentalism mainstream. They forced everyone to pay attention. And in an era where no one was talking about the future of the planet beyond where the next oil rig would go, that was a monumental achievement. But their story is also a reminder that the road to saving the planet is long, full of potholes, and often involves spending an absurd amount of time stuck in parliamentary committees debating the merits of biodegradable coffee cups. Still, someone's got to do it—because no matter how much we recycle or cut down on single-use plastics, if governments don't get their act together on a global scale, we're basically just farting against thunder.

Modern Green Politics: From Activism to Green-washing

Welcome to the age of climate anxiety, where every summer feels hotter than the last[4], and polar bears have become the unofficial mascots of impending doom. We're living in a time where the planet is clearly in trouble, and no matter how much we recycle or reuse our shopping bags, there's a persistent sense that it's just not enough. In recent years, we've seen a revival of environmentalism, largely driven by grassroots movements like *Extinction Rebellion, Just Stop Oil* and *Fridays for Future*. These movements have gone beyond the polite letter-writing campaigns of the past and have thrown environmentalism right into the streets, sometimes quite literally.

There's no denying the impact these movements have had, especially among younger generations. Led by figures like *Greta Thunberg*, they've put the climate crisis front and centre, forcing governments, corporations, and your neighbour with the diesel SUV to at least acknowledge that the planet is warming at an alarming rate. They've inspired millions to take action, whether it's protesting, organising climate strikes, or at least trying to have an awkward conversation with their parents about why they should think twice before booking that third cruise of the year.

But while it's hard not to be impressed by their sheer tenacity and passion, let's also take a step back and be honest about matters for a moment. For every committed activist chaining themselves to a tree, there's a Karen who's swapped her plastic water bottle for a glass one and thinks she's solved climate change. *Weekend activism* is a booming industry. People love nothing

---

4. And this is a genuinely worrying and annoying thing – I moved from the Southern Hemisphere to get away from the heat, now I'm finding myself sweating half to death on packed tubes wishing for unconsciousness in the middle of July while travelling to work. You might not be able to tell, but I am *annoyed*.

more than attending protests, painting their faces with slogans, and posting carefully curated photos on Instagram with hashtags like #ThereIsNoPlanetB. And come Monday morning? They're back to shopping on Amazon, commuting in their petrol-guzzling cars, and planning their next overseas getaway. It's the perfect combination of eco-guilt and eco-convenience.

This isn't to dismiss those who genuinely want to make a difference, but it does raise the question: is *performative activism* helping the planet, or is it just making people feel better about themselves[5] without actually contributing to the systemic change we desperately need? It's the classic case of doing just enough to feel good about yourself without really changing anything. And I can't help but be a little cynical when someone proudly declares they've *"gone zero-waste"*... except, of course, for their weekly Starbucks run, complete with plastic-lined coffee cups that won't biodegrade until the next ice age.

And therein lies the problem. Climate activism is critical—there's no doubt about that—but it *has* to be more than just a hashtag or a weekend protest. We're dealing with a global crisis that can't be fixed with individual actions alone. Don't get me wrong, I will keep doing what I can (when I can), but unless we see changes on a *global scale*, we're all essentially just *farting against thunder*. And while personal actions matter, they're a drop in the ocean when compared to the massive systemic shifts that are needed. The planet isn't going to be saved by your bamboo underwear or your reusable coffee cup (though, hey, every little bit helps); it's going to take governments and corporations stepping up in a big way—and right now, most of them are too busy greenwashing to be of much use.

But who should change?

---

5. And at the same time, giving them the ammunition to make you feel like an awful human being for even *thinking* about a delicious, delicious kebab.

Now let's talk about the real heroes of modern Green Politics—oh, no, wait, I mean villains—corporations. If you thought weekend activists were good at making it look like they're saving the planet, you've clearly never met a corporation in the 21st century. Welcome to the era of *corporate greenwashing*, where slapping an eco-friendly label on something is basically the new marketing strategy. Forget about actually reducing carbon footprints or addressing pollution—just brand yourself as *"sustainable,"* and watch your profits soar.

Walk into any store, and you're bombarded with labels: *"sustainable," "carbon-neutral," "ethically sourced."* From bottled water to fast fashion, consumers are convinced they're saving the planet, one overpriced tote bag at a time. The reality? These labels are usually just marketing ploys to make people feel better about their consumption.

Take *BP*, for example. The oil giant has recently rebranded itself as a leader in green energy, because apparently, if you put the word *"green"* in front of something, it erases decades of environmental destruction. Never mind that they're still making billions[6] off fossil fuels; they've got hastily slapped a wind turbine on their logo, so now they're *totally* on your side[7] . Or look at fast fashion brands that release *"sustainable"* collections while continuing to churn out mountains of cheap, disposable clothing made by underpaid workers in environmentally harmful factories. Nothing says *"green"* quite like a shirt that will fall apart after two washes, right?

And don't even get me started on airlines. They've come up with perhaps the greatest con of all: carbon offsetting. Fly across the world guilt-free because for a small fee, they'll plant a tree on your behalf. Never mind that it'll take decades for that tree

---

6. Upon billions, upon billions...

7. If you haven't watched it, please put this book down RIGHT now and put on *Joe Lycett vs the Oil Giant*. Trust me.

to absorb the carbon you spewed into the atmosphere in one flight, and by that time, the world might be underwater. But hey, at least they're trying, right? This is corporate greenwashing at its finest—giving consumers the illusion that they're part of the solution, while quietly continuing to be a major part of the problem.

The sad reality is that many mainstream political parties have bought into this charade. Desperate to appeal to environmentally-conscious voters, they're more than happy to embrace these corporate-driven narratives of sustainability, without addressing the core issues. We end up with policies that promote "eco-friendly" initiatives while still approving new fossil fuel projects or turning a blind eye to the industries wreaking havoc on the environment. It's like putting a band-aid on a gaping wound and calling it healthcare.

Greenwashing has become such a pervasive part of modern Green Politics that it's easy to get lost in the noise. For every genuine step forward, there's a corporation out there trying to profit off the crisis they helped create. The challenge we face now is cutting through the eco-fluff and focusing on real, systemic change. Because as much as I love the idea of *"sustainable"* shopping, we can't shop our way out of climate change. The planet doesn't care how many trees corporations promise to plant if they keep drilling for oil and pouring toxins into our rivers.

So, the next time you see a product proudly claiming to be *"carbon-neutral,"* ask yourself: is this really helping the planet, or is it just helping someone's bottom line? Because we can't afford to be lulled into complacency by clever marketing strategies when the stakes are this high. Climate change isn't something we can solve with tote bags and branded water bottles—it's going to take a fundamental shift in how we live, how we consume, and most importantly, how we hold corporations accountable.

A Realistic (and Slightly Cynical) Look at Environmentalism

Let's be honest—nobody likes a hypocrite. Yet, for some reason, Green Politics seems to attract them like moths to an LED bulb. Maybe it's the allure of being seen as righteous while secretly indulging in the very habits you publicly shame. It's like the modern version of *do as I say, not as I do*—except instead of Victorian moralising, it's *"use a metal straw while flying first class to a climate summit."* The contradictions are everywhere.

There's the politician who makes sweeping promises about reducing emissions, only to jet off to Davos in a private plane, spewing more carbon into the atmosphere in a few hours than the average person will in a year. Then, of course, there's Karen who we've already mentioned, our lovable Green Politics mascot, who carries her reusable tote bag with pride while her Amazon delivery history reads like a small novel. And don't get me started on influencers. The same folks who post about sustainable fashion while wearing clothes shipped halfway across the world from factories that have a carbon footprint larger than most small countries.

Here's the thing: we're all guilty of a little eco-hypocrisy. I'm certainly not throwing stones from my glass house—yes, I recycle, I try to cut down on plastic, but I'm also human. I buy things online. I travel. The problem is when people start pretending that these contradictions don't exist, or worse, that their small gestures make them an eco-saint.

The hypocrisy isn't just limited to individuals, either. It's baked into the very fabric of modern Green Politics. Politicians stand up and preach sustainability, they smile for the cameras as they hug a tree or ride a bike to work for *exactly* one day of the year, but then they go right back to pushing through infrastructure projects that bulldoze forests or approving oil drilling permits because, well, money. It's easy to talk about reducing emissions when the cameras are rolling, but when it comes down to the fine print of policy? Suddenly, the *"eco-friendly"* rhetoric vanishes, and pragmatism—better known as profit—takes centre stage.

This is why, for many, the environmental movement feels more like a marketing campaign than a genuine revolution. There's a sense that everyone is performing their version of *"going green"* rather than actually making systemic changes. The recycled plastic ad campaigns, the half-hearted promises from politicians, the influencers who fly to a tropical island to talk about coral bleaching—*it's all optics*. At its worst, Green Politics can feel like an elaborate charade, where the appearance of doing something is more important than actually doing anything. And yet, we play along, don't we? After all, it's easier to believe the myth that we can consume our way out of a climate crisis than face the reality that what's really needed is far more radical, and far more uncomfortable, than buying eco-friendly products.

Meat Eaters vs. The Green Police: A Braai and a Quinoa Showdown

Now, let's talk about the *real* controversy in Green Politics already mentioned: *meat*. Specifically, the near-religious fervour around going vegan to save the planet. Look, I get it. The environmental cost of the meat industry is enormous. Cows are farting methane like it's going out of style, and industrial farming is a resource-guzzling nightmare.

You can take away a lot of things from me in the name of sustainability, but I draw the line at my braai. And if we're being really honest here, there are entire cultures around the world where meat is deeply embedded in the way of life. Asking everyone to give it up in the name of saving the planet is not only unrealistic but, frankly, a bit arrogant.

But here's the thing—just because I love a good steak doesn't mean I'm oblivious to the environmental cost. I know the meat industry is one of the worst offenders when it comes to environmental destruction. It's bad—*really bad*. But the conversation around diet and environmentalism has become so polarised, so black-and-white, that there's no room for nuance anymore. It's turned into a kind of morality contest, where you either give up all animal products and saintly ascend to environmental heaven in the hands of bright green angels, or you're the scourge of the Earth, selfishly munching on a burger while glaciers melt.

The truth, as always, is somewhere in the middle. Maybe we can reduce meat consumption without turning the entire world into a quinoa-fuelled morality contest. There's a middle ground here—one that acknowledges the cultural significance of food while also recognising the need for more sustainable practices. Maybe it's about supporting sustainable farming, eating less meat but better quality, and focusing on practices that don't ravage the land. Perhaps it's about choosing local, ethically sourced options, or simply cutting down where we can. You know, baby steps[8].

The environmental movement loves to simplify things into easy binaries, but life—and eating habits—are far more complicated than that. The reality is, most people aren't going to go fully vegan. Not now, not ever. And while a vegan diet can be a great way to reduce your environmental footprint, it's not the only way. We need to make space for discussions about moderation, about changing our consumption habits without turning it into a self-righteous competition. Because, believe it or not, you can still care about the planet without giving up your Sunday roast.

In the end, environmentalism shouldn't be about moralising—it should be about finding practical, workable solutions that fit into the reality of human culture. The world is a big place, with billions of people living vastly different lives. The

---

8. I have started considering chicken not to be a vegetable similar to broccoli.

answer to saving the planet can't be one-size-fits-all. We need to be flexible, realistic, and yes, even a little bit cynical. Because if the only option on the table is an all-or-nothing approach, we'll never get anywhere.

So, Are We Doomed?

So, where does that leave us? Are we destined to sit on our sinking ship, playing *"eco-friendly"* violins while the planet melts around us? Can Green Politics save us from the looming climate catastrophe, or are we already too far gone, sliding headlong into an apocalyptic future where the polar bears are long gone, and Karen's reusable tote bags litter the streets like some kind of tragic irony?

Here's the truth: while there are plenty of genuine efforts being made—by activists, politicians, and even a few corporations—the waters of Green Politics are murky. For every meaningful action, there's a wave of noise, hypocrisy, and a truckload of greenwashing. And yet, despite all the attempts to market environmentalism as something you can buy in a shop, the planet is still warming, and no number of eco-friendly product labels is going to reverse that. We are, as it turns out, in quite a bit of trouble.

Yes, the planet is, indeed, melting. It's a slow burn in some places and a fast one in others, but make no mistake—we're in it *deep*. And no number of recycled straws, bamboo toothbrushes, or Tesla cars is going to change that unless we start addressing the bigger, scarier, and more uncomfortable systemic issues that got us here in the first place. The inconvenient truth[9] is that personal responsibility is all well and good, but without a global-scale overhaul of how we live, consume, and govern, all our efforts are going to be as effective as crochet condom.

---

9. To borrow a phrase from Al Gore.

Now, don't get me wrong, I do care. I care about the planet, and I will keep doing what I can. But I'm also a realist. We can all make small changes, and those do matter, but they're not going to fix everything. If we think saving the world is as simple as driving a hybrid and buying second-hand clothes, we're kidding ourselves. The real work requires governments to get serious, corporations to stop playing PR games, and for all of us to realise that systemic change isn't going to be easy or convenient. It's going to require some real, tangible action—and yes, it's going to involve compromise.

Because, let's face it: Karen's reusable bag isn't going to save the world, but neither is cynicism. Somewhere between the Instagram activism and the climate denialism is a middle ground where real change can happen. It's not glamorous, and it's not going to make anyone feel morally superior, but it's necessary. We need to hold governments accountable, demand better from corporations, and, perhaps most importantly, be willing to rethink how we live on this planet. And sometimes that means looking in the mirror and asking if we're really doing enough, or if we're just part of the noise.

So yes, Karen, keep your reusable bags. Keep trying. Just maybe take a moment to step back and ask if you're focusing on the right fight. The planet needs more than symbolic gestures and performative activism—it needs real action. And that's going to take more than a tote bag. It's going to take systemic change, political will, and yes, maybe even a bit of sacrifice from all of us. Because while we're not doomed yet, if we don't start making some serious moves soon, we might just be headed there faster than we think—and one of those moves could just be taking the Green Party in the UK slightly more seriously.

#IdeologyWars

The Final Showdown

It's been a chaotic mess for years, with the world's greatest ideologies battling it out on Twitter. After all the back-and-forth, one might think things have settled. Not so much.

@NeolibForLife (Milton Friedman) Just deregulate everything, let the markets work their magic We don't need government interference, we need growth! #FreeMarkets #InvisibleHand

@RedsForReal (Karl Marx) The only thing that "invisible hand" has been doing is stealing from the working class! The system's rigged! #WorkersUnite #ClassStruggle

@LiveFree (Ayn Rand) Oh please, more government control? How about you let people actually live their lives without bureaucrats breathing down their necks? #SelfInterestFirst #FreedomIsSelfish

@EcoRevolution (Greta Thunberg) You're all missing the real issue—while you bicker, the planet's burning. Climate action is the only thing that matters. #NoPlanetB #ClimateCrisis

@IronFistFascism (Benito Mussolini) What the world needs is strength None of this market or rights soy-boy nonsense, just strong leadership to bring order! #StrengthThroughUnity #StateAboveAll

@ComradeLenin (Vladimir Lenin) Strength? Please. The real power lies with the people Revolution is the only way forward. #PowerToThePeople #ClassWar

@FriedRich (Friedrich Hayek) Can we just agree central planning destroys freedom? Markets know best #EconomicFreedom #IndividualChoice

The digital shouting match continues, until the thread suddenly goes quiet. A new handle appears in the conversation, unfamiliar yet commanding attention with a simple tweet:

@EquitismRising (Equitism) Okay, stop. Enough with the ideological noise. You've all had your turns, but clearly none of you have the full picture. It's time for something better. #TimeForChange

The ideologues fall silent, collectively blinking in disbelief.

NeolibForLife (Milton Friedman) What's your point? The market will solve everything, just give it time. #Patience

@EquitismRising (Equitism) The market? Right. It's worked out *great*—for the billionaires. Meanwhile, inequality is through the roof, and we're all stuck fighting over scraps. It's not working, Cupcake. #WakeUpCall

@RedsForReal (Karl Marx) FINALLY *someone* gets it. Welcome to the revolution, comrade. #ClassStruggle

@EquitismRising (Equitism) Hold on there. You're not exactly off the hook either *@RedsForReal* Centralised control? That's turned into bureaucratic nightmares more times than we can count. Workers want power, not another layer of red tape. #Balance

@LiveFree (Ayn Rand) Oh, this should be good. Go on, tell us how you're going to fix it with more government handouts #EyeRoll

EquitismRising (Equitism) Handouts? No. But freedom is useless if people are starving. Give them the basics, then let them thrive. It's called equity, Ayn. You should look it up sometime. #BasicsBeforeFreedom

@EcoRevolution (Greta Thunberg) What about the planet? You all seem very focused on people, but we won't have anyone left if the Earth collapses. #ClimateCrisis

@EquitismRising (Equitism) Don't worry, I haven't forgotten. Saving the planet is top priority, *but* we can't do that without saving people too. No point in having a green Earth if no one's around to live on it. #Sustainability

@IronFistFascism (Benito Mussolini) This is all weak cucking. People want strength They want order. You're just rearranging the deck chairs on the Titanic. #WeaknessIsFailure

@EquitismRising (Equitism) Order doesn't mean oppression, Benito. People want dignity, equality—not to be crushed under someone's boot. They want a system where they have a say. #PowerToThePeople #DemocracyMatters

The thread quiets down again as @EquitismRising's messages start gaining retweets. Even the loudest voices seem unsure of what to say.

@NeolibForLife (Milton Friedman) So what's your big solution? Sounds like you're just picking and choosing from all of us

@EquitismRising (Equitism) Exactly. You've all got some good ideas (except @IronFistFascism, you can pop off), but none of you can solve the whole problem on your own. The future isn't about one ideology. It's about combining what works—equity, freedom, sustainability, and yes, a bit of market innovation where it makes sense. #BalancedFuture

The timeline pauses. Even @ComradeLenin seems stumped.

@EquitismRising (Equitism) Look, we can keep shouting into the void, or we can start building something that works for everyone. Your choice. But it's time to stop pretending anyone has all the answers. #BuildTheFuture #TimeForAction

And with that, the thread ends. Silence, for once, falls across Twitter.

Introducing Equitism

Equitism—the love child of ideologies, but raised right. Where each ideology stumbles, Equitism picks up the slack. It isn't about clinging to outdated doctrines or trying to force-fit society into a rigid, one-size-fits-all solution. Equitism is fluid, adaptable, and refuses to be boxed in by past mistakes. It's not afraid to take the best ideas from each system, cut the bullshit, and build a future that actually works. After all, look where all the other -isms have got us: wealth inequality is at an all-time high, climate change is looming like a bad hangover, and democracy is one more scandal away from checking itself into rehab. The world doesn't need another ideological debate—it needs action. And that's where Equitism comes in.

Core Principles of Equitism

Equitism isn't here to declare itself the ultimate -ism like it's competing in some ideological Olympics. No, it's the sensible hybrid—an adaptable, pragmatic approach that picks up where the others left off, blending idealism with real-world practicality. Think of it as a middle child of ideologies, taking the best traits from its siblings without the family drama.

Here's how it works:

Radical Participatory Democracy:

Let's be honest—if democracy were a product, we'd be asking for a refund. Voting once every few years while politicians parade their promises, only to break them faster than a New Year's resolution, feels more like theatre than empowerment. Equitism understands that democracy needs more than a facelift—it needs a full reboot. We need a system where people are constantly engaged, not just as passive voters, but as active participants in governance.

Under Equitism, you won't need to become a full-time politician (don't worry, no one wants that). Instead, through digital platforms, local assemblies, and regular feedback loops, you get a real say—more than a *"like"* on a tweet or a clickbait poll. Imagine real-time referendums on important issues, community-driven decision-making, and yes, perhaps even the occasional meme war to hold leaders accountable.

Governance is not a dusty book of rules but a dynamic process that adapts with the people. This isn't Technocracy's sterile rule-by-numbers approach, nor is it Liberalism's laissez-faire "let them sort it out" mantra. Equitism combines the best of Socialism's collective engagement with the efficiency of modern tech, creating a truly participatory system where your voice matters—without the frustration of waiting for an election cycle to roll around.

Economic Democracy:

Then, the economy—the perpetual tug-of-war between *"let the market decide"* and *"let the government control everything."* Equitism, however, doesn't pick sides in this tired debate. Instead, it hands the power to the people who actually keep the wheels turning: the workers. You know, the ones who do the work while some CEO makes more in a day than they will in a year.

In Equitism's world, worker co-ops, employee-owned business-es, and profit-sharing models are the norm. That's right—no more hoarding wealth at the top while the rest get the scraps. If you're busting your backside day in, day out, you deserve more than just a *"thank you"* email during Employee Appreciation Week. You get *ownership*. You get *profits*. And you get to help make decisions that impact your workplace.

This doesn't mean suffocating innovation with bureaucracy. Libertarianism would argue that too much regulation stifles creativity and growth. Equitism takes that into account, blend-ing Neoliberalism's desire for innovation and entrepreneurial freedom with Socialism's emphasis on fairness and collective ownership. The result? A thriving economy where wealth isn't hoarded by the few, but fairly distributed among those who generate it.

Imagine a world where corporate overlords no longer hoard wealth like Smaug, where Jeff Bezos is just the guy who packs your box himself, and where the term *"minimum wage"* be-comes obsolete because every worker shares in the success of the enterprise.

Sustainable Humanism:

Look, let's not pussyfoot around this—economic growth is great, but growth at all costs is as smart as buying a pet tiger because it's cute (until it eats your face). The planet isn't a bot-tomless pit of resources, and acting like it is will only lead us to an environmental apocalypse that even Netflix can't glamorise.

Equitism brings sustainability to the forefront, making it a *non-negotiable* pillar of society. This isn't just about recycling your tin cans or feeling morally superior about your metal straws. Equitism insists that everything—economics, industry, policy—must be built on the foundation of sustainability. Pic-ture a Green New Deal on steroids, where renewable energy isn't an alternative, but the backbone of global energy policy.

Where circular economies mean that waste becomes fuel for the next cycle, and where sustainable agriculture ensures that we don't turn our soil into dust faster than we can say "climate crisis."

Here, Environmentalism isn't some afterthought tacked onto the end of economic debates—it's at the very core of the conversation. Neoliberalism's obsession with GDP growth for the sake of growth is gently placed in the dustbin of history. Equitism balances human development with planetary limits—a feat no single ideology has quite mastered, despite decades of trying.

Social Equity and Justice:

Now, here's where Equitism steps in with a giant *"DUH"* to every system that has ever left the majority to fight for crumbs. Social equity and justice aren't optional, feel-good policies—they're the backbone of a functioning society. We've had quite enough of the trickle-down economics fairy tale, which is about as real as a Yeti driving a UFO.

Under Equitism, healthcare, education, and housing aren't privileges dangled in front of people to keep them working—these are fundamental human rights. Imagine a world where access to healthcare isn't determined by whether you can afford insurance, where education doesn't bankrupt you before you've even started your career, and where a roof over your head isn't a luxury but a given.

Yes, Socialism and Communism had some good ideas here, but where they fell into authoritarian traps, Equitism avoids the pitfall of turning rights into state-controlled commodities. This isn't also not about government handouts—it's about creating a system where Liberalism's individual freedoms can flourish because the basics are already covered. When people aren't worrying about survival, they can pursue happiness, innovation, and community-building without fear of falling through the cracks.

Technological Integration without Technocracy:

Here's the thing: technology is *the* double-edged sword of our time. Technocracy would have us believe that the world can be governed through data, algorithms, and predictive models. But if the last few years of algorithms messing up everything from elections to social media feeds have taught us anything, it's that we need human oversight, ethics, and empathy.

Equitism embraces technology, but only as a tool for transparency and efficiency—never as a replacement for human decision-making. Think blockchain voting for secure, transparent elections. AI for resource allocation that ensures fairness, not exploitation. Open data platforms where every citizen can see how their tax pounds are spent in real time.

But here's the catch: all of this is guided by human values, not cold, calculating algorithms. Unlike Technocracy, where we'd be at the mercy of the world's biggest nerds (and not the cool kind), Equitism keeps the final say in the hands of the people. Technology helps, but it doesn't rule.

This is democracy 2.0—where the system is smarter but not robotic. It's participatory government with brains, but also with heart.

Cultural Pluralism and Inclusivity:

Monocultures are cute for crops, but they're downright disastrous for societies. Equitism thrives on diversity[1], weaving it into the core of the system. Unlike Fascism and Theocracy, which attempt to enforce uniformity through fear, Equitism knows that cultural pluralism—a society that values different identities, faiths, and backgrounds—is its greatest strength.

---

1. Ignore what people like Suella Braverman, Nigel Farage or Robert Jenrick have to say.

Here, inclusivity isn't just window dressing for political correctness—it's foundational. Whether you're from a historically oppressed group, the global south, or the margins of society, Equitism ensures your rights and opportunities are not just protected but actively championed. Nationalism and xenophobia are seen for what they are: relics of an insecure past.

This isn't about some kumbaya, *"let's all get along"* idealism. It's about policy that ensures equality and fairness for all. When everyone's identity is respected, society isn't just peaceful—it's richer, smarter, and more innovative. That's not just Liberalism's freedom—Socialism's commitment to equality ensures that freedom is meaningful for everyone, not just the privileged few.

Global Cooperation over Corporate Globalisation:

As earthlings, we have to realise that we're in this mess together. Whether it's climate change, trade, or labour rights, these are global issues that can't be solved by competing for the biggest slice of the pie. Equitism recognises that international cooperation is the only way forward, and it promotes treaties and alliances that prioritize human and environmental well-being over corporate profits.

Unlike Neoliberalism, which left the world at the mercy of mega-corporations, Equitism champions a world where fair trade, sustainable development, and labour rights take centre stage. And while Libertarianism would have us believe that fewer restrictions equal freedom, Equitism ensures that freedom doesn't turn into exploitation. Global capitalism is seen for what it is—a vehicle for greed—replaced by global cooperation, where international challenges are met with solidarity, not self-interest.

In Equitism's world, corporate lobbying is a thing of the past. Instead, global agreements are reached with humanity and planetary survival in mind, not profit margins.

Why Equitism Could Actually Work

You're probably rolling your eyes right now[2], thinking, *"Great, another ideological reboot—haven't we heard this song before?"* History is littered with the carcasses of grand ideas that promised salvation but delivered little more than chaos, disillusionment, and perhaps a few overly verbose pamphlets. But Equitism is different. It's not some lofty, top-down theory proclaiming itself the ultimate solution. There are no sacred texts, no self-righteous prophets, and no blind allegiance to abstract principles. Equitism is practical. It's evolving. It responds to the needs of the moment without losing sight of long-term goals.

Here's why it has a real shot at working:

Flexibility Over Dogma:

In the world of political ideologies, dogma is like a bad Tinder date—you know it's not going to work out, but you're stuck paying for dinner anyway. Communism, Fascism, and even Neoliberalism have all fallen into the trap of rigid doctrines. They demand blind loyalty to a set of ideas that are often outdated or unworkable in a complex, ever-changing world. This insistence on ideological purity is why so many of them have failed to adapt to the times. It's like trying to fix a flat tire with a manifesto.

Equitism, on the other hand, has the flexibility of a yoga instructor[3]. It's not about sticking to one rigid script or pretending there's a one-size-fits-all answer to every problem. If a policy works, great! If it doesn't, you don't double down on failure—you adjust, refine, and move forward. Equitism is less

---

2. And believe me, I don't blame you – everyone also says they have the answer, but it very rarely works out that way, does it.

3. And hopefully only half as sanctimonious.

concerned with *"winning"* an ideological argument and more focused on solving real-world problems.

Think of it as a GPS for governance. You set your destination—let's say, a fair and just society—and along the way, you hit a traffic jam. A rigid ideology would keep you stuck in that jam, insisting it's the only way forward. Equitism? It recalculates the route. Maybe it suggests a different path that gets you there faster or smoother. It's not about doggedly following a single road—it's about getting to where we need to go in the most effective way possible.

And unlike Communism's utopian "end of history" or Fascism's iron grip on power, Equitism acknowledges that society's needs will change. What works today might not work in twenty years, and that's okay. Equitism is adaptable. It grows with society, evolves as new challenges emerge, and, crucially, it isn't afraid to admit when it's wrong. A bit of humility in politics? Radical, I know.

Checks and Balances:

Here's something the ideologies of the past always seem to miss: Power corrupts[4]. Left unchecked, power has an uncanny ability to morph into something toxic, whether it's in the hands of a king, a party, or a CEO. The problem with most ideologies is that they concentrate power in the hands of the few, often under the guise of the *"greater good."*

Equitism, however, takes a different approach. It acknowledges that power is necessary to run a society, but it also insists that power must be accountable—at every level. Whether it's the local councillor, a CEO, or the head of state, Equitism's commitment to transparency and continuous citizen engagement ensures that no one gets too comfortable on their throne.

---

4. This isn't a new revelation—Anarchism and Liberalism have been shouting it from the rooftops for years, and they're not wrong.

This is where Technocracy has a point—data can be incredibly useful for ensuring fairness and transparency. But instead of turning society over to algorithms and spreadsheets, Equitism keeps people at the centre of the decision-making process. It's people-powered, not algorithm-driven. Data is a tool, not a tyrant. Leaders are monitored and held accountable through open forums, digital platforms, and community feedback loops, ensuring they can't pull a fast one. Decisions are constantly scrutinised and re-evaluated based on real-world outcomes, not abstract theories or corporate lobbying.

Imagine a world where corruption isn't just something we roll our eyes at but a rare anomaly that's swiftly dealt with because the system is built to expose and eliminate it. Equitism puts the mechanisms in place to ensure power serves the people, not the other way around. And with the continuous participation of citizens, there's no time for complacency. It's governance on a short leash, not the long leash we're currently all too familiar with.

Pragmatic Idealism:

Now, before you start imagining Equitism as some pie-in-the-sky utopian dream, let's be clear: this isn't a fairy tale. There's no magic wand, no revolutionary overnight change. Equitism isn't here to sell you a fantasy where all problems vanish the moment we hit the reset button. Instead, Equitism offers something far more valuable—pragmatic idealism.

What does that mean? It means that Equitism is about bridging the gap between what we want and what we can realistically achieve. It's not pretending that we can suddenly eradicate inequality, fix the environment, or create a perfect society with the stroke of a pen[5]. That's the kind of nonsense that leads to dis-

---

5. And if anyone tells you that they can, look out for the bridge they'll try to sell you shortly thereafter.

appointment and disillusionment when the inevitable human flaws and systemic roadblocks rear their ugly heads.

Equitism isn't offering you a utopia; it's offering you a future where you don't feel like the system is rigged against you. It's about making real, incremental change that brings us closer to the ideals of fairness, justice, and sustainability—without pretending we'll get there overnight. We're not waiting for a glorious revolution to sweep us all off our feet. We're rolling up our sleeves, getting to work, and making the changes that can realistically happen in the here and now.

Think of it like climate action. No one's under the illusion that we can suddenly stop the planet from heating up tomorrow, but every step matters[6] —from reducing emissions to transitioning to renewable energy. Equitism applies that same mindset to governance. We don't need to wait for the perfect conditions to start improving things. We start now, with what we have, and keep pushing forward.

It's idealism grounded in reality. We know where we want to go, but we're not naïve enough to think we'll get there in one leap. It's about incremental, meaningful change—and knowing that every small victory brings us closer to a fairer, more just world. If we keep our eyes on the bigger picture but aren't afraid to get down in the trenches and make those small, necessary adjustments along the way, Equitism stands a real chance of succeeding where others have failed.

In a world that feels increasingly chaotic and polarized, Equitism offers a refreshing middle ground. It's not here to impose some grand, rigid structure on society. It's here to adapt, evolve, and respond to the needs of the people—at every moment. It balances the big ideas we need to tackle the most pressing global issues with the pragmatism necessary to get things done. Equitism isn't just another ideological reboot. It's the flexible,

---

6. Yes, even the stupid paper straws.

transparent, and accountable system we've been waiting for. And, quite frankly, it's about damned time.

Selling Equitism to the Rightfully Sceptical

After decades—no, centuries—of grand promises, political up-heavals, and revolutionary rhetoric, you're probably rolling your eyes so hard they're in danger of getting stuck. Everyone and their dog has come along offering a new system, a new way forward, only for us to end up back where we started—if not worse off. But here's the thing: Equitism isn't about utopia. We're not offering you some unreachable ideal with rainbow unicorns and eternal bliss. We're offering something that's far more realistic—and, dare we say it, much more needed: a system that *listens*. A system that adapts, that changes, and that actually serves the people instead of treating them like disposable cogs in a machine.

Imagine a world where your voice counts for more than a single vote every five years. Where your job isn't just a paycheque but a place where you're valued, a stakeholder in a collective future. A world where government isn't some distant, unreachable entity but a system that's continually checked by its citizens—by you. Where the economy isn't a casino designed for a handful of players, but something that works for everyone. And where the planet isn't just the backdrop to our politics but a living, breathing priority. No, Equitism isn't a utopia—but it's a damn sight better than watching the world burn while we argue over ideological scraps.

And if all that sounds too abstract, here's a more down-to-earth reality check: Equitism is about building systems that serve people. That means listening when the public speaks, adjusting when policies fail, and, most importantly, acting when action is needed. Because the reality is, the world doesn't need another endless debate—it needs a system that works for everyone. And Equitism might just be the best shot we've got.

Breaking Free from the Chains of the Status Quo

Here's the unvarnished truth: the current systems aren't just failing—they're pushing us headlong toward disaster[7] . If you look around, you'll see it everywhere: climate disasters looming on the horizon, extreme inequality, political disenfranchisement, and corporate control tightening like a noose around every public institution.

We can't keep fiddling while Rome burns. And Equitism? It's not about slapping a coat of paint on a sinking ship and calling it good. It's about building a new ship entirely—one that isn't hurtling with gay abandon toward the icebergs of environmental collapse, runaway inequality, and corporate hegemony. Because what we're doing now, the patchwork fixes and half-baked reforms is the ultimate version of rearranging deckchairs on the Titanic. Sure, it might *look* busy and proactive, but let's be honest: the ship is still going down.

But here's the hopeful part: we have the tools, the knowledge, and the collective will to change course. Equitism offers a way to steer us toward something better—a system that doesn't just prioritise the rich, the powerful, or the loudest voices. It prioritises us. All of us.

Yes, it'll be tough to break free from the chains of the status quo—change always is. But Equitism gives us the blueprint, the ship design, if you will, for a future that isn't just about survival, but about thriving. It's not about hoping for the best while continuing with the same broken systems—it's about building a foundation where we can tackle the real problems head-on.

---

7. And somehow it feels like they gain a little bit more momentum every day.

The Future of Equitism

So where do we go from here? Equitism isn't perfect. No system is. But it's infinitely better than the slow, painful slide into oblivion we're facing with the systems we have now. This is a blueprint for something better. For a world where justice isn't a marketing buzzword or a vague aspiration, but a reality we work toward every single day. Where the economy serves everyone, not just the privileged few. And where the planet—our only home—gets a fighting chance at survival.

Is change hard? Absolutely. No one's pretending this will be easy. But what's the alternative? More of the same? Tweaks around the edges while the core of the system rots? Incrementalism won't save us from the disasters looming ahead—environmental collapse, runaway inequality, the hollowing out of democracy. We need bold ideas and the courage to enact them.

And that's what Equitism dares to imagine—a future where we don't just make do with the least-worst option, but build something truly equitable, sustainable, and just. It's not about utopia—it's about setting realistic, achievable goals that lead us to a future we actually want to live in. Where governments are accountable, economies are fair, and people—all people—have a say in shaping their own destiny.

So, no pressure, humanity[8] —but it's time to roll up our sleeves and get to work. Equitism isn't the easy option, but it's the necessary one. After all, as the old saying goes, the definition of insanity is doing the same thing over and over again and expecting different results. Let's not be insane. Let's embrace Equitism.

Because the future? It's ours to shape.

---

8. I lie. There is pressure. A *lot* of pressure.

Appendix

The "-isms"

That Didn't Make The Cut.

Now, I know some of you are chomping at the bit for a deep dive into every political ideology under the sun, but let's be realistic: nobody's got time for a 1,000-page tome, and you didn't sign up for that kind of torture. Think of this as the ideological B-sides—just enough to make you sound clever at a dinner party, but not so much that you have to fake interest.

Absolutism: The political theory that suggests concentrating all power in the hands of a single ruler is a brilliant idea. Because history hasn't already given us enough examples of how absolute power leads to absolute headaches. Under absolutism, the monarch doesn't just rule; they practically own the concept of ruling. Why bother with the messy business of checks and balances when you can have one person making all the decisions? After all, who needs collective wisdom when you've got divine right—or at least a very fancy crown? It's all fun and games until the peasants start sharpening their guillotines.

Authoritarianism: The belief that society runs best when a single leader or small group holds all the power, because who needs things like free speech or democracy when you can have obedience? Under authoritarianism, dissent is squashed, and any form of criticism is treated as a personal insult to the all-powerful ruler. It's a system where "might makes right," and the populace is expected to do as they're told, no questions asked—unless, of course, you enjoy the inside of a prison cell.

Agrarianism: The nostalgic belief that farming is the purest form of human existence. Forget your smartphones and modern conveniences; real virtue is found behind a plough. Advocates long for a return to a simpler time, where communities were tight-knit, and everyone knew how to milk a cow. It's a charming idea until you realise that subsistence farming is backbreaking work, and there's a reason we invented tractors and supermarkets. Plus, let's not forget that moving back to the land en masse might be a bit tricky for the billions crammed into cities.

Capitalism: The economic system that tells you anyone can make it if they just pull themselves up by their bootstraps, ignoring the fact that some people don't even have boots. It's a game of Monopoly where a few players start with hotels on Mayfair and Park Lane, while the rest hope to avoid landing on Income Tax. Proponents argue that free markets lead to innovation and prosperity, and sure, they do—for a select few. Meanwhile, everyone else gets to enjoy the thrill of precarious employment and the gig economy. But remember, if you're not successful, it's definitely because you're not hustling hard enough.

Centrism: The political philosophy that insists the best solution is always found in the middle, even when the middle looks suspiciously like indecision. Centrists believe in moderation, compromise, and meeting halfway, often to the frustration of those who'd like a firm stance on, well, anything. It's a bit like being the Switzerland of politics—neutral, calm, and somehow never quite committing to one side or the other. Critics accuse centrists of being too cautious, while centrists call themselves pragmatists, navigating between extremes with a cup of tea in hand.

Corporatism: The ingenious idea that society should be organised by major interest groups, often led by corporations because they've shown such altruism in the past. Who better to guide public policy than entities whose primary goal is profit? It's like letting the fox guard the henhouse but arguing that the fox has valuable leadership skills. Under corporatism, the lines between government and business blur until you can't tell where one ends and the other begins. So next time you're frustrated with bureaucracy, just remember it could be worse—you could be dealing with McDonald's in charge of healthcare.

Egalitarianism: The radical idea that everyone should be treated equally, regardless of wealth, race, gender, or status. Egalitarians believe in levelling the playing field so that no one is held back by arbitrary distinctions. It's the belief that fairness and equality should be the cornerstones of society, which sounds lovely in theory but tends to send the privileged into a bit of a panic. Egalitarianism promotes a world where opportunities are shared, and success isn't determined by the circumstances of birth—though getting there is another matter entirely.

Elitism: The belief that society should be run by an exclusive, superior class—often those who already have money, education, or both—because apparently, they're the only ones smart enough to make decisions. Elitists hold that the 'best and brightest' (read: the richest and most privileged) should be in charge, dismissing the idea that the general public might know what's good for them. It's the worldview that sees the masses as a bit too messy for power, preferring the well-bred few to keep the world spinning.

Feminism: The audacious belief that women are entitled to the same rights and opportunities as men. Shocking, I know. Despite centuries of progress, feminists still have to point out that gender equality isn't a zero-sum game. It's not about women taking over the world—though, given the current state of affairs, maybe they should consider it. Instead, it's about levelling the playing field, which, apparently, is a controversial stance for those who prefer their hierarchies firmly intact. And yes, feminism also addresses intersectionality, recognising that race, class, and other factors complicate the quest for equality. But who has time for nuance when you can dismiss the whole movement with a sarcastic tweet?

Humanism: The belief that humans, using reason, empathy, and science, can solve their own problems without divine intervention. Humanism puts people first, trusting in logic and ethics to guide society, rather than relying on ancient doctrines or supernatural forces. It's about making the most of this life, focusing on human welfare, and encouraging kindness without needing the threat of eternal damnation. Critics say it lacks the comfort of an afterlife, but humanists are more concerned with improving the here and now—because, well, it's the only life we're sure we've got.

Imperialism: The idea that one country has the right—nay, the *duty*—to expand its power and influence over others, usually by force, and then act surprised when the locals aren't thrilled. Whether through military conquest, economic domination, or cultural imposition, imperialism is about one nation taking control of another, usually to extract resources or bask in the glow of self-righteous superiority. It's the belief that bigger is better, and that colonising half the globe is a perfectly reasonable way to spread 'civilisation,' as long as you're the one defining what 'civilisation' means. And yes, it rarely ends well for the colonised.

Monarchism: The belief that monarchy is the best form of government—because nothing says modern governance like hereditary rule. Monarchists hold that a royal family, by virtue of noble birth and a few genetic disorders, is uniquely qualified to lead a nation. Never mind that their primary activities often include attending ceremonial events and providing fodder for tabloids. And while some monarchies are constitutional, limiting royal power, the taxpayers still foot the bill for palaces and royal yachts. But think of the tourism revenue, they say, as if tourists wouldn't visit historic castles without a living monarchy attached.

Populism: The political approach that champions the "common people" against the "elite," at least in theory. In practice, it's often a convenient tool for ambitious leaders to gain power by tapping into public discontent. Populists excel at grand promises and vague solutions, pointing fingers at shadowy elites while sidestepping their own privileged status. They're the self-proclaimed voice of the people, even if they haven't waited in a queue or taken public transport in years. But hey, as long as they can stir up emotions and gather votes, who cares about consistency?

Progressivism: The belief that society can and should improve through reform, innovation, and government action. Progressives advocate for social justice, environmental protection, and equal rights—you know, all those annoying issues that require long-term thinking and empathy. Critics argue that progressivism leads to excessive government intervention and stifles individual freedom. Because apparently, the freedom to breathe clean air or earn a living wage is less important than the freedom of corporations to maximise profits. Progressives persist, pushing for policies that might make the world a bit more liveable, much to the chagrin of those who prefer the status quo.

Radicalism: The ideology that's all about drastic change—incremental improvements need not apply. Radicals believe the system is so broken that only a complete overhaul will do. Whether they're on the left or the right, they share a common impatience with the moderate middle. Why debate policy nuances when you can advocate for tearing down institutions altogether? Of course, the aftermath of such upheaval is often messy, but that's a problem for another day. For radicals, the cure for societal ills is a strong dose of revolution, side effects be damned.

Republicanism: The ideology that champions a government without monarchs, where the people—or at least their elected representatives—hold sovereignty. It's a lovely idea that aims for a balance between mob rule and autocracy. In theory, republicanism promotes civic virtue and the common good. In practice, it can devolve into partisan gridlock, where elected officials are more interested in scoring political points than governing. Still, it's preferable to absolute monarchy, unless you enjoy the idea of leadership determined by birth order and the whims of royal intermarriage.

Syncretism: The art of blending different beliefs and schools of thought into a cohesive whole—or a muddled mess, depending on your perspective. It's like a philosophical smoothie: throw in a bit of capitalism, a dash of socialism, and a sprinkle of anarchism, and hope it tastes good. Syncretists aim for harmony by reconciling conflicting ideas, which sounds noble until you realise that some ideologies mix about as well as oil and water. But who needs ideological purity when you can have a custom blend tailored to your own preferences?

Tribalism: The instinct to align fiercely with one's own group, often at the expense of others. It's the reason why football fans brawl and why comment sections are a nightmare. Tribalism reduces complex individuals to "us" and "them," making it easier to dismiss, dehumanise, or outright attack those who aren't part of your clan. In the modern world, it manifests in political polarisation, identity politics, and social media echo chambers. It's the ultimate barrier to understanding, ensuring that constructive dialogue is replaced with shouting matches and meme warfare.

Cast of Characters

Aquinas (Saint Thomas Aquinas) A medieval philosopher who tried to reconcile faith with reason, proving that even in the 13th century, people were overthinking things. His major work? Convincing the Church that thinking was, in fact, allowed.

Aristotle Ancient Greece's ultimate overachiever. He wrote on everything from biology to politics and remains the guy everyone pretends to have read when they want to sound clever.

Augustine (Saint Augustine of Hippo) The original sinner-turned-saint, Augustine spent his youth partying and later spent his life telling everyone else why they shouldn't. Classic case of "do as I say, not as I did."

Ayn Rand The queen of selfishness who convinced a generation that greed is good, under the guise of "objectivism." Her philosophy? Help yourself, and if others get trampled, well, that's Libertarianism for you.

Mikhail Bakunin A Russian anarchist who believed that governments were the problem and chaos was the solution. Think of him as the original punk rocker, minus the safety pins and mohawks.

Bob-Bunchanumbers from Twitter That random account with an egg avatar who argues politics online like it's his day job—often with the intellectual depth of a puddle and a love for conspiracy theories.

Edmund Burke The granddaddy of conservatism who believed that tradition was important and that changing things too quickly would make society fall apart. Basically, the guy yelling "slow down!" while everyone else runs for the future.

John Calvin The godfather of puritanical gloom who believed that most of us are destined for hell and that happiness was suspiciously sinful. His idea of a good time? Hard work and eternal damnation.

Cicero (Marcus Tullius Cicero) Ancient Rome's most famous lawyer, politician, and orator. Known for giving long speeches that no one dared interrupt—mostly because they were afraid he'd prosecute them for it.

Nigel Farage The man who made Brexit his life's mission, all while downing pints and pretending to be an ordinary bloke. Spoiler: he's not. Once claimed "independence," but left the rest of us with more paperwork.

Milton Friedman An economist who preached free markets and minimal government interference, conveniently ignoring the fact that real people can't live off theoretical graphs and invisible hands.

Friedrich Hayek Another free-market enthusiast who spent his life warning about the dangers of government control. His ideas helped spawn neoliberalism, making him the spiritual grandfather of austerity and deregulation enthusiasts everywhere.

Thomas Hobbes The philosopher who famously said life without government would be "nasty, brutish, and short," basically implying we'd all be beating each other with sticks if not for the state. He would've loved today's politicians—because they make his grim predictions look optimistic.

Boris Johnson The bumbling former UK Prime Minister who played the fool but knew exactly what he was doing—usually making a mess and leaving others to clean it up. The political equivalent of a tornado in a suit.

Keir Starmer The Prime Minister of the United Kingdom, known for being incredibly reasonable and therefore incredibly boring. He's got the charisma of a wet sock, but hey, at least he's not Boris.

Karen (Environmentalism Karen) Your self-righteous activist friend who screams at anyone using a plastic straw, yet somehow owns three cars and flies to Bali for yoga retreats. Her heart's in the right place, even if her carbon footprint isn't.

John Maynard Keynes The economist who suggested governments should actually spend money during a recession, which sounded so radical that only a global economic meltdown convinced people to listen. He's the guy you wish had been in charge in 2008.

Marine Le Pen France's far-right leader who's really into nationalism, border control, and making you afraid of immigrants. She's like the French version of that aunt who always tells you to lock the door and "watch out for foreigners."

Vladimir Lenin The man who took Marx's ideas, added a dash of revolution, and turned Russia into the world's first communist state. Didn't quite go as planned—unless mass purges were on the agenda all along.

John Locke The philosopher who argued that life, liberty, and property were natural rights, inspiring liberal democracies worldwide. He's basically the founding father of the "you can't tell me what to do" brigade.

Niccolò Machiavelli The guy who wrote *The Prince* and convinced centuries of politicians that being feared is better than being loved. He's the reason your boss keeps asking you to "be a team player" while plotting your downfall.

Karl Marx The bearded philosopher who declared that capitalism was doomed and a worker-led revolution was inevitable. He's still waiting for that revolution, while capitalism keeps chugging along, despite his best predictions.

Giorgia Meloni Italy's current Prime Minister, known for her far-right leanings and love of "traditional values." She's basically Mussolini 2.0 but without the military uniforms—so far.

Angela Merkel Germany's pragmatic former Chancellor who kept Europe stable while everyone else was losing their minds. The political equivalent of a sturdy, sensible pair of shoes—unexciting, but dependable.

Benito Mussolini Italy's original fascist dictator who made trains run on time but also plunged his country into chaos. Proof that punctuality isn't everything.

Viktor Orbán Hungary's Prime Minister who's turned his country into a textbook case of modern authoritarianism—complete with press crackdowns, anti-immigration rhetoric, and enough nationalism to make a flag-waver blush.

Pierre-Joseph Proudhon The French philosopher who famously declared, "Property is theft," which is probably why no one wanted to invite him to their estate for dinner. The original anarchist, but with a flair for economic theories.

Plato The ancient philosopher who imagined a world ruled by philosopher-kings, because, in his mind, only intellectuals knew what was best for everyone. Clearly, he hadn't met modern politicians yet. His *Republic* is a utopia you'd never want to live in.

Ronald Reagan The Hollywood actor turned U.S. president who cut taxes for the rich, deregulated everything, and smiled while telling you it was all for your benefit. A charming grandfather figure who left behind a neoliberal legacy that's still haunting us today.

Jean-Jacques Rousseau The philosopher who believed in the "noble savage" and that society corrupts people. He wanted us all to go back to nature, though he probably would've complained about the WiFi.

Joseph Stalin The Soviet leader who took Lenin's revolution and turned it into one of the most brutal regimes in history. Famously paranoid, he solved most of his problems by purging everyone around him. Who needs friends when you have secret police?

Rishi Sunak The UK's former Prime Minister who is so rich he can't quite figure out why everyone's so upset about the cost of living. Probably thinks "hardship" is when the WiFi is down at one of his many mansions.

Margaret Thatcher The "Iron Lady" who crushed unions, privatised public services, and declared that "there is no such thing as society." If you ever wondered who turned neoliberalism into a British religion, look no further.

Greta Thunberg The teenage climate activist who made grown men in suits very uncomfortable by simply telling them to stop destroying the planet. She's the conscience we desperately need, wrapped in a school uniform and some serious side-eye.

Leon Trotsky The revolutionary with a killer moustache[1] who co-led the Russian Revolution with Lenin, only to be exiled (and later assassinated) by Stalin. Proof that being right about communism doesn't mean you get to survive it.

Liz Truss The UK's Prime Minister for about five minutes, who somehow managed to crash the economy faster than most of us can make a cup of tea. Her leadership skills? Think of a train wreck, but with more tax cuts.

---

1. Grrrrr.

Glossary of Terms

A

Austerity: The government's favourite word when they want to cut public services and blame it on "fiscal responsibility." Essentially, it's starvation, but you're told it builds character.

Anarchy: The political equivalent of throwing all the rules out the window and hoping for the best. Usually leads to chaos, but at least you don't have to fill out forms.

Aristocracy: A group of people who inherited money and titles, convinced they're better than you because someone in their family tree won a battle 400 years ago.

Altruism: The quaint notion that humans can do something nice without expecting anything in return. Politicians like to claim it, but they usually want a knighthood.

Alienation: That lovely feeling of complete disconnection from society, typically caused by a toxic combination of capitalism, social media, and bad politicians.

Asylum: A place of refuge for those fleeing from war, persecution, or famine. Or, as governments like to treat it, a problem to be solved by building higher walls.

B

Brexit: The political equivalent of cutting off your nose to spite your face. A decision driven by nostalgia for an empire long gone, resulting in less money, more paperwork, and national regret.

Bureaucracy: A sprawling mess of forms, procedures, and departments designed to make sure nothing gets done quickly. Usually results in frustration, lost paperwork, and the sudden urge to scream.

Bourgeoisie: The middle class who think they've "made it" but are still terrified of losing it. Their biggest fear is that the working class might one day ask for a raise.

Budget: A government's promise to manage the nation's money, though somehow it always ends with cuts to health and education, but a lovely tax break for billionaires.

Big Government: The bogeyman of conservatives everywhere. It's what they call it when a government actually tries to do anything useful, like regulate banks or provide healthcare.

Balance of Power: A delicate political dance where various branches of government pretend to keep each other in check, but usually end up colluding behind closed doors.

C

Centrism: The art of standing in the middle of the road and pretending you're the sensible one while traffic barrels towards you. A favourite among people who fear commitment.

Communism: The political dream of equality that, when attempted, tends to collapse into totalitarianism. It's like trying to bake a perfect cake and accidentally setting the kitchen on fire.

Coup d'état: The dramatic moment when someone decides that elections are for losers and seizes power, usually with tanks and lots of shouting. Dictators love them.

Cronyism: The fine art of giving your mates jobs they're hopelessly unqualified for. A common practice among governments that talk about "meritocracy" but can't spell it.

D

Democracy: A system where you vote for people to make decisions, only for them to ignore you the minute they're elected. It's a nice idea, though, and occasionally works.

Dictatorship: A political system where one person calls all the shots and everyone else pretends to be thrilled about it. If you're not thrilled, there's a prison cell with your name on it.

Diplomacy: The art of pretending to be polite to countries you'd rather bomb. Involves a lot of handshakes, smiles, and backroom deals you'll never hear about.

Disinformation: A fancy word for lies, often spread by governments and corporations to confuse people. The internet made it easier, but to be fair, humans have been doing this forever.

Division of Labour: When society decides some people will do all the dirty, difficult jobs, while others sit in air-conditioned offices and make PowerPoint presentations about it.

Debt: The magical invention that keeps entire countries (and most of their citizens) in a constant state of financial anxiety. A tool for control, dressed up as a fact of life.

Detente: A temporary easing of tensions between countries that hate each other but are tired of all the shouting. Usually ends when someone says something stupid.

Deficit: What happens when governments spend more than they earn, which is always, because cutting billionaire tax loopholes would be too radical.

Decentralisation: A political buzzword that means spreading power around but often results in the same people in charge, just with different titles.

E

Economics: The science of making life harder for poor people while explaining why rich people need to get richer. Its complexity is directly proportional to its unfairness.

Equality: The ideal that everyone should be treated the same, no matter their race, gender, or background. Governments love to say they support it, but rarely do anything about it.

Elections: The one day every few years where you feel powerful as you cast your vote, only to realise a week later that nothing's changed except the names on the door.

Egalitarianism: The philosophy that people should have equal rights and opportunities. Sounds lovely on paper, but in practice, it's usually dismissed as "naive."

F

Freedom: The most overused political term in existence. It usually means the right to do what you want, as long as it doesn't upset the people in charge.

Foreign Aid: The practice of wealthy countries giving money to poorer ones, often with strings attached. A bit like giving a gift, but making them pay for shipping and handling.

Free Speech: The right to say whatever you want, until some-one important gets offended, at which point you'll quickly discover how "free" it really is.

Free Market: The economic fantasy that if businesses are left alone, everything will magically work out. What actually happens is a handful of monopolies form and everyone else suffers.

Franchise: The right to vote, which politicians like to pretend is an empowering act, even though your choices are usually between terrible and slightly less terrible.

G

Gentrification: The process of making a neighbourhood more expensive by kicking out the poor and moving in people who really enjoy artisanal bread. It's like urban colonisation, but with more yoga studios.

Globalisation: The interconnectedness of the world, where goods, services, and people flow freely, unless you're a migrant, in which case you're stopped at the border while corporations skip through without a passport.

Gerrymandering: A clever trick used by politicians to redraw electoral districts so they can win elections without getting more votes. It's democracy's equivalent of cheating on your homework.

Greenwashing: When companies pretend to care about the environment by slapping a green label on something deeply unsustainable. It's like painting a landfill green and calling it a park.

Gunboat Diplomacy: The charming practice of sending in warships when you don't get your way. Because nothing says "peaceful negotiation" like a few cannons aimed at your shores.

H

Hegemony: The dominance of one group over others, often disguised as "leadership" or "influence." Think of it as the political version of the cool kid at school who bullies everyone but still gets invited to all the parties.

Human Rights: The basic rights every human should have, unless you're inconvenient to the government, in which case you'll discover just how "optional" they are.

Hyperinflation: When a country prints so much money that it's worth less than toilet paper. Economists love to talk about it like it's an abstract concept, but you'll notice it when your bread costs £1,000.

House of Lords: A delightful relic of the UK's past where unelected aristocrats and life peers make decisions about your future. It's like giving your grandad control over your Spotify playlist and pretending it's still relevant.

Humanitarian Intervention: The noble-sounding reason governments give for invading another country. In theory, it's about helping people. In practice, it's usually about oil, power, or whatever they can get away with.

Habeas Corpus: Latin for "you shall have the body," which in legal terms means the right not to be thrown in jail without a trial. In political terms, it's a rule that gets ignored whenever inconvenient.

I

Ideology: A set of beliefs that people cling to despite overwhelming evidence that they're wrong. Politicians love to use ideology to justify terrible decisions, even when everyone else can see the train wreck coming.

Inflation: The gradual rise in prices that makes your money worth less, unless you're rich, in which case it's just another opportunity to buy property and pretend you're still "middle class."

Isolationism: The belief that your country should mind its own business and ignore the rest of the world. It works great until you realise your entire economy relies on imports.

Interventionism: The practice of stepping into other countries' affairs, usually uninvited. Often results in prolonged wars, economic disasters, and a lot of hand-wringing at the United Nations.

J

Justice: The noble concept of fairness that sounds great in theory but in practice is more like a lottery, where rich people buy the winning tickets and the rest of us end up with jury duty.

Jingoism: Over-the-top patriotism, usually involving flag-waving, chest-thumping, and the belief that your country can do no wrong. It's the political equivalent of singing karaoke after too many pints.

Judicial Review: The process by which courts check if the government is following the law, which is useful until the government decides to change the law to make everything they do legal.

Jargon: The language politicians and economists use to make simple problems sound impossibly complicated. It's designed to make you feel stupid and stop you from asking too many questions.

Joint Venture: A partnership between two companies or governments that always starts with promises of mutual benefit and usually ends with one side realising they got the short end of the stick.

Jubilee: A celebration of a monarch's reign that's less about their achievements and more about the chance for a bank holiday and some bunting. It's like a royal birthday party, but the whole country gets invited.

K

Kleptocracy: A form of government where those in power use their position to steal as much as they can. It's like running a country as a smash-and-grab operation, and the people are always the ones footing the bill.

Keynesianism: The economic theory that governments should spend money to get out of a recession, as opposed to the usual tactic of just cutting everything and hoping for the best.

Kickback: A polite term for bribery, where politicians or officials get a little something extra for looking the other way. It's corruption in a suit, pretending it's just "business as usual."

Kangaroo Court: A mockery of justice where the outcome is already decided, and the trial is just a formality. If you're in one, don't bother with a lawyer—just prepare for the inevitable.

L

Lobbying: The practice of paying politicians to listen to your ideas and pretend they're their own. It's basically legalised bribery, but with better catering.

Left Wing: The side of the political spectrum that believes in social equality, wealth redistribution, and occasionally scaring the rich. They're the ones calling for revolution, but usually end up settling for more taxes.

Laissez-Faire: The economic theory that the government should stay out of business and let the market do whatever it wants. It's beloved by CEOs and loathed by anyone who's had to live through a financial crisis.

Labour Party: A UK political party that used to fight for the working class but now spends most of its time trying to convince middle-class voters it's not too radical. If it had a slogan, it'd be "We promise we won't scare you too much."

Landslide: An election victory so overwhelming that even the losing side can't pretend they had a chance. Usually followed by four years of gloating and a lot of bad policy decisions.

Lynching: A term used historically for the violent and unlawful killing of someone by a mob. Today, it serves as a grim reminder of the brutal power dynamics that persist beneath civilised society's polite veneer.

M

Marxism: The political theory that the working class will eventually overthrow the ruling class and seize control of the means of production. In practice, it mostly involves long meetings, confusing pamphlets, and endless debates over the true meaning of revolution.

Meritocracy: The idea that success is based on talent and hard work, which is great if you're already successful and want to ignore how much your wealth and privilege helped.

Monarchy: A system where power is handed down through a single family, whether or not they've earned it. It's like winning the lottery every generation but pretending it's because you're special.

Multilateralism: The idea that countries should work together to solve global problems. Sounds lovely, until you realise that most countries would rather go it alone and blame each other when things go wrong.

Military-Industrial Complex: The cosy relationship between governments and the arms industry, where wars and conflicts are good for business, and peace is a bit of a nuisance.

Mixed Economy: An economic system where both the government and the private sector are involved in running things, resulting in a constant tug-of-war over who gets to keep the profits.

Mutually Assured Destruction (MAD): The delightful concept that if everyone has enough nuclear weapons to destroy the planet, no one will actually use them. It's the ultimate in bad ideas with a catchy acronym.

N

NATO: The North Atlantic Treaty Organization, a military alliance that exists to defend the West from its enemies—mostly by spending vast amounts of money on weapons and pretending it's all about peace.

Non-Governmental Organisation (NGO): A group that exists to do the things governments should be doing but aren't, like providing aid or protecting the environment. Loved by idealists, ignored by politicians.

Nationalisation: The process of taking private industries and making them public, which sounds great until the government gets involved and runs them like a particularly inefficient post office.

O

Oligarchy: A system where a small group of rich people control everything, usually behind the scenes. It's like democracy, but with fewer votes and more yachts.

Oppression: The systematic denial of rights, opportunities, and freedoms to certain groups, all while pretending it's for their own good. Usually justified by outdated laws and bad excuses.

Outsourcing: The practice of hiring people in other countries to do the jobs that were once done locally, all in the name of saving money. It's globalisation's favourite cost-cutting trick.

Open Market: A market where anyone can trade freely, with minimal restrictions. Sounds nice, until you realise that "anyone" mostly means corporations that can crush smaller competitors.

Overreach: When governments or organisations use their power far beyond what's necessary, often resulting in a mess of regulations, lawsuits, and general discontent.

Opposition: The political party that pretends to fight the ruling party but often just agrees with them on everything important. They exist to keep up appearances, not actually change anything.

P

Plutocracy: A system where the rich run the show, using their wealth to influence politicians, laws, and basically everything else. It's what happens when capitalism stops pretending.

Protest: The act of publicly disagreeing with the government, usually met with eye-rolls, tear gas, and a patronising speech about how "everyone's voice matters."

Privatisation: The process of selling off public services to private companies, who immediately make them worse and more expensive. It's like putting a fox in charge of the henhouse, then charging the hens rent.

Protectionism: The economic idea that you can help your country by keeping out foreign competition, often resulting in higher prices and lower quality products. It's a bit like building a moat around your economy, only to realise you're the one trapped inside.

Q

Quango: Quasi-Autonomous Non-Governmental Organisation. A government body that isn't really part of the government, but still somehow manages to spend your tax money. Like an unnecessary middleman with a nice office.

Quorum: The minimum number of people needed to make a meeting official. It's the political equivalent of "we need enough warm bodies in the room before we can pretend to be productive."

Quantitative Easing: A fancy term for printing more money, which somehow helps the economy while making everything more expensive. Economics at its most baffling.

R

Referendum: A political tool where the public is asked to vote directly on an issue, often used by politicians who want to avoid making tough decisions themselves. The results are usually regretted within weeks.

Recession: A period of economic decline, caused by rich people making terrible decisions that the rest of us have to suffer for. It's the financial version of a hangover, except everyone's drunk except you.

Regulation: The rules that governments impose to make sure businesses don't destroy everything. They're often watered down by lobbyists, ensuring that corporations can still do whatever they want, just more quietly.

Revolution: The dramatic overthrow of a government or system, usually involving a lot of angry people, a few guillotines, and the hope that the new system will be better. Spoiler: it's often not.

Rhetoric: Fancy words and clever speeches used by politicians to distract you from the fact they're not actually doing anything. Think of it as verbal smoke and mirrors.

Redistribution: The radical idea that rich people should pay more taxes to help the poor, often dismissed as "socialism" by those with very full bank accounts.

Reform: The process of making changes to a political system, though it's often more like rearranging deck chairs on a sinking ship. Real reform scares politicians, so they usually opt for the cosmetic kind.

S

Socialism: The political belief that people should share things more equally, like wealth and resources. To conservatives, it's communism's more palatable cousin. To socialists, it's the only thing stopping society from imploding.

Spin: The art of taking bad news and making it sound positive, usually by changing a few words and hoping no one notices. Spin doctors are like magicians, except they make facts disappear instead of rabbits.

Sovereignty: The idea that a country should be able to do whatever it wants without interference from other nations. It's often used as an excuse for terrible policies, disguised as "taking back control."

Sanctions: Economic punishments imposed on a country to make them behave, though they mostly make ordinary people suffer while the leaders carry on as usual.

Sedition: The crime of speaking out against the government, often used by authoritarian regimes to silence dissent. It's what happens when free speech gets inconvenient.

Surveillance State: A government that watches your every move, all in the name of "security." They promise it's for your safety, but it's really just so they can keep tabs on you.

State of Emergency: When the government decides things are so bad, they need to break their own laws to fix them. Conveniently, these emergencies often last just long enough to suspend your rights.

T

Terrorism: The use of violence and fear to achieve political aims. Governments love to use it as a reason to pass new laws that have nothing to do with actually stopping terrorism.

Trade War: An economic fight between countries, where tariffs are the weapons and the casualties are usually small businesses and consumers. It's like a fistfight in a shop, where everyone loses except the politicians.

Taxes: The money you pay so the government can provide services like healthcare and education, but somehow ends up in the pockets of big corporations and military contractors.

Treaty: A formal agreement between countries that's supposed to keep the peace. In reality, it's usually a way for the powerful to get what they want without starting a war—yet.

Tyranny: The oppressive rule of a government or leader who has absolute power and uses it poorly. If democracy is a messy kitchen, tyranny is the chef burning everything on purpose.

U

Universal Basic Income: A radical idea where everyone gets free money from the government, which makes conservatives clutch their pearls and billionaires very nervous. It's welfare, but without the guilt trips.

Unemployment: When people can't find work, usually blamed on laziness by those who've never had to apply for a job in their life. Governments like to fiddle with the numbers to make it look better, but the queues for benefits tell a different story.

Utopia: An imagined perfect society that politicians promise but never deliver. It's a land of peace, equality, and happiness, which, unfortunately, exists only in campaign speeches and science fiction.

V

Veto: The political power to say "no" to a law, idea, or proposal, usually wielded by someone in a position of authority. It's democracy's version of "I'm not listening, la la la."

Vote of No Confidence: When parliament decides they're so disappointed in the leader that they want to kick them out. It's the political equivalent of a workplace firing, but with more shouting and handshakes.

Voter Apathy: The widespread disinterest in elections, caused by the realisation that no matter who you vote for, the same problems persist. It's the ultimate "what's the point?" attitude, which politicians love because it keeps them in power.

Vaccine: A medical breakthrough that can prevent diseases, but somehow became a political football kicked around by conspiracy theorists and politicians desperate for a win.

Venture Capitalism: The practice of throwing large amounts of money at start-up companies in the hope that one of them will succeed, while conveniently ignoring the wreckage of the ones that fail.

Voluntary Sector: Charities and non-profits that do the work governments should be doing, but don't. It's where well-meaning people go to clean up society's mess, unpaid and underfunded, of course.

W

Welfare State: A system where the government provides support to its citizens in the form of healthcare, education, and benefits. Conservatives see it as a necessary evil; socialists see it as basic human decency.

Weapons of Mass Destruction: The imaginary excuse for wars that turns out to be real, but never in the country we're invading. It's like looking for your car keys in someone else's house, with tanks.

Woke: Originally a term for being socially aware, but now used by certain politicians to describe anything they don't like. It's basically their way of saying, "How dare you care about other people?"

Whistleblower: The brave individual who leaks government or corporate secrets, only to be vilified by the same people they're exposing. Governments say they protect them, right before destroying their lives.

World Trade Organisation (WTO): The global body that makes sure international trade is as free and fair as possible, though "fair" usually means whatever benefits the richest countries.

X

Xenophobia: The irrational fear and hatred of foreigners, frequently stoked by politicians looking to distract you from their own incompetence. It's nationalism's uglier, more aggressive sibling.

X-Ray Politics: A term I just made up to describe political transparency, which, like an X-ray, is something you only get when things are badly broken.

Y

Youth Vote: The political Holy Grail—everyone talks about it, few actually get it. Politicians court young voters with promises of change, only to forget about them as soon as they're elected.

Yellow Journalism: Sensationalist media that sacrifices truth for catchy headlines and scandal. Think of it as clickbait for the 19th century, still thriving today in tabloids everywhere.

Yes-Man: The political lackey who agrees with everything the leader says, regardless of how idiotic it is. Their job is to nod and look obedient, hoping it'll earn them a promotion.

Yuppie: The young, urban professional who emerged in the 1980s with a love for big money, bigger egos, and brand-new suits. They're the foot soldiers of capitalism, always chasing the next bonus.

Z

Zero-Hour Contract: A brilliant invention where employers don't have to guarantee you any work, but you have to be available whenever they feel like it. Flexibility for them, anxiety for you.

Zeitgeist: The spirit of the times, often used to describe the cultural mood or general vibe of a particular period. Right now, the zeitgeist is "existential dread, with a dash of impending doom."

Bibliography

Adams, Douglas. *The Hitchhiker's Guide to the Galaxy.* Pan Books, 1979.A reminder that in the vast absurdity of the universe, human politics is just one more cosmic joke.

Chomsky, Noam and Herman, Edward. *Manufacturing Consent: The Political Economy of the Mass Media.* Pantheon Books, 1988.A deep dive into how governments and corporations control the media narrative, leaving you wondering if free speech is anything more than a quaint theory.

Fanon, Frantz. *The Wretched of the Earth.* Grove Press, 1963 .Required reading if you want to understand the psychology of colonialism and why empires never truly die, they just rebrand.

Foucault, Michel. *Discipline and Punish: The Birth of the Prison.* Vintage Books, 1977.Where you'll discover that modern society isn't that far removed from a prison, except now we pay rent for our cells and subscribe to Netflix.

Harvey, David. *A Brief History of Neoliberalism.* Oxford University Press, 2005.A delightful romp through the ways neoliberal policies have destroyed the public good and turned everything into a commodity. Spoiler alert: it's all worse than you thought.

Hobbes, Thomas. *Leviathan.* Andrew Crooke, 1651.A must-read for anyone who enjoys imagining life as "nasty, brutish, and short" unless we have a massive state to keep us all in line.

Keynes, John Maynard. *The General Theory of Employment, Interest and Money.* Palgrave Macmillan, 1936.Because what's more exciting than trying to fix capitalism with a set of complicated equations? Even Keynes couldn't stop people from misinterpreting him, but bless him, he tried.

Machiavelli, Niccolò. *The Prince.* Antonio Blado d'Asola, 1532.A timeless guide for politicians everywhere, proving that it's better to be feared than loved—as long as you're still invited to the right parties.

Marx, Karl, and Engels, Friedrich. *The Communist Manifesto.* Penguin Classics, 1848.The pamphlet that launched a thousand revolutions, or at least a lot of angry student protests. Still, a great read if you're into smashing the state and abolishing capitalism.

Mill, John Stuart. *On Liberty.* John W. Parker and Son, 1859.An optimistic take on how individual freedom is the cornerstone of a happy society—unless, of course, you live in the 21st century, where freedom comes with asterisks.

Orwell, George. *1984.* Secker & Warburg, 1949.A charming little novel about a dystopia where the government spies on everything you do and rewrites history. Not at all relevant to modern politics, of course.

Piketty, Thomas. *Capital in the Twenty-First Century.* Harvard University Press, 2014.A doorstopper of a book that will make you question why the rich keep getting richer while the rest of us fight over table scraps. Spoiler: it's by design.

Rousseau, Jean-Jacques. *The Social Contract.* Marc-Michel Rey, 1762.A philosophical masterpiece that imagines a world where the will of the people governs society. Clearly, Rousseau hadn't met the people yet.

Smith, Adam. *The Wealth of Nations.* W. Strahan and T. Cadell, 1776.The founding text of modern economics, written by someone who didn't anticipate the rise of billionaires hoarding wealth while the rest of us debate whether to buy groceries or pay rent.

Thatcher, Margaret. *The Downing Street Years.* HarperCollins, 1993.A personal account of how one woman taught a generation to hate the word "society" and love privatisation. It's a nostalgic read for anyone who enjoys economic devastation.

Zinn, Howard. *A People's History of the United States.* Harper & Row, 1980.For when you need a history lesson that isn't written by the winners. It's everything your school textbooks left out, and trust me, it's not pretty.